D1420438

MILTON'S VISUAL IMAGINATION

Imagery in Paradise Lost

To tell the story of humankind's Fall requires the description of much that has never been seen – from the war in Heaven, to life in Eden before the first sin. In *Milton's Visual Imagination*, Stephen B. Dobranski discovers new allusions and previously ignored contexts that show how Milton enriches his biblical source text with acute and sometimes astonishing visual details. He contends that Milton's imagery – traditionally disparaged by critics – advances the epic's narrative while expressing the author's heterodox beliefs. In particular, Milton exploits the meaning of objects and gestures to overcome the inherent difficulty of his subject, and to accommodate seventeenth-century readers. Bringing together Milton's material philosophy with an analysis of both his poetic tradition and cultural circumstances, this discerning study is a major contribution to our understanding of early modern visual culture as well as Milton's epic, the preeminent work of the English literary canon.

Stephen B. Dobranski is Distinguished University Professor of early modern literature and textual studies at Georgia State University. He is the author of several books, including *Milton, Authorship, and the Book Trade* (Cambridge University Press, 1999); *Readers and Authorship in Early Modern England* (Cambridge University Press, 2005); *A Variorum Commentary on the Poems of John Milton: "Samson Agonistes"* (2009); and *The Cambridge Introduction to Milton* (Cambridge University Press, 2012).

MILTON'S VISUAL IMAGINATION

IMAGINATION

Imagery in Paradise Lost

STEPHEN B. DOBRANSKI

Georgia State University

CAMBRIDGE
UNIVERSITY PRESS

CAMBRIDGE
UNIVERSITY PRESS

32 Avenue of the Americas, New York NY 10013-2473, USA

Cambridge University Press is part of the University of Cambridge.

It furthers the University's mission by disseminating knowledge in the pursuit of
education, learning and research at the highest international levels of excellence.

www.cambridge.org
Information on this title: www.cambridge.org/9781107094390

© Stephen B. Dobranski 2015

First published 2015

A catalogue record for this publication is available from the British Library

ISBN 978-1-107-09439-0 Hardback

for John Rumrich

Contents

List of illustrations   *page* viii
Acknowledgments   xi
List of abbreviations   xiii

1   Introduction: Of things invisible   1

2   Free will and God's scales   36

3   Heaven's gates   62

4   Pondering Satan's shield   90

5   What do bad angels look like?   108

6   Transported touch   135

7   Clustering and curling locks   153

8   Images of the future and the Son   176

9   Postscript   204

Index   213

Illustrations

All illustrations are used with permission.

2.1 Francis Quarles, *Emblemes* (London, 1635), B4v. Folger
Shakespeare Library. *page* 59

3.1 Example of automata from John Bate, *The Mysteryes
of Nature, and Art* (London, 1634). Folger Shakespeare
Library. 71

3.2 Another example of automata from Bate, *The Mysteryes
of Nature, and Art* (London, 1634). Folger Shakespeare
Library. 72

3.3 Temple doors opened by fire on an altar, Hero of Alexandria,
Gli Artificiosi, e Curiosi Moti Spiritalidi Herone, trans.
Giovanni Battista Aleotti (Bologna, 1647). Photo reproduced
under the GNU Free Documentation License. 73

4.1 Greek amphora depicting warriors with shield. Louvre
Museum. Photo reproduced under the GNU Free
Documentation License. 97

4.2 Richard Corbould, "Forthwith upright he rears from off the
pool, / His mighty stature...," in Milton, *Paradise Lost*, 2
vols. (London, 1796). Robert J. Wickenheiser Collection of
John Milton, Irvin Department of Rare Books and Special
Collections, University of South Carolina Libraries,
Columbia, S.C. 99

4.3 Michael Burgesse, illustration opposite page 1, in Milton,
Paradise Lost (London, 1688). Robert J. Wickenheiser
Collection of John Milton, Irvin Department of Rare Books
and Special Collections, University of South Carolina
Libraries, Columbia, S.C. 100

5.1 John Martin, illustration for book I, line 192, in *The "Paradise
Lost" of Milton with Illustrations, Designed and Engraved by*

John Martin (London: Septimus Prowett, 1825–1827). Robert J. Wickenheiser Collection of John Milton, Irvin Department of Rare Books and Special Collections, University of South Carolina Libraries, Columbia, S.C.   127

5.2 John Martin, illustration for book I, line 314, in *The "Paradise Lost" of Milton with Illustrations, Designed and Engraved by John Martin* (London: Septimus Prowett, 1825–1827). Robert J. Wickenheiser Collection of John Milton, Irvin Department of Rare Books and Special Collections, University of South Carolina Libraries, Columbia, S.C.   128

6.1 George Wither, *A Collection of Emblemes, Ancient and Moderne* (London, 1635), P3r. Harry Ransom Center, The University of Texas at Austin.   142

6.2 John Speed's "Genealogies of the Holy Spirit," in *The Holy Bible* (London, 1611), A1v. Harry Ransom Center, The University of Texas at Austin.   145

7.1 Anthony Van Dyck, *Charles I, King of England, from Three Angels*, 1636. Oil on canvas. Royal Collection, Windsor Castle, Berkshire. Photo reproduced under the GNU Free Documentation License.   155

9.1 Raphael Sanzio, *The Creation of the Animals*, 1518–1519. Fresco. Photo reproduced under the GNU Free Documentation License.   205

Acknowledgments

I am pleased to thank publicly the many friends and colleagues who helped to make this book possible. Some of the chapters grew out of conference papers and invited talks, and I am grateful for the encouragement and questions that I received from audiences at the Conference on John Milton, the International Milton Symposium, the Modern Language Association Convention, and the Renaissance Society of America Conference. The chapter on Adam and Eve's hair began as a Newberry Library Seminar in 2007. The seminars' participants – especially Stephen Fallon, Christopher Kendrick, David Loewenstein, Michael Lieb, and the late John Shawcross – bolstered my confidence to undertake a study of Milton's imagery and offered timely advice.

The chapter on God's golden scales grew out of a paper for a symposium sponsored by the Texas Institute for Literary and Textual Studies in 2010. I wish to extend special thanks to the symposium's directors, Frank Whigham and Wayne A. Rebhorn, as well as David Anderson, J. K. Barret, Mary Blockley, Douglas Bruster, Todd Butler, Joseph A. Campana, Kimberly Coles, Brooke Conti, Kasey Evans, Daniel Gibbons, Jane Grogan, Kenneth Hodges, Jenna Lay, Eric Mallin, Joseph Navitsky, Anita Sherman, and Hannah Wojciehowski. The conversations and friendships begun at this week-long event have proven gratifying as my research on early modern religious conflict continues to develop.

Shorter versions of chapters 4, 6, and 7 first appeared in, respectively, *English Literary Renaissance* 35 (2005); *Milton, Rights, and Liberties*, ed. Christophe Tournu and Neil Forsyth (Peter Lang, 2007); and *PMLA* 125 (2010). I am grateful to the publishers for permitting me to draw upon my earlier work and to the readers for each of these publications who offered insightful suggestions. In particular, I wish to thank Michael Schoenfeldt and Catherine Gimelli Martin. The anonymous readers for Cambridge University Press provided additional recommendations for revision that greatly improved both the book's overarching organization and several of the individual sections. This project has also benefited from the time and effort of Ray Ryan and Caitlin Gallagher at Cambridge; Ray enthusiastically supported this project early on, and both he and Caitlin gently guided the book through to press.

In the later stages of researching and writing, I received a Provost Faculty Fellowship from Georgia State University, which provided much needed time and resources. Two Summer Research Awards from the Department of English at Georgia State also allowed for concentrated periods away from the classroom. I am fortunate to teach and work in such a genial and supportive department and am grateful to colleagues, past and present, for their contributions to my thinking and writing – in particular, Wayne Erickson, Scott Lightsey, Randy Malamud, Matthew Roudanè, and Paul Schmidt. My own students continue to challenge and inspire, and I have learned a great deal over the years while working with, among others, Karen Dodson, Mary Grace Elliott, Pitt Harding, Sarah Higinbotham, Judith Irvine, Matthew McIntyre, and Lisa Ulevich.

In the field of Milton studies, I have benefited from the advice and scholarship of a wide range of critics. A necessarily incomplete list includes Sharon Achinstein, Gregory Chaplin, Dennis Danielson, Karen Edwards, Thomas Fulton, Wendy Furman-Adams, Edward Jones, Paul Klemp, Laura Knoppers, Barbara Lewalski, William Shullenberger, Paul Stevens, and Joseph Wittreich. I am especially indebted to Stephen Fallon and Joad Raymond, who generously read sections of the manuscript in progress. Their astute suggestions and corrections helped me to improve matters, both large and small. The late, great Stella Revard read an early version of one chapter and over the years was consistently encouraging as the book's argument gradually took shape. She is much missed.

John Rumrich, with characteristic acuity and goodwill, also offered detailed responses to two chapters. These sections and the book as a whole are better for John's thoughtful advice. For his countless kindnesses, his friendship, and his abiding influence on my work, I have dedicated this book to him.

Finally, for helping me first to conceive this project during our many summer strolls in Gorizia, and then, years later, for reading the entire manuscript back in Atlanta – at times sacrificing sleep to read new drafts – I am especially grateful to my wife, Shannon. I thank her for her unwavering support, and for so much else. This book also benefited in less direct but no less important ways from the influence of our daughter, Audrey. She continues to provide us with indelible images of joy and grace. The mistakes that remain are my own.

Abbreviations

CPEP *The Complete Poetry and Essential Prose of John Milton*, ed. William Kerrigan, John Rumrich, and Stephen M. Fallon (New York: Modern Library, 2007).

CPW *The Complete Prose Works of John Milton*, gen. ed. Don M. Wolfe, 8 vols. (New Haven: Yale University Press, 1953–1982).

Fowler Alastair Fowler, ed., *Paradise Lost*, by John Milton, 2nd edn. (London: Longman, 1998).

OED *The Oxford English Dictionary*, 2nd and 3rd editions.

Citations and line numbers for Milton's poetry, unless otherwise noted, are taken from *CPEP*. Citations to classical works are to the Loeb editions published by Harvard University Press; citations to the Bible are taken from the King James (Authorized) Version.

CHAPTER I

Introduction: Of things invisible

His eyes are said never to have been bright; but if he was a dexterous fencer, they must have been once quick.

– Samuel Johnson[1]

When Milton in *Paradise Lost* complains that blindness has separated him irrevocably from nature – what he calls "the book of knowledge fair" (III.47) – critics have tended to take the author at his word. Whereas some twenty-five years earlier, in *Lycidas*, Milton had sought consolation for the death of a friend by meditating on nature's cycles, he now emphasizes his isolation from the physical world:

> Thus with the year
> Seasons return, but not to me returns
> Day, or the sweet approach of ev'n or morn,
> Or sight of vernal bloom, or summer's rose,
> Or flocks, or herds, or human face divine;
> But cloud instead, and ever-during dark
> Surrounds me, from the cheerful ways of men
> Cut off, and for the book of knowledge fair
> Presented with a universal blank
> Of Nature's works to me expunged and razed,
> And wisdom at one entrance quite shut out.   (III.40–50)

Here the sequence of hard enjambments dramatizes the speaker's sense of disconnection – "returns / Day," "dark / Surrounds," and "ways . . . / Cut off." The abrupt line-breaks underscore the pain of the speaker's separation from the visible world, while the comprehensiveness of "universal blank" and "ever-during dark" reinforces the finality of "expunged," "razed," and "shut out."

Yet even in these lines, which provide a glimpse into Milton's personal experience, the apparent poignancy of the specific things that the speaker

---

[1] *Lives of the English Poets*, ed. George Birkbeck Hill, 3 vols. (New York: Octagon, 1967), I: 151.

can no longer see seems to be undermined by the list's conventionality. Milton already sounds detached from his physical world as he turns from an unspecified "vernal bloom" to "flocks, or herds," a group of images that sound more like standard pastoral topoi than parts of Milton's lived experience in seventeenth-century London. Perhaps also tellingly, he figures the natural world in this passage as a book instead of granting nature its own reality. If Matthew Arnold criticized William Wordsworth because the Romantic author "should have read more books," Milton, we might worry, may have read too many.[2] Even Milton's most personal self-expressions appear to be mediated through poetic tradition instead of firsthand knowledge.

Samuel Johnson was among the first readers to highlight this potential problem in *Paradise Lost*. Whereas Joseph Addison had praised Milton's "Multitudes of Beauties ... especially in the Descriptive Parts of his Poem," Johnson was dissatisfied with the epic's visual images, in particular, the depiction of the war in heaven.[3] Johnson criticized the poem's design because it "requires the description of what cannot be described, the agency of spirits," and he wished that Milton had kept "immateriality out of sight" instead of "unhappily perplex[ing] his poetry with his philosophy."[4] Johnson also found fault with the epic's natural imagery because, he felt, it was unrealistic. He complained that Milton's "images and descriptions of the scenes or operations of Nature do not seem to be always copied from original form, nor to the have the freshness, raciness, and energy of immediate observation."[5] Johnson admired Milton's "accumulation of knowledge ..., fermented by study and exalted by imagination," but he maintained that the imagery's "original deficience cannot be supplied" and "The want of human interest is always felt."[6]

In this book, I wish to challenge Johnson's disparaging assessment of the epic's "images and descriptions." Examining visual representations in *Paradise Lost* in relation to what Johnson dismissed as the poem's "confusion of spirit and matter," I argue that Milton's epic contains acute and sometimes astonishing images that grew out of his reading and imagination but were also influenced by his contemporary culture.[7] Specifically, I am

---

[2] Matthew Arnold, "The Function of Criticism at the Present Time," in *Lectures and Essays in Criticism*, ed. R. H. Super (Ann Arbor: University of Michigan Press, 1962), pp. 258–85 (p. 262).

[3] Joseph Addison, *Criticism on Milton's "Paradise Lost,"* ed. Edward Arber (London, 1869), p. 75. In contrast to Johnson, Addison went on to praise specifically Milton's depiction of the war in heaven for its "Pregnancy of Invention" and "Strength of Imagination" (pp. 93–94).

[4] Johnson, *Lives of the English Poets*, I: 184.

[5] Johnson, *Lives of the English Poets*, I: 178.

[6] Johnson, *Lives of the English Poets*, I: 183.

[7] Johnson, *Lives of the English Poets*, I: 185.

analyzing Milton's depictions of material objects and physical reality in light of his materialist philosophy. Milton depends on this imagery, I argue, to advance his poem's narrative and express his theological beliefs. I am accordingly concerned with three related questions: How does Milton's imagery contribute to the meaning of both individual episodes and *Paradise Lost* as a whole? How does Milton combine poetic tradition and seventeenth-century culture to render the invisible visible? And, how does material culture find expression in a text that explicitly theorizes the etiology of the material from which all things are created?

Admittedly, to announce that this book focuses on Milton's imagery may at first seem old-fashioned or, given the wealth of superb readings of *Paradise Lost* that have been published over the past decades, redundant. But whereas Rosemond Tuve attempted to identify "great central figurative conceptions" around which *Paradise Lost* "organizes" itself, and Theodore Banks assembled a taxonomy of image clusters with the expectation, as Banks puts it, "that the imagery reveals Milton the man," the aim of this book is more specific. I wish to discover inductively the epic's visual strategies by spotlighting previously neglected or misunderstood images that strike me as either surprisingly incongruous or especially significant.[8] By "imagery" I thus do not mean poetic language that conveys the "sensuous qualities of experience," nor am I looking at figurative language in general, which the term "imagery" came to encompass within the New Criticism.[9] Instead, I am looking more narrowly at visual representations in Milton's epic – what T. S. Eliot presumably intended when he referred to the poem's "visual imagination."[10]

Yet Eliot famously followed Johnson in faulting this aspect of *Paradise Lost* and went further, blaming Milton for a so-called "dissociation of sensibility" in English verse beginning in the 1600s. After Milton and Dryden, according to Eliot, "the language [of poets] became more refined, the feeling became more crude."[11] Although subsequent critics have dispelled Eliot's canard about a rupture of thought from sensation in seventeenth-

---

[8] Rosemond Tuve, *Images and Themes in Five Poems by Milton* (Cambridge: Harvard University Press, 1962), p. 4; and Theodore Howard Banks, *Milton's Imagery* (New York: Columbia University Press, 1950), p. xiii.

[9] Rosemond Tuve, *Elizabethan and Metaphysical Imagery: Renaissance Poetic and Twentieth-Century Critics* (Chicago: University of Chicago Press, 1947), p. 3; and Cleanth Brooks, Jr., and Robert Penn Warren, *Understanding Poetry* (New York: Holt, 1938), p. 555. For an application of this latter definition of "imagery," see Caroline Spurgeon, *Shakespeare's Imagery, and What It Tells Us* (1935; Cambridge: Cambridge University Press, 1965).

[10] T. S. Eliot, "Milton I [1936]," in *On Poetry and Poets* (New York: Farrar, Straus, and Giroux, 1957), pp. 156–64 (p. 158).

[11] Eliot, "The Metaphysical Poets," in *Selected Essays*, 3rd edn. (London: Faber and Faber, 1972), pp. 281–91 (p. 288).

century poetry, the lack of visual detail in Milton's verse – his epic's "generic" or "archetypal imagery" – has become a commonplace in early modern scholarship.[12] F. R. Leavis, for one, detected "a certain sensuous poverty" in Milton's poetry and found Milton in *Paradise Lost* "focussing [*sic*] rather upon words than upon perceptions, sensations or things."[13] Leland Ryken countered that the epic's scenes do carry "sensuous force," but the "sensory impressions belong to the apocalyptic senses of smell and hearing rather than to the everyday world of visual details."[14] One still widely accepted assumption is that Milton's visual descriptions declined as his own sight began to fail. Surveying Milton's imagery, Banks, for example, proposed that Milton's "visual sense . . . weakened, but his other senses – smell, hearing, and touch – became more quick and sharp."[15] Samuel Taylor Coleridge's disparaging assessment of Milton's imagery also seems to assume a connection between the author's blindness and a lack of visual detail. Milton, Coleridge felt, was among those writers who, instead of portraying "*individual* objects as actually present to his Senses," settled for "*classes* of things, presented by the memory and generalized by the Understanding."[16]

Underlying both Banks and Coleridge's critiques, however, is the false assumption that a reliance on memory dulls a writer's visual acuity. Recent scholarship on perceptions of the past in early modern England shows that personal and popular memory was often closely associated with visible things and features, and psychologists have concluded that a person who goes blind after the age of seven does not experience a decline in mental imagery or visual memory.[17] Milton, in other words, would not have been hampered in envisioning the world of his epic simply because he could no

[12] William Riley Parker, *Milton: A Biography*, ed. Gordon Campbell, 2nd edn., 2 vols. (Oxford: Clarendon, 1996), p. 594. For a contrary view, see John Ruskin, who complained that Milton's imagery was "too far detailed." *The Works of John Ruskin*, 39 vols., ed. E. T. Cook and Alexander Wedderburn (London: George Allen, 1903–1912), IV: 250.

[13] F. R. Leavis, "Milton's Verse," *Scrutiny* 2 (1933): 123–36; rpt. in *Revaluation: Tradition and Development in English Poetry* (London: Chatto and Windus, 1936), pp. 42–67 (pp. 47, 49). Leavis adds that Milton "exhibits a feeling *for* words rather than a capacity for feeling *through* words; we are often, in reading him, moved to comment that he is 'external' or that he 'works from the outside'" (p. 50).

[14] Leland Ryken, *The Apocalyptic Vision in "Paradise Lost"* (Ithaca and London: Cornell University Press, 1970), p. 229.

[15] Banks, *Milton's Imagery*, p. 137. Eleanor Gertrude Brown, for example, offers a similar interpretation in *Milton's Blindness* (1934; New York: Octagon, 1968), p. 136.

[16] Samuel Taylor Coleridge, "Letter to an Unknown Correspondent, 1820," in *Coleridge on the Seventeenth Century*, ed. Roberta F. Brinkley (Durham: Duke University Press, 1955), pp. 599–600. And, in the same volume, see Coleridge's "Lecture on Milton and the Paradise Lost," pp. 572–79. E. M. W. Tillyard similarly describes Milton's imagery as "a composite of several recollections or imaginings not the reproduction of something seen and intensely apprehended in every-day life." Tillyard, *The Miltonic Setting: Past and Present* (1938; New York: Barnes and Noble, 1966), p. 99.

[17] Daniel Woolf, *The Social Circulation of the Past: English Historical Culture, 1500–1730* (Oxford: Oxford University Press, 2003), pp. 360–61; Stephen Michael Kosslyn, *Ghosts in the Mind's Machine: Creating*

longer see his own. Instead, following cultural tradition, the author might have clung more tenaciously to images he recalled from experience as a way of staying mnemonically connected to his forty-three years of sight.

Yet Eliot's belittling of *Paradise Lost*'s visual sense has had far-reaching influence. Eliot emphatically asserted that "At no period is the visual imagination conspicuous in Milton's poetry," and he ultimately described Milton's imagination as "purely auditory," adding that even before Milton went blind he "may be said never to have seen anything." "Indeed," Eliot writes, "I find, in reading *Paradise Lost*, that I am happiest where there is least to visualize."[18]

Various scholars since have attempted to answer Eliot's rebuke and to defend Milton's visual imagination. Most notably, Roland Frye, in *Milton's Imagery and the Visual Arts*, demonstrated that the author of *Paradise Lost* was responding to and borrowing from an array of traditional representations in order to render more vividly the epic's scenes and characters. As Frye notes, "Without a knowledge of the visual lexicon available to Milton and his contemporaries, it is all too easy to find in him a blindness that is really our own."[19] Much of my study accords with Frye's premise that Milton's "use of visual allusions was consciously directed to reinforce and undergird both his poetic and his religious purposes."[20] But whereas Frye's monumental book situates Milton's verbal depictions within the context of Western art – "the great panorama of paintings, mosaics, and sculptures"[21] – I return repeatedly to the blending of poetic knowledge and lived experience, and am specifically interested in the ways that Milton's articulation of the epic's philosophy and religion often depends on his visual descriptions.

Regarding the relevance of Milton's firsthand experiences, critics have tended to privilege the young poet's thirteen-month continental journey instead of the possible effects of his life in England. Marjorie Nicolson, for example, suggested that Milton's visit to the volcanic Phlegraean Fields near Naples informed *Paradise Lost*'s description of Hell's burning land-scape, while other commentators, as I discuss in chapters 3 and 5, have

and Using Images in the Brain (New York and London: Norton, 1983), pp. 77–79; and Alan Baddeley, *Human Memory: Theory and Practice*, rev. edn. (Boston: Allyn and Bacon, 1990), pp. 71–77.

[18] Eliot, "Milton I," pp. 158, 162. In a later essay, Eliot amplified this argument: "Milton's weakness of visual observation ... was always present – the effect of his blindness may have been rather to strengthen the compensatory qualities than to increase a fault which was already present." See Eliot, "Milton II [1947]," in *On Poetry and Poets*, pp. 165–83 (p. 177).

[19] Roland Mushat Frye, *Milton's Imagery and the Visual Arts* (Princeton: Princeton University Press, 1978), p. 7.

[20] Frye, *Milton's Imagery and the Visual Arts*, p. 8.

[21] Frye, *Milton's Imagery and the Visual Arts*, p. 3.

proposed Roman and Tuscan influences on, respectively, the descriptions of Pandemonium and the fallen angels.[22] More often, examinations of the epic's imagery focus on Milton's likely artistic and literary reminiscences. Diane McColley uncovered medieval and Renaissance topoi that shed light on Milton's depiction of Adam and Eve's prelapsarian and regenerate experience, while Stella Revard concentrated on the literary context of Milton's spiritual creatures.[23] Revard showed in particular how Milton's vision of the war in heaven appropriates and redeploys imagery from other sixteenth- and seventeenth-century epics so as to discredit the classical heroic ethic.[24] Douglas Bush offered a related but broader defense of what he called Milton's "suggestive visual images."[25] Highlighting the opening description of Satan in Hell and the account in book VII of the world's creation, Bush emphasized that in *Paradise Lost* "the solid and literal continually merge with the metaphorical and symbolic," and he concluded that even the poem's most abstract ideas have a tangible quality to lend Milton's cosmos "a substantial solidity."[26]

The last phrase – "substantial solidity" – seems to allude to John Keats' observation that Milton in *Paradise Lost* "is not content with simple descriptions" but relies on "stationing" his characters in relation to solid objects. Keats' language – he refers to both "stationing" and "statuary" – grows out of nineteenth-century theories of visual art and nineteenth-century paintings in which figures stand within a particular scene or are "caught in a suspended, significant moment."[27] Writing about the surviving marginalia that Keats jotted in his copy of *Paradise Lost*, Beth Lau has determined that the Romantic author largely experienced Milton's epic as a visual, almost cinematic work – "as a series of still shots, whether medium-range views of complete figures or close-ups of revealing facial expressions."[28]

More generally, as evidence of Milton's ability to create rich visual details, we might note the more than 150 artists who have illustrated

---

[22] Marjorie Hope Nicolson, *John Milton: A Reader's Guide to His Poetry* (New York: Farrar, Straus, and Giroux, 1963), pp. 194–95.

[23] Diane Kelsey McColley, *A Gust for Paradise: Milton's Eden and the Visual Arts* (Urbana and Chicago: University of Illinois Press, 1993).

[24] Stella Purce Revard, *The War in Heaven: "Paradise Lost" and the Tradition of Satan's Rebellion* (Ithaca and London: Cornell University Press, 1980), p. 197.

[25] Douglas Bush, *John Milton: A Sketch of His Life and Writings* (New York: Collier, 1964), p. 157.

[26] Bush, *John Milton*, pp. 173, 172.

[27] Nancy M. Goslee, "'Under a Cloud in Prospect': Keats, Milton, and Stationing," *Philological Quarterly* 53 (1974): 205–19, especially pp. 205–06. See also Goslee, *Uriel's Eye: Stationing and Statuary in Blake, Keats, and Shelly* (University, AL: University of Alabama Press, 1985); and Ian Jack, *Keats and the Mirror of Art* (Oxford: Clarendon, 1967), especially pp. 48, 141.

[28] Beth Lau, *Keats's "Paradise Lost"* (Gainesville: University Press of Florida, 1998), pp. 38–39.

Paradise Lost, from the first illustrated edition in 1688 to works by such diverse artists as Gustave Doré, William Blake, J. M. W. Turner, and Salvador Dali. The more than three centuries of vivid and evocative drawings, engravings, and paintings based on *Paradise Lost* would seem to give the lie to Johnson's and Eliot's critical characterization of the epic's imagery.[29] As early as 1668, in *An Idea of the Perfection of Painting*, an anonymous reader has written in the margin that he deemed "ye Paradise Lost of Milton" one of the "Books of advantage to a Painter," and most recently the cinematic adaptation of Milton's epic in production at Legendary Pictures promised, in one producer's words, to "make extensive use of digital effects" and emphasize the epic's visual qualities.[30]

Yet, Johnson's original observation that *Paradise Lost* "requires the description of what cannot be described" is nevertheless incisive because it captures one of the crucial challenges that Milton knew he faced: how to depict what has never been and can never be seen. In the invocation to book III, Milton appeals to his muse for inner illumination as compensation for the "universal blank" imposed by his blindness (line 48), but he also explains that he needs assistance from his muse so that he "may see and tell / Of things invisible to mortal sight" (lines 54–55). Milton, I will show, also sought other, more practical solutions to describing the epic's invisible scenes and characters, and drew on the works of his predecessors and contemporaries as well as his seventeenth-century culture. In contrast to Johnson, who cordons off Milton's reality from "worlds where only imagination can travel," I argue that the two are related in important ways in *Paradise Lost* and that the poet's real experience often enriched his imaginative portrayal.[31] Whereas Johnson objected that Milton's "knowledge" and "study" diminished the impact of his natural imagery, I wish to show how Milton imbricates poetic tradition and cultural experience to add sometimes subtle implications to the things he depicts. As a young man, Milton claimed not to have finished his poem "The Passion" because he found "This subject . . . to be above the years he had when he wrote it" (*CPMP* 33). Perhaps he nevertheless published "The

---

[29] Wendy Furman-Adams has examined in depth Milton's artistic legacy. See, for example, her essay, co-authored with Virginia James Tufte, "Ecofeminist Eve: Artists Reading Milton's Heroine," in *Ecofeminist Approaches to Early Modernity*, ed. Jennifer Munroe and Rebecca Laroche (New York: Palgrave, 2011), pp. 55–83.

[30] *An Idea of the Perfection of Painting . . . Translated by J. E.* (1668), cited in Michael Lieb and John T. Shawcross, "Preface," *"Paradise Lost": A Poem Written in Ten Books*, ed. Lieb and Shawcross (Pittsburgh: Duquesne University Press, 2007), pp. ix–xv (p. xiv); and Michael Joseph Gross, "It's God vs. Satan. But What About the Nudity?" *New York Times* (4 Mar. 2007): Arts 18. The film's production was halted in early 2012 due, at least in part, to escalating costs.

[31] Johnson, *Lives of the English Poets*, I: 178.

Passion" in its incomplete form in 1645 and 1673 because it had taught him a valuable lesson – namely, to match his writing to his experience.

In addressing the historical context of Milton's imagery, I am also building on recent work in object studies in several of the chapters and examining what material things can reveal about the culture that produced and used them and the authors who, consciously or unconsciously, appropriated and alluded to these objects' social values and moral significance.[32] But I am not researching the diachronic trajectory or "life history" of a specific artifact, nor am I offering a Marxist critique of commodification and subject/object relations.[33] Instead, this book focuses on what Patricia Fumerton has helpfully called the "everyday," a category which focuses on familiar things, but includes social practices and collective values.[34] Specifically, I am investigating how Milton combined and exploited the meaning of cultural and poetic objects and gestures in an effort to overcome the inherent limitations of his epic's subject. What associations might readers have had with scales or shields during the seventeenth century, for example? What did it mean to Milton and his readers to wear long hair? Simply put, if we return to Johnson's complaint about the war in heaven, I am analyzing how Milton uses *things* in *Paradise Lost* to help him render the invisible visible. While critics have long acknowledged the classical and scriptural traditions that inform the epic's imagery, the following chapters examine the various ways that he combines this knowledge with the more immediate experience of living in seventeenth-century London.

Imagistic traditions

Discussions of imagery in early modern literature often begin with Horace's well-known formulation that "A poem is like a picture" (*Ut pictura poesis*).[35] Horace may have been influenced in turn by the poet Simonides of Ceos who, centuries earlier, according to Plutarch,

[32] See, for example, Catherine Richardson, *Shakespeare and Material Culture* (Oxford: Oxford University Press, 2011).
[33] For these alternative approaches to object studies, see, for example, the essays in *Subject and Object in Renaissance Culture*, ed. Margreta de Grazia, Maureen Quilligan, and Peter Stallybrass (Cambridge: Cambridge University Press, 1996). For the concept of an object's "life history," see Arjun Appadurai, *The Social Life of Things: Commodities in Cultural Perspective* (Cambridge: Cambridge University Press, 1986), p. 34.
[34] *Renaissance Culture and the Everyday*, ed. Patricia Fumerton and Simon Hunt (Philadelphia: University of Pennsylvania Press, 1999), pp. 4–5; see also Jules David Prown, "Mind in Matter: An Introduction to Material Culture Theory and Method," in *Art as Evidence: Writings on Art and Material Culture* (New Haven and London: Yale University Press, 2001), pp. 69–95.

had asserted that "painting is inarticulate poetry and poetry articulate painting."[36] But Horace, in *Ars Poetica*, develops this relation more fully – although not, as is often thought to be the case, as a general aesthetic theory. Primarily, Horace compares the diversity of critical evaluations that poetry and painting can prompt, and argues that both poets and painters should pursue simple and consistent visual depictions. Both have the freedom of their imagination, he asserts, "but not so far that savage should mate with tame, or serpents with birds, lambs with tigers."[37]

Writing roughly three hundred years earlier, Plato and Aristotle had also compared poetry and painting. Aristotle used the analogous relation between the two art forms to explain the potency of imaginative imitation or *mimesis*, whereas Plato emphasized the resemblance between poetry and painting to underscore the limitations of the same aesthetic theory.[38] Socrates, in the *Republic*, accordingly concludes that poets, like painters, create merely "phantoms" or "a dim adumbration" of nature which appeal "to the inferior part of the soul."[39] Although a poet may seem to be well informed about his subject, he actually knows "nothing but how to imitate." He "lays on . . . the colours of the several arts" in such a fashion that only "others equally ignorant, who see things only through words, will deem his words most excellent."[40]

But if Socrates finds fault with both painting and poetry for being far removed from nature and human excellence, Horace's comments imply that painting holds a privileged position over poetic expression because the visual arts more effectively resemble natural objects and allow for the instantaneous perception of what they portray. When, for example, Horace, in his discussion of drama, asserts, "Less vividly is the mind stirred by what finds entrance through the ears than by what is brought before the trusty eyes," he is referring to the oracular experience of play-going and suggesting that hearing – and thus reading – are inferior to seeing because language introduces an added level of mediation.[41] During the

---

[35] Horace, *Ars Poetica*, trans. H. Rushton Fairclough (Cambridge: Harvard University Press, 1999), lines 361–65 (p. 481).

[36] Plutarch, *Moralia*, ed. and trans. Frank Cole Babbitt, et al., 16 vols. (Cambridge: Harvard University Press, 1927–1969), IV: 346 (p. 501). Plutarch goes on to explain that artists and writers "differ in the material and the manner of their imitation; and yet the underlying end and aim of both is one and the same; the most effective historian is he who, by a vivid representation of emotions and characters, makes his narration like a painting" (IV: 347).

[37] Horace, *Ars Poetica*, lines 11–13 (p. 451).

[38] See, for example, Aristotle, *Poetics*, ed. and trans. Stephen Halliwell (Cambridge: Harvard University Press, 2005), IV, 1450a (p. 53); II, 1448a (p. 33); and VI, 1450a (p. 51).

[39] Plato, *The Republic*, 2 vols., trans. Paul Shorey (Cambridge: Harvard University Press, 1980), book X, sec. VI, II, VI (vol. II: pp. 459, 427, 457).

[40] Plato, *The Republic*, book X, sec. IV (vol. II: pp. 442–43).

Renaissance, Leonardo da Vinci explained this idea in physiological terms. Most likely influenced by ancient theories of optics that described vision as coming from objects emitting copies of themselves, he proposed that to understand a painting involves less work than reading poetry because the visual arts transmit their subjects directly to spectators – "with the same truth as is possible with nature." By comparison, he argued, poetry, because it occurs in the writer's mind and imagination, presents information "more confusedly" and requires that readers study its meaning over time.[42]

A similar argument about the force and immediacy of the visual arts occurs in many of the ancient rhetorical treatises that Milton would have first encountered as part of the humanist curriculum at St. Paul's School. Echoing Horace's discussion of drama and visual cognition, Cicero, for example, writes:

> that the keenest of all our senses is the sense of sight, and that consequently perceptions received by the ears or by reflexion can be most easily retained in the mind if they are also conveyed to our minds by the mediation of the eyes, with the result that things not seen and not lying in the field of visual discernment are earmarked by a sort of outline and image and shape so that we keep hold of as it were by an act of sight things that we can scarcely embrace by an act of thought.[43]

Here Cicero argues that direct oracular perception allows viewers to comprehend and retain what they perceive, in contrast to language, which conveys only "a sort of outline and image and shape." He goes on to recommend that orators try to incorporate imagery in their speeches – an "almost visual presentation of events" – both for "stating a case" and "explaining and amplifying the statement."[44] The best an orator can do, in other words, is to emulate the act of sight.

This long-standing assumption about the relative statuses of painting and poetry may help to explain the controversy over religious imagery that erupted during the seventeenth century in England. If pictorial representations were thought to affect viewers directly, then visual depictions of

---

[41] Horace, *Ars Poetica*, lines 180–82 (p. 465).
[42] Leonardo da Vinci, *Leonardo on Painting*, ed. Martin Kemp, trans. Martin Kemp and Margaret Walker (New Haven and London: Yale University Press, 1989), pp. 37, 23. In Leonardo's words, painting "presents its essence to you in one moment through the faculty of vision by the same means as the *imprensiva* receives the objects in nature," whereas poetry "presents the same thing but by a less noble means than by the eye, conveying it more confusedly to the *imprensiva*" (p. 23). By *imprensiva*, Leonardo seems to mean a "receptor of impressions."
[43] Cicero, *De Oratore*, 2 vols., trans. E. W. Sutton (Cambridge: Harvard University Press, 1948), II. lxxxvii.357 (vol. I, pp. 468–69).
[44] Cicero, *De Oratore*, III.liii.202 (vol. II, pp. 160–61).

Christian belief – frescoes, statuary, and stained-glass windows – could have a more powerful influence on parishioners than the mediated transmission of God's word in, say, pamphlets and sermons. Thus, when Archbishop William Laud insisted on the "Beauty of Holiness" to justify the restoration of pre-Reformation ceremonies and architecture, he was positing an intimate connection between ecclesiastical forms and spiritual belief. As Laud explained at his trial, "I found that with the Contempt of the Outward Worship of God, the Inward fell away apace, and Profanness began boldly to shew it self."[45]

In contrast, opponents of Laud objected that material images of the divine were merely superficial, earthly manifestations. Following Paul's admonishment that man should not "[intrude] into those things which he hath not seen, vainly puft up by his fleshly mind" (Col. 2:18), Calvin had most forcefully declared that any type of visual depiction of the Divine corrupted God's glory. Calvin writes in his *Institutes* that "God himselfe is the onely convenient witnes of himselfe," and he explains that the Divine "rejecteth all images, pictures, and other signes. . . . For when men thought that they beheld God in images, they did also worship him in them . . . This is alway idolatrie."[46] Milton, in his early prose writings about church governance, similarly complains that high-church ceremonies and icons – what he dismissed as the "new-vomited Paganisme of sensuall Idolatry" (*CPW* I: 520) – not only impeded the individual's pursuit of truth, but also threatened to supplant it. Milton uses the metaphor of a diseased body in his tracts opposing an episcopal hierarchy to emphasize how Laudian ceremony was corrupting true religion: "all the inward acts of *worship* issuing form the native strength of the SOULE, run out lavishly to the upper skin, and there harden into a crust of Formallitie" (*CPW* I: 522).

Such contempt for the external signs of religious worship in favor of inward acts of the spirit corresponds to an alternative aesthetic and rhetorical theory that treated language as uniquely transcendent. Instead of physical embodiment in sculpture or painting, verbal expression – including verbal imagery – could best convey even invisible truths. In terms of religion, the idea finds its most acute expression in the Protestant belief in the almost sacramental authority of scripture. According to the doctrine of *Sola scriptura*, the Bible contains the direct, immediate, and freely accessible Word of God. Here we might also recall Augustine's

---

[45] *The History of the Troubles and Tryal of the Most Reverend Father in God and Blessed Martyr, William Laud* (London, 1695), X3v.

[46] John Calvin, *The Institution of Christian Religion*, trans. Thomas Norton, 2nd edn. (London, 1611), D4v, D5r, E1r (book 1, chap. 11).

conversion of faith as he perused a section from Paul's Epistle to the Romans: "At once, with the last words . . . , it was as if a light of relief from all anxiety flooded into my heart. All the shadows of doubt were dispelled."[47] Reformers during the Renaissance similarly insisted that, instead of turning to church authority or outward signs of faith, believers need only rely on the scriptures and their individual conscience for all matters related to salvation and holiness.

Yet claims for the transformative capability of language were not limited to sacred texts. Some secular ancient writers also emphasized a linguistic vitality that could emotionally and intellectually inspire authors and readers – although these writers, by stressing the visual capacity of language, once again seemed to privilege the image over the word. Quintilian, in *Institutio oratoria*, for example, includes "*vivid illustration*" or ὑπούυπωσις in his catalogue of the most powerful rhetorical figures.[48] This style of writing, Quintilian explains, can take various forms:

> There is . . . one form of vividness which consists in giving an actual word-picture of a scene, as in the passage beginning, "Forthwith each hero tiptoe stood erect" [*Aeneid* V.426]. Other details follow which give us such a picture of the boxers confronting each other for the fight, that it could not have been clearer had we been actual spectators . . . Is there anybody so incapable of forming a mental picture of a scene that . . . he does not seem not merely [*sic*] to see the actors in the scene, the place itself and their very dress, but even to imagine to himself other details that the orator does not describe?[49]

This explanation echoes Cicero's discussion of the rhetorical advantages of using verbal imagery, but Quintilian goes further as he highlights the emotional and imaginative absorption that could be inspired by vivid illustration or *enargeia*, as it is sometimes called. Ideally, readers will become so engaged in an intensely described passage that the object or gesture is reproduced before their eyes, and readers can then supplement the writer's portrayal and fill in any missing parts.[50]

In the Renaissance, Henry Peacham, the elder, similarly praised the use of verbal imagery in speeches because it could move listeners and prompt

---

[47] Augustine, *Confessions*, trans. Henry Chadwick (Oxford: Oxford University Press, 1998), VIII.29.

[48] Quintilian, *Institutio oratoria*, 4 vols., trans. H. E. Butler (Cambridge: Harvard University Press, 1959), IX.II.40 (vol. III, p. 397), VIII.III.61 (vol. III, pp. 244–45).

[49] Quintilian, *Institutio oratoria*, VIII.III.63–64 (vol. III, pp. 246–47).

[50] *Enargeia* should not be confused with the related but more specific figure *ekphrasis*, a type of "verbal pictorialism," as Claire Preston helpfully defines it, most often applied to descriptions of works of art but also used for images of landscapes, bodies, and artifacts. An ekphrasitic description – or *descriptio rei*: literally, "a description of the thing" – can be heavily or lightly detailed; typically, it

them to think. An orator, Peacham explains, should "expresse and set forth a thing so plainly and lively, that it seemeth rather painted in tables, then declared with words, and the mind of the hearer therby so drawen to an earnest and stedfast contemplation of the thing described, that he rather thinketh he seeth it then heareth it."[51] Peacham suggests that such images of external reality, by encouraging "contemplation," help the orator achieve an intelligible truth: an orator who "imitateth the cunning painter ... compoundeth as it were complexion with substance and life with countenance" so that the images in a speech "do not onely make a likely shew of life" but also express "the inward spirite and affection."[52]

Other ancient and early modern writers made even stronger claims in extolling the potency of verbal imagery to move beyond the physical world. Longinus in *On the Sublime*, for example, refers to the emotional impact of *enargeia*, as had Quintilian, but Longinus also emphasizes that such descriptions require a writer's spiritual engagement with the object or scene being described. Citing, among other examples, two passages depicting Furies from Euripides' works, he concludes that "Weight, grandeur, and urgency in writing are very largely produced ... by the use of 'visualizations' (*phantasiai*)" – that is, by "passages where, inspired by strong emotion, you seem to see what you describe and bring it vividly before the eyes of your audience."[53] Longinus then turns to Euripides' description of Phaethon's fatal chariot ride to illustrate the imaginative participation required of a writer who visualizes such things: "Would you not say that the writer's soul is aboard the car, and takes wing to share the horses' peril?"[54] Longinus proposes that an author's soulful engagement emotionally involves readers; a speech that includes such vibrant descriptions, he concludes, "not only convinces the audience, it positively masters them."[55]

Early modern treatises about writing reflect the influence of both Longinus and Horace as both writers' works became canonical texts widely used and cited by imitators ranging from Petrarch to Ben Jonson and George Sandys. In particular, Horace's formula that "A poem is like a picture,"

---

is a discrete passage that egregiously interrupts the narrative in order to demonstrate the poet's skill and ambition. See Claire Preston, "Ekphrasis: Painting in Words," in *Renaissance Figures of Speech*, ed. Sylvia Adamson, Gavin Alexander, and Katrin Ettenhuber (Cambridge: Cambridge University Press, 2007), pp. 115–29 (p. 117); and Murray Krieger, *Ekphrasis: The Illusion of the Natural Sign* (Baltimore: Johns Hopkins University Press, 1991), pp. 93–115.

[51] Henry Peacham, *The Garden of Eloquence*, 2nd edn. (London, 1593), T3v.
[52] Peacham, *The Garden of Eloquence*, T3v.
[53] Longinus, *On the Sublime*, trans. W. H. Fyfe, rev. Donald Russell, 2nd edn. (Cambridge: Harvard University Press, 2005), 15.1–2 (pp. 215–17).
[54] Longinus, *On the Sublime*, 15.4 (p. 219).
[55] Longinus, *On the Sublime*, 15.9 (p. 223).

stripped of its immediate rhetorical context, was applied loosely throughout the sixteenth and seventeenth centuries by English and continental critics who wished to substantiate a strong visual emphasis in poetry and rhetoric.[56] Published in the same year as *Paradise Lost* but written thirty years earlier in 1637, Charles Alphonse Du Fresony's *De Arte Graphica*, for example, became popular in England in the late seventeenth century and was translated into English by, among others, John Dryden (in 1695) and Daniel Defoe (in 1720). But while Du Fresony's Latin poem begins by positing a reciprocal relation between painting and poetry – "*Ut pictura poesis erit; similisque poesi / Sit pictura*" ("Let poetry be like painting; and let painting resemble poetry") – ultimately Du Fresony offers a fairly limited pictorial aesthetic.[57] He continues to hold up the representation of nature as the chief end of art and, by then concentrating on the resemblance between painting and natural perception, implies that the visual arts depict things more immediately and faithfully than language. As Murray Krieger has observed, Du Fresony also never explains how writing should, like painting, attempt to "imitate nature well."[58]

Yet, alongside such a conservative pictorial aesthetic – what commentators have come to call a natural sign theory[59] – other early modern writers, following Longinus, argued that words were not limited to natural signs and could thus better express complex, abstract ideas. Longinus' treatise, in particular, laid the groundwork for mimetic theorists in the Renaissance to reconcile poetry and painting but to reverse the privileged position of the material arts.[60] While poetry resembled painting in its ability to reproduce sensible objects and experience, poets were not restricted to imitating a finite external reality and could transcend nature by making the intelligible visible. As W. J. T. Mitchell notes, one of the fundamental assumptions behind arguments for the superiority of linguistic imagery was that nature is a "lower region" and thus natural signs can communicate "only a limited and relatively inferior sort of information."[61]

Philip Sidney in *The Defense of Poesy* probably attributes more power to poetic imagery than any of his English contemporaries. Following Julius

---

[56] Krieger, *Ekphrasis: The Illusion of the Natural Sign*, pp. 79–80.

[57] Charles Alphonse Du Fresony, *The Art of Painting [De Arte Graphica]*, trans. William Mason (York, 1783), lines 1–2 (A1r); and see Krieger, *Ekphrasis: The Illusion of the Natural Sign*, pp. 80–81.

[58] Krieger, *Ekphrasis: The Illusion of the Natural Sign*, p. 81. Krieger also discusses how Dryden's preface to Du Fresony's treatise does not explain in what ways writing should imitate visual art. See John Dryden, "A Parallel of Poetry and Painting," in *Essays of John Dryden*, ed. W. P. Ker, 2 vols. (Oxford: Clarendon, 1900), II: 115–53 (especially p. 136).

[59] See W. J. T. Mitchell, *Iconology: Image, Text, Ideology* (Chicago and London: University of Chicago Press, 1986), pp. 42–46, 60.

[60] Krieger, *Ekphrasis: The Illusion of the Natural Sign*, p. 120.

[61] Mitchell, *Iconology: Image, Text, Ideology*, p. 79.

Caesar Scaliger's insistence on the poet's superiority over the historian and philosopher, Sidney, too, argues that imaginative writing surpasses not just painting but all of the other language arts. Only a poet, he maintains, can create a "perfect picture" by bringing together an abstract idea with a specific example that appeals to the reader's intellect: "A perfect picture I say, for he yieldeth to the powers of the mind an image of that wherof the philosopher bestoweth but a wordish description, which doth neither strike, pierce, nor possess the sight of the soul so much as that other doth."[62] Here Sidney reinforces the ideal of classical *enargeia* as his specific language – "strike, pierce," and "possess" – indicates the almost rapturous effect of a vivid image.[63] Working presumably from Horace's formula and Aristotle's mimetic theory, Sidney more generally defines poetry as "an art of imitation," which he explains as "a representing, counterfeiting, or figuring forth – to speak metaphorically, a speaking picture – with this end, to teach and delight."[64] But instead of accepting Horace's sense of poetry's limitations, as Sidney's metaphor might imply, the *Defense* directly challenges the Socratic critique of artistic imitation and emphasizes that imaginative writers are not bound by nature. They can thus achieve expressions that transcend the finitude of mimesis:

> Only the poet, disdaining to be tied to any such subjection, lifted up with the vigor of his own invention, doth grow in effect into another nature, in making things either better than Nature bringeth forth, or, quite anew, forms such as never were in Nature, as the Heroes, Demigods, Cyclops, Chimeras, Furies, and such like: so as he goeth hand in hand with Nature, not enclosed within the narrow warrant of her gifts, but freely ranging only within the zodiac of his own wit.[65]

That Sidney in this passage still says a poet "goeth hand in hand with Nature" suggests the need for imaginative writers to draw from their experiences. But clearly Sidney believed that poets should not be restricted by reality – as he puts it, "not enclosed within the narrow warrant of her gifts." Instead, he echoes Longinus' emphasis on authorial inspiration and

[62] Philip Sidney, *An Apology for Poetry* or *The Defence of Poesy*, ed. Geoffrey Shepherd, rev. R. W. Maslen, 3rd edn. (Manchester and New York: Manchester University Press, 1989), p. 90.

[63] George Puttenham, in *The Art of Poesy* (1589), also addresses *enargeia*. But, while he explains that this device "giveth a glorious luster and light" and acknowledges that the term derives from the Greek word for "bright" (*argos*), he idiosyncratically converts *enargeia* into an aural – as opposed to visual – figure, one that aims "to satisfy and delight the ear only by a goodly outward show set upon the matter with words and speeches smoothly and tunably running." See Puttenham, *The Art of English Poesy*, ed. Frank Whigham and Wayne A. Rebhorn (Ithaca and London: Cornell University Press, 2007), p. 227.

[64] Sidney, *An Apology for Poetry* or *The Defence of Poesy*, p. 86.

[65] Sidney, *An Apology for Poetry* or *The Defence of Poesy*, p. 85.

draws on the idea of the artist as emulating nature's creative process, an idea which had emerged in the Renaissance under Neoplatonic influence. Creative writers, according to Sidney, are limited only by their "own invention" and "wit," and must "lift up" and "grow" what they perceive in the natural world.

In the case of *Paradise Lost*, I would not insist that Milton consciously followed a specific poetic theory in imagining the epic's actions, scenes, and characters. But by piecing together the poem's broader aesthetic and rhetorical context, we can appreciate how Milton's visual depictions work. Most often, his method seems in accord with Quintilian's and Longinus' ideas about vivid illustrations: Milton expresses the conceptual scenes and characters that his epic subject requires by incorporating striking visual details that invite readers to imagine what he describes and to fill in the missing parts. More generally, Longinus' idea of the sublime, as David Norbrook has argued, would have suited Milton poetically and politically in its opposition to smooth-sounding harmony and easy resolution.[66] But that Longinus specifically praised "things so widely different ... by a strange artifice brought together" so as to "advance Eloquence and render it illustrious" might describe how Milton used ideas and objects from his contemporary culture to illustrate his supernatural subject.[67] Again and again, *Paradise Lost* engages readers through such evocative visual details. So Milton includes a brief but arresting image as Satan in Hell addresses his fallen compatriots: "Seest thou yon dreary plain, forlorn and wild, / The seat of desolation, void of light, / Save what the glimmering of these livid flames / Casts pale and dreadful?" (I.180–83). Or, when Adam and Eve leave Paradise "hand in hand with wand'ring steps and slow" (XII.648), Milton enhances the powerful image of the couple's departure with yet another visual passage, this one analogously as the good angels come to guard the eastern gate: "all in bright array / The Cherubim descended; on the ground / Gliding meteorous, as ev'ning mist / Ris'n from a river o're the marish glides, / And gathers ground fast at the laborer's heel / Homeward returning" (XII.627–32). In each of these instances – as we might anticipate of a narrative that takes place in heaven, hell, chaos, and Paradise – Milton does not adhere to a strict natural sign theory – the false expectation, I think, behind Johnson's and Eliot's

---

[66] David Norbrook, *Writing the English Republic: Poetry, Rhetoric and Politics, 1627–1660* (Cambridge: Cambridge University Press, 1999), p. 138. Norbrook argues that the sublime had a "distinctly republican accent" in the seventeenth century (p. 137).

[67] Here, following Norbrook, I am quoting the translation of Longinus by Milton's friend and disciple, John Hall: *Peri Hypsous, or Dionysius Longinus of the Height of Eloquence*, 2nd edn. (London, 1652), D3v, D3r. Cf. Fyfe's translation in Longinus, *On the Sublime*, 10.3 (p. 201).

critiques of the epic's imagery. Instead, Milton blends concrete and abstract details so as to form in readers' minds what Phyllis MacKenzie called "an unforgettable picture which the physical eye could never see."[68] Milton, as the following chapters will show, turns repeatedly to the natural world for his descriptions, but he then aspires to transcend the real by combining it with the mythic and imaginary.

Like angel, like author

Within *Paradise Lost*, Milton dramatizes the difficulty of his narrative endeavor through the angel Raphael. Attempting to describe the war in heaven and explain his life as a spiritual being, Raphael wonders whether he can communicate in a language that Adam and Eve will comprehend: "how shall I relate / To human sense th' invisible exploits / Of warring spirits" and "how . . . unfold / The secrets of another world, perhaps / Not lawful to reveal?" (V.564–66, 568–70). The imagistic approach that the angel settles on reveals Milton's own poetic strategy: "what surmounts the reach / Of human sense, I shall delineate so, / By lik'ning spiritual to corporal forms, / As may express them best" (V.571–74). Milton in *Paradise Lost* similarly turns to the corporeal to depict "invisible exploits" that transpire in hell, heaven, and Paradise. The theological doctrine behind such a poetics is called *accommodation* – that is, the translation of infinite truths for a finite understanding through anthropomorphism and anthro-popathy. As with Longinus' claims about the efficacy and affect of visual images, the theory of accommodation holds out the possibility that inspired language, transcending the literal and figurative, can express a higher reality and make the invisible visible.[69]

Milton discusses the doctrine of accommodation in *De Doctrina Christiana* as he emphasizes God's unknowableness – "When we talk about knowing God, it must be understood in terms of man's limited

---

[68] Phyllis MacKenzie, "Milton's Visual Imagination: An Answer to T. S. Eliot," *University of Toronto Quarterly* 16 (1946–1947): 17–29 (p. 22).

[69] Writing about Raphael's accommodating language in *Paradise Lost*, N. K. Sugimura seems to mistake the acknowledgment of the doctrine's limitations as an indication of its failure. She repeatedly suggests that Raphael's analogies and images are "self-destructive" (p. 221) because they are not literally true and thus, instead of explaining the similarity between angels and humans, they merely "confirm the initial separation" (p. 198). Yet missing from such an assessment is the understanding that accommodating language by definition is always inadequate literally and depends on a prophetic speaker to convey something greater than what mere words express. Once again, accommodation aspires to transcend the literal and figurative and to communicate a higher reality through inspired language. Thus, as Sugimura ultimately concedes, the type of imagery deployed by Raphael and Milton is essential for conveying the epic's subject even as the material images necessarily fall short of the divine: "Meaning itself may defy definition (as does

powers of comprehension" (*CPW* VI: 133). Yet, he accepts the authority of scriptural passages that depict God in human terms. Milton observes, for example, that God in the Bible endures grief (Gen. 6:6), feels refreshed (Exod. 31:17), and experiences fear (Deut. 32:27). He concludes that we should not hesitate to accept such human-sounding qualities if God assigns them to himself, but we should not assume that such emotions are the same for human beings as they are for the Divine: "what is imperfect and weak in us is, when ascribed to God, utterly perfect and utterly beautiful" (*CPW* VI: 136). Milton's was thus a limited theory of accommodation, no doubt stemming from his underlying belief in the sufficiency of Scripture, and he adamantly objects to efforts by exegetes to assign additional human qualities to God to make the Divine easier to understand. God in the Bible might at times condescend to make himself conceivable to us, but "he has brought himself down to our level expressly to prevent our being carried beyond the reach of human comprehension, and outside the written authority of scripture, into vague subtleties of speculation" (*CPW* VI: 133–34).

Many of the accommodating poetic forms in Milton's verse can be traced back to the scriptures themselves or, as various commentaries have observed, to literary works by Milton's predecessors or contemporaries. One of this book's central claims is that Milton also imbues his biblical and poetic sources with details from his own contemporary culture – what Johnson presumably meant when he referred to the relation between the epic's imagery and Milton's own "immediate observation." Johnson, as we have seen, asserted that this latter element was missing in *Paradise Lost*, but I wish to show, on the contrary, that Milton sometimes uses his and his readers' experience of seventeenth-century London to tell the story of the Fall, just as Raphael appeals to Adam and Eve's experience in the garden to render the invisible visible.

Another quality of Milton's epic imagery that I emphasize in several of the following chapters concerns his theory of matter. Part of what makes Milton's (and thus Raphael's) poetic method so powerful is that physical reality – that is, the objects and gestures depicted in *Paradise Lost* – cannot be treated as merely material but always includes spiritual potential. While Milton, as we have seen, insisted on the separation of external worship and spiritual truth in his opposition to Laudian ritual, by the time he wrote

God), but the tenor still needs its vehicle" (p. 229). See Sugimura, *"Matter of Glorious Trial": Spiritual and Material Substance in "Paradise Lost"* (New Haven and London: Yale University Press, 2009). For a corrective overview of the scholarly debate about accommodation and prophetic insight, especially in relation to the depiction of angels, see Joad Raymond, *Milton's Angels: The Early-Modern Imagination* (Oxford: Oxford University Press, 2010), pp. 162–88.

Paradise Lost he had come to espouse a heterodox concept of matter that stressed the continuity of the material and spiritual. Rejecting the centuries of Christian tradition that supported a dichotomous view of existence, he adopted instead a monistic ontology; that is, he believed that God created everything from the same substance – "one first matter all," as Raphael succinctly states in *Paradise Lost*, "Endued with various forms, various degrees / Of substance, and in things that live, of life" (V.472–74).[70] This account allows Milton to articulate how the material cause of creation ("one first matter") comes from God, but all created beings are still separate from God's essence. Or, as Raphael puts it at the start of his reply to Adam, "one Almighty is, from whom / All things proceed," yet all things will "up to him return" only "If not depraved from good" (V.469–71). Here the words "If not depraved from good" point up the implications of Milton's monism: this conditional phrase indicates that "first matter" is inherently good, but individual beings must freely preserve that goodness.[71]

Raphael goes on to introduce a metaphor of a plant to explain more fully the epic's ontology. Like the parts of a flower, God's creations are "more refined, more spiritous, and pure, / As nearer to him placed" (V.475–76): the least refined creations resemble a plant's roots, while more spiritous creations correspond to the green stalk, even more spiritous creations correspond to the leaves, and so on. The continuum of nature that Raphael posits helps to clarify the relationship that Milton envisions between angels and humans: angels resemble humans in some ways – both, for example, have shapes, eat, and blush – but angels are incorporeal, "more spiritous, and pure" than their earthly counterparts. Whereas humans rely on discursive knowledge, angels more often use intuition; and whereas Adam and Eve enjoy a loving physical relationship, angels have a more spiritual sex life.[72] Raphael thus sums up the similarity and separateness of angels and humans, "Differing but in degree, of kind the same" (V.490).

Most immediately, Raphael offers his plant comparison in an attempt to explain how he can "convert ... / To proper substance" Adam and Eve's "earthly fruits" (V.492–93, 464) and how the couple can similarly transform

---

[70] Phillip J. Donnelly contends that Milton's monism is "implicit in the biblical narrative" and thus does not actually represent a radical departure from the Bible. See Donnelly, "'Matter' versus Body: The Character of Milton's Monism," *Milton Quarterly* 33.3 (1999): 79–85 (p. 82).

[71] Phillip J. Donnelly, *Milton's Scriptural Reasoning: Narrative and Protestant Toleration* (Cambridge: Cambridge University Press, 2009), p. 93.

[72] As Raphael shyly explains, "Whatever pure thou in the body enjoy'st / ... we enjoy / In eminence, and obstacle find none / Of membrane, joint, or limb, exclusive bars: / Easier than air with air, if spirits embrace, / Total they mix, union of pure with pure / Desiring; nor restrained conveyance need / As flesh to mix with flesh, or soul with soul" (VIII.622–29).

their own material "nourishment" into "vital spirits" that enable motion and thought (V.483, 484). But the dynamic nature of Raphael's metaphor also applies more generally to all of God's creations, who can rise or descend on the "scale of nature" based on their moral choices (V.509). Just as human beings or angels can turn their physical food into sustenance, so in the hierarchy of existence God's creations can, within limits, improve (or decline) in their material form, "Till body up to spirit work, in bounds / Proportioned to each kind" (V.478–79). Raphael accordingly raises the possibility that Adam and Eve will one day ascend to heaven if they remain faithful to God: "from these corporal nutriments perhaps / Your bodies may at last turn all to spirit, / Improved by tract of time, and winged ascend / Ethereal" (V.496–99). Conversely, as I argue in chapters 4 and 5 when Satan and his followers rebel and turn away from God, they become less spiritous and pure through their depravity – "now gross by sinning grown," as Raphael explains (VI.661).

Milton's *De Doctrina Christiana* more plainly explains the material and spiritual implications for human beings of the angel's account of creation *ex deo*. Humankind, Milton writes, "is not double or separable: not, as is commonly thought, produced from and composed of two different and distinct elements, soul and body. On the contrary, the whole man is the soul, and the soul the man: a body, in other words, or individual substance, animated, sensitive, and rational" (*CPW* VI: 318). Milton thus distinguishes between body and soul, but insists on their inseparability within each person – a crucial point to which I return in the examination of Adam and Eve's hand-holding and hair in, respectively, chapters 6 and 7. We can trace this inseparability to the common origin of spirit and matter that Raphael describes and the paradox of conjunction and distinction that Raphael's account of "one first matter" implies for the relation between God and all created beings.

In offering this explanation of Milton's ontology, I am indebted to Stephen Fallon's ground-breaking study of the poet's monism. Answering Johnson's charges against the war in heaven in *Paradise Lost*, Fallon illustrated how all creation in Milton's epic derives from a single, dynamic substance; as Fallon puts it, matter is "merely more gross and less vital spirit," a metaphysical premise that allows for the depiction of both spiritual and corporeal beings.[73] In particular for my purposes, Fallon's analysis of Milton's angels serves as the starting point for the discussion of Satan and his followers in chapters 4 and 5. But whereas Fallon argued that Milton ingeniously facilitated the narrative action of the war in heaven by

---

[73] Stephen M. Fallon, *Milton among the Philosophers* (Ithaca: Cornell University Press, 1991), p. 102.

endowing angels with "subtle material bodies," I propose that even Milton's bad angels remain incorporeal but are falling into materiality, as expressed in both Satan's reliance on physical things and images of the rebels' still changing appearance.[74]

I have also benefited from more recent work on Milton's ontology by Phillip Donnelly and N. K. Sugimura, both of whom offer qualifications for parts of Fallon's argument. Donnelly, for example, helpfully distinguishes between Raphael's reference to "first matter" and its possible corporeal forms. As Donnelly explains, both spiritual and corporeal beings in *Paradise Lost* "consist of that first matter (as it is endued with form)," but they "are differentiated out of the one first matter." Thus, the original creative substance is not exactly the same as either spiritual or corporeal substance.[75] Sugimura has gone further, rejecting what she calls Fallon's "monist rarefaction model" and asserting that Milton's use of "first matter" is "not straightforwardly material."[76] When Raphael refers to "one first matter all," Sugimura argues, the angel cannot mean something entirely material because, according to Raphael's explanation, it is "a mysterious substrate" – she also calls it "formless and characterless stuff" and a "strange force field" – that possesses "a power all its own to translate and transform."[77]

But, regardless of whether one accepts Fallon's reading of a gradually rarefying material as the basis for all of God's creation (as I do), or Sugimura's claim that the plant metaphor Raphael uses to explain creation is "implicitly dualist," both interpretations emphasize (in Sugimura's words) the "continuity between ... material and spiritual substance" in *Paradise Lost*.[78] Whereas Fallon acknowledges that Milton in places "struggles ... to articulate monism with a vocabulary tempered by centuries of dualism," Sugimura suggests that Milton's epic pits "various philosophical ideas in conflict with one another."[79] And whereas Fallon offers a cohesive reading as he describes a gradual scale of density and rarefaction of God's

---

[74] Fallon, *Milton among the Philosophers*, p. 145.

[75] Donnelly, "'Matter' versus Body," p. 83.

[76] Sugimura, *"Matter of Glorious Trial,"* pp. 50, 43. To make this case, Sugimura pursues what she judges to be "fluid intermediaries" in Milton's explanation of his concept of matter, so that, for example, she concedes "the overriding monist tenor" of Raphael's plant metaphor and admits that Fallon's reading is "indeed confirmed by Raphael's process of 'thinned out' materiality." But she insists that Fallon's model is "shattered" by the subsequent reference to "reason" as "her [the soul's] being" (V.487), which means, she proposes, that the soul is non-material and thus implies a latent dualism. By comparison, Fallon reads the soul in these lines as a more rarefied form of the originative matter: he reads "soul" as synonymous with "intellectual spirits" and thereby "save[s] the coherence of this passage." See Sugimura, *"Matter of Glorious Trial,"* pp. xvii, 44, 50; and Fallon, *Milton among the Philosophers*, pp. 102–05.

[77] Sugimura, *"Matter of Glorious Trial,"* pp. 52, 44, 54.

[78] Sugimura, *"Matter of Glorious Trial,"* pp. 126, 54.

"first matter," Sugimura seeks out passages that seem to resist such an overarching materialist explanation. She accepts that earthly substance can become spiritual substance in Milton's epic, but she ultimately finds the poetic description of this transformation "mysterious."[80]

It is the underlying dynamic unity – whether physical (Fallon) or irreducibly mystical (Sugimura) – that, I think, informs Milton's imagery and that I return to in the following chapters. That the cosmos depicted in *Paradise Lost* has symbolic meaning may be a commonplace of Christian theology, but Milton's theory of matter provides a philosophical foundation for reading the epic's images as representations of things that are inseparably both material and spiritual. In this book, I accordingly focus on the spiritual implications of his depiction of material reality, especially as the epic's imagery is, as Sugimura also emphasizes, necessarily enriched by Milton's dense and subtle poetic style.[81]

That Milton refers to Adam and Eve themselves as *images* helps to illustrate the dynamic unity of the physical and spiritual in the poem's various material forms.[82] Even as Milton's diction was shaped by the language of scripture, the repetition of *image* in *Paradise Lost* neatly expresses the couple's inseparably material and non-material nature: *image* during the early modern period could mean both an abstract "idea" or "conception" and a physical "semblance" or "likeness."[83] When accordingly God compliments Adam for requesting a mate and "Expressing well the spirit within thee free, / My image, not imparted to the brute" (VIII.440–41), *image* is likely a synonym for Adam's inner "spirit," which God did not impart to animals. But *image* could just as well refer to Adam as a man, a noun in direct address modified by the participial phrase "Expressing well" (with "not imparted to the brute" still modifying man's free inner "spirit"). Similarly, Raphael remembers how God told the Son, "'Let us make now man in our image, man / In our similitude'" (VII.519–20), and, closely following Genesis 1:27, the angel goes on to explain to Adam that God

> formed thee, Adam, thee O man
> Dust of the ground, and in thy nostrils breathed
> The breath of life; in his own image he

[79] Fallon, *Milton among the Philosophers*, p. 102; Sugimura, *"Matter of Glorious Trial,"* p. xvi.

[80] Fallon, *Milton among the Philosophers*, p. 80; Sugimura, *"Matter of Glorious Trial,"* p. 54.

[81] Sugimura, *"Matter of Glorious Trial,"* p. xvii.

[82] Or, as Donnelly usefully puts this idea, "corporeal reality" in the epic is repeatedly "subsumed within spiritual reality." Donnelly, *Milton's Scriptural Reasoning*, p. 63.

[83] *OED*, s. v. "image," defs. 5a, 2a. In *Tetrachordon*, Milton explains that he thinks the phrase "Image of God" in Genesis means "Wisdom, Purity, Justice, and rule over all creatures" (*CPW* II: 587).

> Created thee, in the image of God
> Express, and thou becam'st a living soul.   (VII.524–28)

In all such passages, *image* remains meaningfully equivocal, referring to potentially both humanity's physical likeness and spiritual resemblance, to both an outward appearance and an inward state. Given that God mostly stays out of sight in *Paradise Lost* – sitting invisibly in the "pure empyrean . . . / High throned above all highth" (III.57–58), as I discuss in chapter 2 – we might hesitate to assign physical significance to the word *image* in such contexts, but Milton's God, while ultimately unknowable, is not all spirit: as the origin of the epic's monist universe, he is also the material cause of creation and contains "dark materials" (II.916) and "Matter unformed and void" (VII.233). As Milton reasons in *De Doctrina Christiana*, God must at least possess "bodily force in his own substance, for no one can give something he has not got" (*CPW* VI:309). Moreover, following the early theologian Chrysostom, Milton in the above passage clearly describes a two-step creation for Adam – body first, then spirit – which further obscures the subsequent use of "image": it seems to encompass both stages of Adam's creation, both his physical and spiritual selves.[84]

The details that Eve recollects about her creation also suggest the importance of Milton's explanation of the spiritual and material for interpreting the epic's visual imagery. In one of the poem's best known scenes, she is initially attracted to her own "shape" reflected in the "wat'ry gleam," until a voice informs her that she is gazing at herself and promises to bring her to one "Whose image thou art" (IV.461, 472). Here Milton contrasts the physicality of "shape" with the more ontologically inclusive meaning of "image": whereas the water's rippling surface physically presents only a single, superficial vision, Eve and Adam share both a physical and spiritual bond, and together, as the voice explains, will ultimately create innumerable other images, "Multitudes like thyself" (IV.474).[85]

---

[84] In like manner, when Satan first spies the couple, we are told that Adam and Eve "In naked majesty seemed lords of all, / And worthy seemed, for in their looks divine / The image of their glorious Maker shone, / Truth, wisdom, sanctitude severe and pure, / Severe but in true filial freedom placed" (IV.290–94). *Image* in this context sounds like a physical resemblance between creator and created, but the subsequent list of virtues – "Truth, wisdom, sanctitude severe and pure" – suggests God and humankind's spiritual similarity. As W. J. T. Mitchell has observed, the meaning of "looks" here also seems equivocal, referring to either the couple's outward appearance or the "quality of their gazes, the character of their 'expressions.'" See Mitchell, *Iconology: Image, Text, Ideology*, p. 36.

Such an account of Eve's creation resonates in various ways throughout the epic, but on one level it helps to clarify the choice that Milton himself faced: we can understand the episode as dramatizing the rejection of a natural sign theory (as symbolized by Eve's rejection of her superficial reflection) in favor of a transformative imagistic tradition (as represented by Eve and Adam's physical and spiritual marriage).[86] Just as Milton in *Paradise Lost* does not seek to represent the natural world as in a mirror but instead pursues visual imagery that also expresses intelligible truths through inspired language, so Eve is led by a divine voice, walks away from her watery shape, and chooses instead the more profound and productive nuptial bond that the material and non-material senses of "image" convey. As Adam will later articulate, Eve's status as his image means that the couple has a deep and intimate connection, "one flesh, one heart, one soul" (VIII.499).

"Fruit of fairest colors mixed"

To take another, more extended example: we can appreciate the impact of both Milton's personal experience and material philosophy for the epic's visualizations by comparing apples to, well, apples. Milton says little about the appearance of the fruit that Adam and Eve are forbidden to taste or touch. We read repeatedly that the Tree of Knowledge and its fruit are "fair" (for example, IX.661, 777, 798, 972, 996), a description that punningly suggests both the fruit's beauty and God's justice. Milton also emphasizes the fruit's appealing appearance in the temptation scenes. As the serpent seduces Eve, "Fixed on the fruit she gazed, which to behold / Might tempt alone" (IX.735–36), and earlier, when Satan approaches Eve in her sleep, we learn that the fruit looked enticing: Eve recollects that it seemed "fair . . . / Much fairer to my fancy than by day," which also suggests that in her dream she imaginatively enhanced the fruit's physical appeal (V.52–53).

Yet Milton adds few other visual details about the Tree of Knowledge, and readers are left to wonder exactly what the fruit looks like. If, as Karen

---

[85] As Donnelly also notes, the category of "carnal" for Milton referred to "a condition of the whole person" and not just to the body (p. 65). Donnelly examines Milton's different uses of "inward" and "outward" in relation to his view of religious toleration, and concludes that the terms do not imply a dualist ontology. Milton instead distinguishes between brute outward force, which he condemns, and verbal persuasion, which he condones and allies with inward prompting. See Donnelly, *Milton's Scriptural Reasoning*, pp. 65–69.

[86] That Eve later refers to her shape as a "smooth wat'ry image" (IV.480) might seem to complicate the distinction I'm drawing, but the specific qualifiers of "smooth" and "watery" still emphasize the reflection's ontologically inferior status: it is superficial and fragile.

Edwards has shown, Milton in *Paradise Lost* "consistently uses botanical terms with precision and care," then the lack of information about the poem's central natural object seems significant.[87] Again and again, he tacks from sight to smell, as if deflecting questions about the tree's appearance, first as Eve's attention shifts from the fruit's beauty to its "pleasant savory smell" that "quickened appetite" (V.84, 85), and later as Adam notices the "fairest fruit" and almost simultaneously discerns its "ambrosial smell" (IX.851, 852). Perhaps most remarkably, when Satan leads Eve to the Tree of Knowledge, not only does the fruit's appearance attract her gaze, but also "An eager appetite, raised by the smell / So savory of that fruit, which with desire, / Inclinable now grown to touch or taste, / Solicited her longing eye" (IX.740–43). Here the fruit's aroma provokes a gustatory and tactile desire that then appeals to Eve visually, a synesthetic description that recalls the plant metaphor Raphael uses to illustrate creation *ex deo*. Just as Raphael explains that a plant's "green stalk" consists of the same "first matter" as the "Spirits odorous" that the "bright consummate flow'r" breathes (V.480–82, 472), so Milton, by mixing the forbidden fruit's visual, tactile, and olfactory qualities, suggests the dynamic relation between all of its sensual properties.

But while the conflation of the fruit's physical traits may help to account for the lack of specifically visual information that Milton provides about the Tree of Knowledge, we also need to consider that Milton's reticence might itself be purposeful. If we return to Eve's perception that the fruit seems "Much fairer to my fancy than by day" (V.53), her comparison could suggest Milton's own poetic method, as he appeals to his fit readers to imagine, like Eve, a fruit more beautiful than any they had ever seen. Why should we need to know more? As William Poole has shown, early modern interpretations of the story of Genesis were overwhelmingly literal.[88] But within the narrative, the Tree of Knowledge is symbolic – "The pledge of thy obedience and thy faith," as God pronounces to Adam (VIII.325) – and so specific details about the fruit's physical appearance are superfluous. The point is not even the type of fruit, but that God has forbidden Adam and Eve to taste or touch it. The prohibition allows God to measure Adam and Eve's obedience; the prohibition matters, not the specific thing that God has prohibited.

Only Satan in his fallenness, as critics have long observed, refers to the fruit on the Tree of Knowledge as apples. Twice he uses this specific name:

---

[87] Karen L. Edwards, *Milton and the Natural World: Science and Poetry in "Paradise Lost"* (Cambridge: Cambridge University Press, 1999), p. 145.

[88] William Poole, *Milton and the Idea of the Fall* (Cambridge: Cambridge University Press, 2005), p. 68.

first as he tempts Eve in the form of the serpent ("tasting those fair apples, I resolved / Not to defer," IX.585–86) and later in Hell as he exults over his success ("him by fraud I have seduced / From his Creator, and the more to increase / Your wonder, with an apple," X.485–87). In both of these instances, Satan's naming of the fruit could punningly reveal his ill intent: because the classical Latin word *malum* signifies both "apple" and "evil," a post-biblical tradition emerged identifying the forbidden fruit as such.

But that only Satan calls the fruit apples also indicates the arch-fiend's material debasement: he reduces the evocative and unique *fruit* to a specific thing – an apple – and, especially when he uses the name a second time, he has so fully sundered the physical from the spiritual that he seems to misunderstand the Tree's symbolic power. He concludes his announcement in Hell with the mundanity of *apple*, holding it out like a punch line to amplify the magnitude of his success: "and the more to increase / Your wonder, with an apple" (X.486–87). Even if we suppose that *apple* in this passage need not refer to a specific fruit and signifies, more generally, "any of various fruits (and vegetables), esp. those thought to resemble the apple," this latter meaning would still set physical limits on the Tree of Knowledge.[89] In contrast, all of the other references in *Paradise Lost*, like those in the Bible and Talmud, emphasize the Tree's symbolic significance by leaving uncertain the type of fruit that Adam and Eve consumed (the Talmud, for example, identifies it variously as grapes, figs, or wheat).[90]

Satan's ontologically diminished perspective also finds expression in the detail with which he describes the Tree of Knowledge. He does not just name the fruit, but also provides the most complete account of its visual appearance, as if to suggest that he can no longer see or think beyond a superficial physical reality:

> A goodly tree far distant to behold
> Loaden with fruit of fairest colors mixed,
> Ruddy and gold: I nearer drew to gaze;
> When from the boughs a savory odor blown,
> Grateful to appetite, more pleased my sense
> Than smell of sweetest fennel or the teats
> Of ewe or goat dropping with milk at ev'n,
> Unsucked of lamb or kid, that tend their play.   (IX.576–83)

Here again Milton adheres to the epic's monistic premise and combines the fruit's appearance and aroma so that "fruit of fairest colors mixed" quickly

---

[89] *OED*, s. v. "apple," def. I.2a.

[90] On Rabbinical attempts to determine what species of fruit Adam and Eve were forbidden to eat, see J. M. Evans, *"Paradise Lost" and the Genesis Tradition* (Oxford: Clarendon, 1968), pp. 45–46.

merges with "a savory odor blown." Satan allies the fruit's fair coloring with smells of wholesome nourishment.[91] Yet the specific detail that Satan offers of the fruit's mixed coloring has troubled commentators for its apparent unreality. As early as 1753, Joseph Warton cited Milton's reference to gold fruit among the epic's indefensible descriptions. Neither beautiful nor accurate, according to Warton, it would "only please those who, when they read, exercise no faculty but fancy, and admire because they do not think."[92] Centuries later, critics continued to object to such strange fruit: T. S. Eliot dismissed the details of Adam and Eve's surroundings as among the epic's least visual and thus least enjoyable passages; A. Bartlett Giamatti found "something sinister in the idea of 'vegetable Gold,' something unnatural and unhealthy"; G. Stanley Koehler complained of a "suspicious complexity" in the fruit's mixture of red and yellow; F. R. Leavis emphasized Eden's gold fruit to show that Milton's poetry is "incompatible with sharp, concrete realization"; and Leland Ryken proposed that the two adjectives are not colors but instead convey a "visual" quality and a "textural hardness of surface."[93] Ryken concluded that the gold fruit belongs among what he calls "mystic" oxymora – that is, images "whose contradiction is real and cannot be resolved in terms of ordinary experience."[94]

But if we apply Occam's razor and look for the simplest and most elegant explanation, it is exactly Milton's ordinary experience that, I think, helps to resolve Satan's account of the Tree of Knowledge. The description of the fruit that Adam and Eve consume is noteworthy, not because it seems unnatural or complex, as its detractors maintain, but because, on the contrary, it sounds so normal. As Roland Frye has shown, golden flowers, fruits, and vegetables were portrayed widely in early

---

[91] Edwards, *Milton and the Natural World*, adds that serpents, according to ancient lore, loved fennel and milk from the teat (p. 146).

[92] Joseph Warton, letter, *Adventurer* 101 (23 October 1753), rpt. in *Milton: The Critical Heritage*, ed. John T. Shawcross, 2 vols. (New York: Barnes and Noble, 1970; London and Boston: Routledge and Kegan Paul, 1972), II: 226–30 (p. 227).

[93] Eliot, "Milton I [1936]," p. 162; A. Bartlett Giamatti, *The Earthly Paradise and the Renaissance Epic* (Princeton: Princeton University Press, 1966), p. 308; G. Stanley Koehler, "Milton's Use of Light and Color," *Milton Studies* 3 (1971): 55–81 (p. 60); Leavis, *Revaluation*, p. 50; and Ryken, *The Apocalyptic Vision in "Paradise Lost,"* p. 87.

[94] Ryken, *The Apocalyptic Vision in "Paradise Lost,"* p. 88. The image of gold-and-red fruit in *Paradise Lost* has found defenders, most notably Alastair Fowler who tried to smooth out the apparently inconsistent coloring by suggesting that "gold used often to be *ruddy*." Certainly in Latin *luteus* could represent both shades; editors of Milton's Latin poem *Mansus*, for example, variously translate the reference to "lutea mala" (line 39) as "yellow," "red," "rosy," and "flame-colored." Yet, *pace* Fowler, the use of "mixed" in the passage from *Paradise Lost* indicates that the fruit's two colors are not the same. The English word *gold* during the early modern period referred more narrowly to a "bright golden yellow" or "a beautiful yellow color," whereas *ruddy* designated a "red," "reddish," or "rosy" hue. See Fowler, p. 503; and *OED*, s. v. "gold," defs. 1 and 5, and "red," defs. A and B.

Christian art and Renaissance paintings. Frye also points out that *pomidoro*, the Italian word for tomato, literally means "apple of gold," and, more immediately, when Milton attended Christ's College in Cambridge, he would have daily seen the ornate heraldic carving with gold-painted fruit above the doorway to the Master's Lodge.[95]

I would add that Milton could have also been drawing on his firsthand knowledge of nature, which may have been surprisingly richer than a modern reader's experience in the produce section of a supermarket. By the end of the sixteenth century, more than 120 varieties of apples were being raised in Europe, and the new varieties, aided by improved methods of storage and horticulture, meant that apples were available in England for about ten months out of the year, from late July until the end of the following spring.[96] When Charles I purchased Wimbledon Manor for Henrietta Maria in 1639, he commissioned his gardener, John Tradescant the Younger, to design and create extravagant gardens, which ultimately contained a ten-acre orchard and over 1,000 fruit trees with more than 150 kinds of pears and apples.[97] Charles II's administration also invested heavily in orchards: when the manufacture of cloth became less profitable after the civil wars, owners of commercial gardens found that apples, able to thrive in most counties in England, provided a reliable alternative source of revenue.

In *Paradisi in Sole* (1656) the English herbalist John Parkinson lists more than sixty varieties of apples that he thought worth cultivating, of which only three were not then grown in England. Parkinson describes apples of a wide range of shades and colors – "red," "Russet," "green," "greenish," "yellowish green," "yellow," "Golding," "whitish," "spotted," and, no doubt most striking, "black sooty."[98] He also mentions apples containing mixed colors that specifically recall Satan's account of the forbidden fruit in *Paradise Lost*, such as the "Marligo," which Parkinson describes as "a middle sized apple, very yellow on the outside, shadowed over as it were with red, and more red on one side."[99]

---

[95] Frye, *Milton's Imagery and the Visual Arts*, pp. 252–53. We also cannot dismiss the fruit's coloring as mere satanic invention. In four other passages, Milton's narrator similarly refers to vegetables as "gold" or "golden" to convey the bounty of Paradise: "Blossoms and fruits at once of golden hue" (IV.148), "fruit / Of vegetable gold" (IV.219–20), "fruit burnished with golden rind" (IV.249), and flowers "specked with gold" (IX.429).

[96] Joan Morgan and Alison Richards, *The Book of Apples* (London: Ebury, 1993), pp. 46, 48; and Joan Thirsk, *Food in Early Modern England: Phases, Fads, Fashions 1500–1760* (London: Hambledon Continuum, 2007), p. 300.

[97] *Parliamentary Survey of Wimbledon* [Nov. 1649], in Evelyn Cecil, *A History of Gardening*, 2nd edn. (London: Bernard Quaritch, 1896), pp. 315–27 (p. 323).

[98] John Parkinson, *Paradisi in Sole* (London, 1656), Ccc6r-v.

Knowledge of these various apples was not restricted to specialists during the sixteenth and seventeenth centuries. Most notably, miniature apple trees bearing gold-colored fruit were popular in private gardens throughout Europe; these so-called Paradise trees were most commonly planted in Stuart England along walks or set in pots on balconies or around ornamental flower beds.[100] The custom of holding lavish outdoor feasts in both royal and private gardens, despite the vagaries of English weather, would have also brought people in contact with various types of fruit trees: some estate owners had separate banqueting houses constructed, to which dinner guests would retire after the meal to enjoy fruit and sweet wines with a view of the surrounding orchards. Most famously, of course, in the year before *Paradise Lost* was published, Isaac Newton recounted how he had been drinking tea "under the shade of some appletrees" in his mother's garden when "the notion of gravitation came into his mind."[101]

And if during the civil wars significant collections of fruit trees were established by disenfranchised royalists, such as Thomas Hanmer, who retreated to their country estates literally to cultivate their own gardens, we should also note that supporters of commonwealth encouraged improved planting practices during the same period. Milton's friend Samuel Hartlib, working on behalf of the Interregnum government, published in 1652 *A Designe for Plentie*, which called on all landowners to cultivate fruit trees in imitation of *"the Garden of God"* and for "the benefit and publike relief of this whole Nation" and "the prevention of famine in time to come."[102] The tract singles out apples as providing "a good and wholesome drink from the juice" and being "good for hot stomacks, for all inflammations, tempering melancholy humours; good for diverse diseases."[103] Other contemporary accounts suggest how widely apples had become a part of England's early modern food culture. Apples of various kinds were used in ciders and served as table fruit. John Evelyn in 1664, for example, lauded the "rare effects" of hard apple cider, which he called the "most eminent" of all

---

[99] Parkinson, *Paradisi in Sole*, Ccc6r. Another English herbalist, John Rea in *Flora* (1665), lists more than twenty varieties of apples suitable for gardens, while acknowledging that "many other good *Apples*" are "proper to be planted at large in Orchards." Like Parkinson, Rea includes mixed-colored apples that resemble the fruit that Satan offers Eve, such as the *"Winter Queening,"* a "fair red-striped *Apple*"; the *"Juniting,"* "a small, yellow, red-sided *Apple*, upon a wall ripe in the end of *June*"; and, perhaps most relevant for Satan's account, the *"Margaret,* or *Magdalen Apple,"* "a fair and beautiful fruit, yellow, and thick striped with red, early ripe, of a delicate taste, sweet scent, and best eaten off the Tree." See Rea, *Flora: Seu De Florum Cultura. Or, A Complete Florilege* (London, 1665), Fff1v, Fff1r.

[100] Morgan and Richards, *The Book of Apples*, pp. 18, 48.

[101] William Stukeley, *Memoirs of Sir Isaac Newton's Life*, ed. A. Hastings White (1752; London: Taylor and Francis, 1936), pp. 19–20.

[102] *A Designe for Plentie, By an Universall Planting of Fruit-Trees* (London, 1652), C1v, B2v.

[103] *A Designe for Plentie*, B3v–B4r.

beverages[104], and the expression "as American as apple pie" isn't entirely true. Laborers brought apple pies to work in the fields, and, writing in the late seventeenth century, the diarist Celia Fiennes recalled with special fondness "an apple pye with a custard all on the top" that she enjoyed in Cornwall: "it's a sort of clouted creame as we call it, with a little sugar, and soe put on the top of the apple pye."[105]

My point in turning to these cultural details is not that Satan's description of the Tree of Knowledge is based on any of the fruit that Milton might have seen while strolling through an orchard or garden near Cambridge or in Hammersmith or Horton. Instead, I wish to emphasize how our knowledge of Milton's range of possible experiences, combined with an understanding of biblical and poetic tradition, helps to clarify the epic's imagery. Certainly also relevant for Satan's description of the Tree of Knowledge is Ovid's account of the gold fruit in the garden of Hesperides, "trees whose glittering leaves of gold / Clothed golden apples under golden boughs."[106] Milton's image of the fruit's coloring might reflect as well, for example, the bountiful orchard that Odysseus spies outside the court of King Alcinous which contains – in addition to figs, pears, and pomegranates – "apple trees with their glossy burden."[107] But, as with Milton's other imagery in *Paradise Lost*, the forbidden fruit that Satan offers seems to bring together scriptural lore, poetic tradition, and firsthand knowledge within a heterodox materialist context. In the case of "fruit of fairest colors mixed," Satan's description need not have sounded sinister or even unrealistic to the epic's seventeenth-century audience; on the contrary, the fruit's coloring, when viewed in relation to contemporary culture, is much more evocative than critics have previously realized. The use of an everyday, thoroughly *English* object could have helped Milton's readers not just to enter the extraordinary scene imaginatively, but also to ally themselves

---

[104] John Evelyn, *Pomona, Or an Appendix Concerning Fruit Trees in Relation to Cider*, in *Sylva, Or a Discourse of Forest-Trees, and the Propagation of Timber* (London, 1664), A2r.

[105] Thirsk, *Food in Early Modern England*, p. 152; and *The Illustrated Journeys of Celia Fiennes, 1685–1712*, ed. Christopher Morris (London and Sidney: Macdonald, 1982), p. 204. Fiennes in her travels through southwest England in the late seventeenth century remarked that "In most parts of Sommer-setshire it is very fruitfull for orchards, plenty of apples and peares," and surveying the West Midlands, she added that the country of Herrifordshire was "very full of fruite trees etc., . . . the apple pear trees etc., are so thick even in their corn fields and hedgrows" (pp. 41, 64).

[106] Ovid, *Metamorphoses*, trans. A. D. Melville (Oxford and New York: Oxford University Press, 1987), p. 93 (IV.637–38). On this likely allusion, see Richard J. DuRocher, *Milton and Ovid* (Ithaca and London: Cornell University Press, 1985), p. 34; and Davis P. Harding, *Milton and the Renaissance Ovid*, Illinois Studies in Language and Literature, vol. 30, no. 4 (Urbana: University of Illinois Press, 1946), pp. 79–80.

[107] Homer, *The Odyssey*, trans. A. T. Murray, rev. George E. Dimock, 2 vols. (Cambridge: Harvard University Press, 1995), I: 254–55 (book VII, lines 112–16).

further with the unsuspecting Eve. Satan's initial temptation is all the more disarming, for readers as for her, because the ruddy-and-gold fruit that the devil describes sounds appealing but not unusual.

Satan's description of the fruit thus also illustrates his deviousness: like the quotidian choice of *apples*, the coloring that Satan highlights fits his rhetorical strategy of making the fruit seem tempting but innocent. The devil wants to convince Eve that he is talking about merely apples, just as he wants her to think he is merely a snake. As John Leonard has shown, Satan carefully times when he reveals to Eve that the "goodly fruit" he describes hangs on the Tree of Knowledge (IX.576).[108] So Satan begins his temptation "far distant" from the tree (IX.576) and downplays the fruit's significance by emphasizing its ordinary appearance before Eve realizes that he is referring to the one fruit God has forbidden.

More subtly, the description of an ordinary piece of fruit, found in countless English gardens and kitchens during the early modern period, echoes the proem to book IX, in which Milton meditates on the relation between his epic and its medieval and classical forbears. There he insists that he pursues a "higher argument" (IX.42) and an "argument / Not less but more heroic" (IX.13–14). Yet, as Milton reflects on his current circumstances, he also worries whether a seventeenth-century English epic by a sixty-year-old poet is viable – whether, in other words, "an age too late, or cold / Climate, or years damp my intended wing / Depressed" (IX.44–46). The incorporation of an identifiable contemporary object as the mechanism of humankind's punishment captures this ambivalence: Milton makes the genre of epic his own by grounding the image of the forbidden fruit in his own time and place, but by also striving to write for all times, he in effect disavows such a familiar image by putting the description of red-and-gold apples in the mouth of the devil.

The challenge that today's readers face in interpreting the poem's descriptive passages begins with a willingness to accept an amalgamation of possible influences and precursors instead of searching for a single source or assuming that the epic's imagery derives exclusively from books – what Rosemund Tuve once called the next to last infirmity of noble minds.[109] As I show in the following chapters, the encyclopedic quality of *Paradise Lost*

---

[108] John Leonard, *Naming in Paradise: Milton and the Language of Adam and Eve* (Oxford: Clarendon Press, 1990), p. 207. Evans adds that Satan's strategy is to begin the temptation proper with Eve already in "a mood of frustrated anticipation." See Evans, *"Paradise Lost" and the Genesis Tradition*, p. 277.

[109] See Rosemond Tuve, *Allegorical Imagery: Some Mediaeval Books and Their Posterity* (Princeton: Princeton University Press, 1966), p. 79.

extends from the poem's wide-ranging generic features to the broadly inclusive foundation of even its briefest images.

If we return to the specific case of the forbidden fruit, Satan's misguided naming and colorful description are not the only information in *Paradise Lost* about the appearance of the Tree of Knowledge. After Adam and Eve disobey God and eat the fruit, Milton provides a few additional details that not only help readers to picture the tree but also continue to reveal its symbolic significance. As a fallen Eve returns to Adam, for example, she brings "in her hand / A bough of fairest fruit that downy smiled, / New gathered, and ambrosial smell diffused" (IX.850–52). Here again Milton associates the fruit's visual and olfactory qualifies, but the image of "bough" also indicates Eve's new corruption. She greedily carries back to Adam not just a piece or two of fruit, but a large limb.[110] Apparently, she pried or ripped off a whole branch, in contrast to God's interdiction that she and Adam are not even to touch the fruit.

The added detail of "downy smiled" in the same scene combines the tactile sense of, say, a peach's soft flesh with the abstract notion of fruit that smiles. Most obviously, this specific account means that the forbidden fruit had an agreeable physical appearance, but the idea of a downy smile also seems symbolic: it contrastively anticipates the dreadful consequences that consuming the fruit will bring – tears, lamentation, and death.[111] Such a disjunctive description suggests a new Satanic rupture in the couple's experience; their physical perceptions no longer correspond to spiritual reality. Based on this passage, Robert Appelbaum has argued that after the Fall the nature of the fruit has changed from an apple to a peach.[112] But I think the description more likely reflects Eve's new, fallen perspective, especially if we consider that "downy" need not mean literally covered with down; during the seventeenth century it often meant "soft as down" and, based on Milton's syntax, could just as plausibly describe the "bough" in Eve's hand as the "fairest fruit."[113] The emphasis in this passage falls on Eve's tactile perception, which overtakes her acceptance of the fruit's status as a sign of obedience.

Milton repeatedly stresses this epistemological shift in Adam and Eve after they eat the fruit: they "each the other viewing, / Soon found their eyes how opened, and their minds / How darkened" (IX.1052–54). Here

---

[110] *OED*, s. v. "bough, *n.*," def. 3a.

[111] Christopher Ricks, *Milton's Grand Style* (Oxford: Oxford University Press, 1967), also discusses the "ominous possibilities" of nature's smile here, heartlessly indifferent to humanity's ruin (pp. 58–59).

[112] Robert Appelbaum, *Aguecheek's Beef, Belch's Hiccup, and Other Gastronomic Interjections* (Chicago and London: University of Chicago Press, 2006), p. 198.

[113] *OED*, s. v. "downy," def. 4.

again the physical is sundered from the spiritual as the couple's visual sense now seems superficial, divorced from their intellectual understanding, as "minds / How darkened" implies. Whereas a diabolic reading of Milton's epic would stress that the name of the forbidden tree indicates what God denies Adam and Eve – that is, knowledge of good and evil – Milton, as he shows here and explains more fully in *De Doctrina*, does not believe the fruit materially contains any knowledge. Instead, its name derives from "what happened afterwards [*ab eventu*]" (*CPW* VI: 352), when God punishes the couple for their transgression. Eating puts them in the dark and allows them to see only surfaces.

After the Fall, Adam and Eve first express their new state through their eyes: "that false fruit / Far other operation first displayed, / Carnal desire inflaming; he on Eve / Began to cast lascivious eyes, she him / As wantonly repaid; in lust they burn" (IX.1011–15). Milton again emphasizes the physiological effects of eating the forbidden fruit in visual terms. Whereas prelapsarian love, as I discuss in chapters 6 and 7, combines spiritual and physical reality, the couple's lust sounds much more limited, based on a superficial experience, as both "displayed" and "cast[ing] ... eyes" imply. After the Fall, the fruit appears "false," as opposed to its prelapsarian status as "fair," and now Adam also wrongly calls it "Bad" (IX.1073), a punning transliteration of Satan's use of *apples* (Latin: *mala*), which seems to ignore the tree's status as a symbol. Adam and Eve's choice to eat the fruit was false and bad, not the Tree itself.

When Adam and Eve then see themselves as naked, Milton follows Genesis in having them turn to another tree and cover themselves with fig leaves. But this superficial clothing proves a "vain covering if to hide / Their guilt and dreaded shame" (IX.1113–14). The shift from the fruit's *gold* to the couple's newfound *guilt/gilt* subtly suggests the loss that comes with disobedience. Even if we hesitate to accept that Milton intended such a pun, the contrast between this passage and the description of the tree before the Fall implies a loss of imagistic unity. The physical and symbolic fruit that Adam and Eve consumed has become merely apples.

* * *

The following chapters explore other images in *Paradise Lost* that similarly combine Milton's poetic knowledge and cultural experience. And I concentrate on other vivid images of things or gestures enriched by the epic's philosophy of matter – what we might call "provoking objects," to borrow a suggestive phrase from *Areopagitica*, because they are of greater significance than they initially seem (*CPW* II: 527).

So as to illustrate how thoroughly Milton's visual imagination informs his epic theodicy, I have divided the book into three sections and devoted one to each of the poem's primary locations: heaven, hell, and Paradise. Beginning with the least physical realm, I show how Milton deploys sparse but strong visual images to depict God's power and grace. In chapter 2, I specifically examine the golden scales that appear in the sky as Satan and Gabriel confront each other. Analyzing the image in the context of the Arminian controversy, epic precedent, and seventeenth-century balances, I argue that God's scales do not limit Satan and the angels' choices but instead express heavenly justice and angelic freedom. Chapter 3 then focuses on the frequently repeated image of heaven's walls and gates. Comparing contemporary accounts of urban and residential fortifications, I argue that heaven's physical architecture, although another apparent symbol of limitation, also enacts God's potency and benevolence.

The next pair of chapters shifts from the divine to the diabolic and addresses images that Milton uses to portray Satan and his followers. I first examine Satan's shield as a physical expression of his damaged heroic status and his fall into materiality. The subsequent chapter looks at the imagery that Milton uses to describe the fallen angels' liminal status and ongoing transformation. Whereas Milton indicates Satan's moral fall with the archfiend's newfound preoccupation with hardened things, the shapes of the devil's followers are themselves declining and will ultimately degenerate into pagan idols.

Chapters 6, 7, and 8 turn at last to the human and emphasize the way that Milton visually depicts Adam and Eve's experience in Paradise. First, I show that Adam and Eve's hand-holding is more than symbolic. The couple's loving, tactile connection signifies not only their marital state but also enables their spiritual joining, both to each other and to God. I then examine Milton's detailed descriptions of Adam and Eve's intertwining tresses. Drawing on seventeenth-century hair culture, Milton repeatedly uses the couple's vibrant locks to underscore the reciprocity of prelapsarian love and to suggest the physical and spiritual consequences of disobedience. I conclude with a discussion of postlapsarian imagery in the epic's final two books. Milton enhances his overview of sacred history with vivid snapshots of the mundane, drawn in part from his contemporary culture. These descriptions in turn set off the mysterious and thus unseen incarnate Son, whom Milton portrays only at a distance through substitute images of the angel Michael.

All of these chapters attempt to correlate Milton's imagery, narrative, theology, and philosophy. Just as the poem treats the spiritual and the material as different degrees of a common original substance, so Milton combines both literary tradition and cultural experience for a common purpose – to advance his ideas visually. When after the Fall God sends Michael to "reveal / To Adam what shall come in future days" (XI.113–14), the angel begins with an emphatically imagistic form of revelation. He tells Adam, "now ope thine eyes, and first behold / Th' effects which thy original crime hath wrought" (XI.423–24). Milton describes in perhaps surprising detail the physiological process by which Michael initiates his ocular proof:

> to nobler sights
> Michael from Adam's eyes the film removed
> Which that false fruit that promised clearer sight
> Had bred; then purged with euphrasy and rue
> The visual nerve, for he had much to see;
> And from the Well of Life three drops instilled.
> So deep the power of these ingredients pierced,
> Even to the inmost seat of mental sight,
> That Adam now enforced to close his eyes,
> Sunk down and all his spirits became entranced.   (XI.411–20)

While the purging of mortal sight occurs in other epics – most notably in the *Iliad* and *Aeneid*[114] – Milton's more detailed account sounds literal. He similarly described his own diminishing sight in a letter to his friend Leonard Philaras: "the mist which always hovers before my eyes both day and night" (*CPW* IV: 869). In this book, I am concerned with other instances in which Milton's blending of personal experience and poetic knowledge seems to have informed the way that he visualized his epic's scenes and characters. The following chapters show that Milton devised a uniquely cohesive imagistic strategy in *Paradise Lost* as he attempted, like Michael, to reach "the inmost seat of mental sight" and depict things that no one had previously described.

---

[114] In Homer's epic, Athena thus aids Tydides, "Look, I've lifted the mist from off your eyes / that's blurred them up to now – / so you can tell a god from man on sight" (V.140–42). And Virgil similarly portrays Venus telling Aeneas, "Behold – for all the cloud, which now, drawn over thy sight, dulls thy mortal vision and with dark pall enshrouds thee, I will tear away" (*aspice namque omnem, quae nunc obducta tuenti / mortalis hebetat visus tibi et umida circum / caligat, nubem eripiam* II.604–06). See Homer, *Iliad*, trans. Robert Fagles (New York: Penguin, 1991); and Virgil, *Aeneid*, trans. H. R. Fairclough (Cambridge: Harvard University Press, 1986).

CHAPTER 2

Free will and God's scales

> Their fortunes both are weigh'd;
> In your lord's scale is nothing but himself,
> And some few vanities that make him light.
> — Shakespeare, *Richard II*[1]

Something strange happens in *Paradise Lost* as Satan confronts Gabriel and his angelic squadron on the western point of Paradise: God intercedes. As the two sides brace for battle, a surprising image appears in the sky: "Th' Eternal to prevent such horrid fray / Hung forth in Heav'n his golden scales," and "in these he put two weights / The sequel each of parting and of fight" (IV.996–97, 1002–03). Milton's use here of a deus ex machina, although arguably necessary for preserving the epic's narrative structure, seems to encroach on Satan's and the angels' free will. If we accept the Arminian premise at the core of the theodicy – that God created not only human beings but also "all th' ethereal Powers / And spirits" as "authors to themselves in all" (III.100–01, 122) – we would not expect the Creator to provide such a timely and telling visual preview of where Satan's choices might lead. God insists of Adam and Eve's Fall that "if I foreknew, / Foreknowledge had no influence" (III.117–18), but as Gabriel and Satan gaze at God's scales, divine foreknowledge seems to do exactly that – influence Satan's and the angels' decisions. We can only imagine, by way of comparison, what would have happened if God's scales had suddenly appeared in the sky just before Adam or Eve chose to eat the forbidden fruit.

Yet, aside from this abrupt imagistic intrusion, the deity in *Paradise Lost* more often remains invisible. The narrator establishes God's inaccessibility early on as the angels acclaim – and distinguish between – the Son's mercy and the Father's justice:

---

[1] William Shakespeare, *King Richard II*, ed. Peter Ure (London and New York: Routledge, 1994), III.4.84–86.

Thee Father first they sung omnipotent,
Immutable, immortal, infinite,
Eternal King; thee Author of all being,
Fountain of light, thyself invisible
Amidst the glorious brightness where thou sitt'st
Throned inaccessible, but when thou shad'st
The full blaze of thy beams, and through a cloud
Drawn round about thee like a radiant shrine,
Dark with excessive bright thy skirts appear,
Yet dazzle Heav'n, that brightest Seraphim
Approach not, but with both wings veil their eyes.   (III.372–82)

This passage effectively encapsulates the chief characteristics of Milton's God – all-powerful, undying, infinite, and ultimately beyond human understanding. Even when God sits behind a cloud, as the narrator here explains, the highest angels must cover their eyes to approach God's dazzling brilliance. In these lines, Milton is already suggesting both the audacity and inherent limitation of his divine portrayal. He dares to include God within his epic but indicates that God defies the metaphysical reality of the poem's narrative and is largely a theological construct, almost always glimpsed, as Alastair Fowler has observed, through the perspective of a different character – Satan, Adam, Eve, Raphael, or Michael.[2]

The passages in which God appears accordingly contain some of the poem's most abstract and least sensuous language. Milton strips away the rich imagery of hell, chaos, and Paradise in an attempt to evoke a divine presence mostly through dialogue and a few metonymic details – a voice, an ear, an eye, or a throne. Addressing the angels about the Son's exaltation, for example, God appears only "in orbs / Or circuit inexpressible" and "Amidst as from a flaming mount, whose top / Brightness had made invisible" (V.594–95, 598–99). Or, when God congratulates the angel Abdiel for refusing to follow Satan, Raphael describes how the other angels celebrate God's servant, but God himself remains unseen. The angels present Abdiel "Before the seat supreme; from whence a voice / From midst a golden cloud thus mild was heard" (VI.27–28).

This chapter and the next focus on two of the few substantial images that Milton deploys to depict the divine in *Paradise Lost*: God's scales and heaven's gates and walls. Given God's status as a construct more than a character, any material things with which he is associated would seem especially significant. Why does Milton sometimes resort to visual images of physical reality to depict an invisible God, and why does he use these specific objects?

---

[2] Fowler, pp. 39–40.

In the case of God's scales, critics have traditionally been bothered not that Milton uses the image of a balance to represent divine authority, but that the trays' decisive action seems to deny Satan's and the angels' agency at the conclusion of the scene. John Peter, finding fault with much in *Paradise Lost*, criticized Milton's insertion of God's scales as "underhand and unfair."[3] William Empson similarly inferred that the episode proved that Milton's "God was determined to make man fall," and Marjorie Nicolson complained that the "scene fails ethically as well as artistically." Nicolson added, "I can only . . . wish that when . . . [Milton's] ama[n]uensis read this passage aloud to him, he had shaken his head, and said: 'Strike out that ending.'"[4]

Building on the work of more recent scholars who have defended Milton's depiction of God's scales by examining the image in terms of astrological constellations and Renaissance emblem books, I discuss, first, the implications of God's balancing act for Milton's concept of military valor.[5] Whereas much of the critical commentary on this scene attempts to justify God's intervention by interpreting the scales in human terms – Virginia Mollenkott, for example, suggests that the heavenly balance symbolizes the internal battle within each "authentic Christian"; and Mindele Anne Treip argues that the scales allegorize Adam and Eve's "mental weighing of alternatives and their consequences"[6] – I wish to emphasize the impact of God's golden scales for Satan and the good angels as armed combatants. The subsequent sections of this chapter address how Milton's imagery engages with both his seventeenth-century culture and the works of Homer and Virgil to dramatize the tension between angelic authority and divine will. Instead of accepting that the scene between Gabriel and Satan somehow compromises the theodicy's Arminian premise or that the image of scales needs to be recouped by applying it to Adam and Eve's moral decision-making, I suggest that this episode has the contrary effect: it illustrates that, even among the celestial powers, divine foreknowledge does not inhibit free will.

[3] John Peter, *A Critique of "Paradise Lost"* (New York: Columbia University Press, 1960), p. 25.

[4] William Empson, *Milton's God*, rev. edn. (London: Chatto and Windus, 1965), p. 112; and Marjorie Hope Nicolson, *John Milton: A Reader's Guide to His Poetry* (New York: Octagon, 1971), p. 244.

[5] See, for example, John T. Shawcross, *With Mortal Voice: The Creation of "Paradise Lost"* (Lexington: University Press of Kentucky, 1982), pp. 79–80; and Mindele Anne Treip, "'Reason Is Also Choice': The Emblematics of Free Will in *Paradise Lost*," *Studies in English Literature* 31 (1991): 147–77.

[6] Virginia R. Mollenkott, "The Wheat, the Chaff, and the Aborted Duel," *Concerning Poetry* 6.2 (1973): 38–43; and Treip, "Reason Is Also Choice," p. 168.

"War wearied"

Satan's conflict with Gabriel is not the first battle that the arch-fiend narrowly averts. Standing at the gates of hell, Satan squares off against Death – "Each at the head / Leveled his deadly aim," Milton writes (II.711–12) – until Sin rushes between these "mighty combatants" and explains that they are father and son (II.719). That she also prevents their fighting by reminding them of God's "justice, . . . / . . . which one day will destroy ye both" (II.733–34) anticipates the sudden appearance of God's scales as Satan opposes Gabriel. Both interruptions seem to indicate the futility of Satan's efforts in the presence of divine righteousness.

But if Satan and Death are evenly matched in this earlier confrontation, Satan appears to have the upper hand when he encounters Gabriel's squadron. The good angels at first look truculent; they respond to Satan's taunts by turning "fiery red, sharp'ning . . . / Their phalanx," porting their spears, and "hem[ming] him round" (IV.978–79). But the subsequent simile encourages us to question their resolute posture. Bearing their spears aloft, the angels resemble "a field / Of Ceres ripe for harvest" that "waving bends / Her bearded grove of ears, which way the wind / Sways them" (IV.980–83). This same comparison, as John Leonard has observed, describes not ferocious champions but demoralized armies in the works of Homer, Tasso, Ariosto, and Apollonius Rhodius.[7]

Milton depicts Satan, "On th' other side," as "alarmed" (IV.985), a term that during the early modern period could convey "disturbed" or "excited by the prospect of danger," but could also mean simply "called to arms."[8] Here Milton emphasizes the arch-fiend's size, strength, and stubbornness. "Collecting all his might," Satan "dilated stood," as "unremoved" as the mountains of "Teneriffe or Atlas" and just as large: "His stature reached the sky, and on his crest / Sat Horror plumed" (IV.986–89). Lest we ignore the seriousness of the military threat that Satan poses, Milton then briefly catalogues the "dreadful deeds" that "Might have ensued" if Gabriel and Satan had fought:

> nor only Paradise
> In this commotion, but the starry cope
> Of Heav'n perhaps, or all the elements

---

[7] John Leonard, ed., *John Milton: The Complete Poems* (London: Penguin, 1998), p. 773. John Rumrich, Stephen Fallon, and William Kerrigan, however, suggest that Milton's simile departs from epic precedent because the angels have begun to "hem" Satan "round" (IV.979) and thus their spears do not ultimately indicate the angels' weakness. The shafts merely resemble stalks of grain in that they slant in various directions (*CPMP* 415).

[8] *OED*, s. v. "alarmed," defs. 1, 2.

                        At least had gone to wrack, disturbed and torn
                        With violence of this conflict.   (IV.991–95)

While Empson objected to these lines because they suggest that God lets
Satan go free for the sake of the scenery, I would propose that the passage
reflects Milton's rejection of traditional heroism and his acute awareness
of the costs of warfare.[9] Raphael uses the same expression, "Had gone
to wrack" (VI.670), when justifying God's intervention on the third day
of the war in heaven – that is, God had to send forth his Son or else
"all Heav'n / Had gone to wrack" (VI.669–70). Similarly, if Satan and
Death had fought at the gates of hell, we are told, "great deeds / Had been
achieved, whereof all Hell had rung" (II.722–23). Milton, by deploying
the same Homeric contra-factual construction in each passage, seems to
join these scenes of averted battles so as to undermine Satan's bluster.[10]
At the end of book IV, the point is not that Satan might have defeated
Gabriel but that, as with both the war in heaven and Satan and Death's
conflict, the potentially ruinous consequences of battle warrant God's
intercession.

    We can also read Milton's emphasis of the destructiveness of armed
conflict in the context of Britain's civil wars and seventeenth-century
pamphlet literature in which both sides sought to defend military action
as a victory for Christ. In *A Treatise of Civil Power* (1659), Milton clearly
accepts that violent action is sometimes justified. Although he acknowledges that "the kingdom of Christ [is] not governd by outward force; as
being none of this world," he insists that "a Christian commonwealth may
defend it self against outward force in the cause of religion as well as in
any other" (*CPW* VII: 256–57). Milton, in his unpublished theological
treatise *De Doctrina Christiana*, also endorses the use of force; he argues
that "There is no reason why war should be any less lawful now than it was
in the time of the Jews" and culls various passages from scripture to show
that Jesus, too, "conquers and crushes his enemies" so as to fulfill his
"kingly function" (*CPW* VI: 803, 435–37). Milton goes on to stipulate
what constitutes a just war: for example, "it is to be undertaken only after
extremely careful consideration," "it is to be waged knowledgeably and
skilfully [*sic*]," and it should be conducted "with moderation" and "in
holiness" (*CPW* VI: 802). Christopher Hill has traced the foundation
for Milton's acceptance of violent action to a broad Protestant tradition

---

[9] Empson, *Milton's God*, p. 113.
[10] Bruce Louden examines ten contra-factual constructions in *Paradise Lost* in relation to antecedents
in the *Iliad* and *Odyssey*. See Louden, "Milton and the Appropriation of a Homeric Technique,"
Classical and Modern Literature 16.4 (1996): 325–40.

of treating the hatred of God's enemies as a duty, an idea that Milton would have presumably heard early and often, the first time as a boy in the sermons of Richard Stock, his parish minister.[11]

But even late in life, after witnessing the failure of the civil wars and the censure and execution of many of his friends and collaborators, Milton continued to support the legitimacy of violence. Most notably, in *Samson Agonistes*, Samson pulls down the pillars "heroic'ly," in the words of Manoa, and "hath finished / A life heroic, on his enemies / Fully revenged" (lines 1710–12). Similarly, in *Paradise Regained*, the poem published with *Samson* in 1671, Milton depicts a Jesus who, in considering how best to quell "Brute violence" (I.219), never rules out the need for force. Instead, Jesus resolves "At least to try" to "make persuasion do the work of fear" (I.223–24). Later, when Satan tries to tempt him with "projects deep / Of enemies, of aids, battles and leagues," Jesus explains that the "cumbersome / Luggage of war" remains "Plausible to the world, [though] to me worth naught" (III.391–93, 400–01). While "cumbersome" certainly sounds pejorative, "plausible" could mean either genuinely laudable or merely appearing so.[12] Jesus may be acknowledging that such "projects" sometimes deserve approval (although they are useless for him), or he may be implying that warfare sometimes seems worthwhile but only when judged by worldly standards.

Less ambiguous is Jesus' earlier concession, "the stubborn only to *destroy*" (I.226, emphasis added), which seems to validate unequivocally Samson's climactic action in "destroy[ing]" the Philistines (line 1587). Only after turning to the list of errata in the 1671 volume would readers discover that "destroy" in *Paradise Regained* is to be replaced with "subdue," a change that substantially mitigates without entirely eliminating Jesus' threat of violence.[13] In the corrected text, Jesus no longer will annihilate "proud tyrannic power" (I.219), but he still holds out the possibility of bringing such tyrants into subjection by intimidating or conquering them.[14] This apparently last-minute revision suggests that more than ten years after the Restoration Milton was still grappling with

---

[11] Christopher Hill, "*Samson Agonistes* Again," *Literature and History*, 2nd ser., 1 (1990): 24–39; and *Dictionary of National Biography*, s. v. "Stock, Richard."

[12] *OED*, s. v. "plausible," defs. A.1–2, A.3.a.

[13] *Paradise Regain'd. A Poem. In IV Books. To which is added Samson Agonistes* (London, 1671), P4r.

[14] Another possible late revision to the 1671 volume are the ten lines labeled *Omissa* and printed on the page opposite the list of errata. Readers are instructed to insert the missing text in *Samson Agonistes* as Manoa and the Chorus listen to Samson off-stage destroying the Philistines. I discuss the *Omissa* and its implications for Milton's response to the British civil wars in Dobranski, *Readers and Authorship in Early Modern England* (Cambridge: Cambridge University Press, 2005), pp. 183–209.

the question of violence and trying to decide how far Jesus goes in extolling its use.

But if in *Paradise Lost* Milton also accepts the legitimate use of force – so that, for example, God orders the angels "to subdue / By force" Satan and his followers (VI.40–41) – Milton qualifies such passages by repeatedly repudiating the value of military conflict. Not only does the narrator announce that his poetic subjects of "patience" and "martyrdom" are "better" than the "tedious havoc" depicted in other epic poems (IX.30–32), but also God tells Abdiel that the angel has "fought / The better fight" by opposing Satan's "revolted multitudes" with "word mightier than they in arms" (VI.29–32). Dispatching the Son on the third day to end the angels' conflict, God concludes that "War wearied hath performed what war can do" (VI.695), a clear indication of the limited success that can be achieved on a battlefield. "Wearied" suggests Milton's own disillusionment with military conflict after the Restoration, especially given that we have now seen "what war can do": the first two days of the war in heaven essentially accomplish nothing. Just as Jesus in *Paradise Regained* distinguishes between mundane and divine perceptions of warfare, so Michael explains to Adam that men in the future who are "styled great conquerors" should be "Destroyers rightlier called and plagues of men" (XI.695, 697).

Milton's reference to an angelic "Intestine" war (VI.259) also directly challenges the language that some contemporary writers used to justify Britain's recent civil conflicts. Both before and after the Restoration, Puritan saints and Commonwealthmen turned to biblical accounts to help understand contemporary experiences.[15] Whereas Royalists attacked Puritans as "new Luciferists" or allied themselves with anointed kings such as David and Solomon,[16] Puritans borrowed from the Book of Revelation to cast the civil wars in terms of a heavenly battle between devils (the Royalists) and Christ's angels and saints (supporters of Parliament). Thus, in 1652 Peter Sterry, a preacher to the Council of State, exhorts his readers, "*O Christians, you* fight not with Flesh and Blood, but Principalities and Powers, spirituall wickednesses in Heavenly forms."[17] Sterry argues that the country's recent conflicts should be viewed as part of a grander, spiritual battle: "Every *Good*, and *Evill* is *Spirituallized* in the midst of us. . . . While *Men* fight, *Angels* fight: *Michael*, and his Angels, with the *Dragon*, and his

---

[15] See Blair Worden, "Milton, *Samson Agonistes*, and the Restoration," in *Culture and Society in the Stuart Restoration*, ed. Gerald MacLean (Cambridge: Cambridge University Press, 1995), pp. 111–36.

[16] Stella Purce Revard, *The War in Heaven* (Ithaca: Cornell University Press, 1980), p. 113.

[17] Peter Sterry, *England's Deliverance from the Northern Presbytery, Compared with Its Deliverance from the Roman Papacy*, 2nd edn. (London, 1652), A4v.

Angels."[18] Henry Lawrence, the President of the Council of State under Cromwell's Protectorate, offers a similar interpretation of Britain's civil wars. Writing in "an age . . . when warre is become almost the profession of all men," he explains the country's recent conflicts as occurring within "an irreconcileable, and everlasting warre" between "the good Angels" and "the divell and his Angells."[19] As Stella Revard has argued, the similarities between the warring angels in *Paradise Lost* and the warfaring saints in contemporary political tracts are significant: "For embattled Christians and loyal angels alike the war is . . . a struggle they cannot win: none but the Son of God possesses the power to crush Satan."[20]

In this context, we might recall the medieval and Renaissance visual tradition of *Christus in statera*, which combines the image of Christ on the cross with a pair of scales to symbolize the union of divine mercy and divine justice. The presence of such "disguised symbolism," as Eugene Cunnar has argued, would illustrate in the scene with Gabriel and Satan that "God's justice is effected through Christ's mercy."[21] And the fact that the scales God holds forth at the end of book IV are the same ones "Wherein all things created first he weighed" further connects this "celestial sign" with the Son, for we later learn that God created the world through his Son: "by thee / This I perform, speak thou, and be it done" (IV.999, 1011; VII.163–64). Milton may thus be using the image of God's scales – in which Satan is "weighed" and found wanting (IV.1012) – to suggest that, as with the war in heaven, the Son of God must end the conflict. The golden scales might accordingly have Revelational implications. As with the specific description that the Son enters God's chariot by "Ascend[ing]" on the third day of the war in heaven and anticipating "when in the end" his Father "shalt be all in all" (VI.711, 731–32), Milton with the evocative image of justice at the end of book IV might be tipping the scale to foreshadow more subtly the day when the Son will vanquish both Satan and death.

The possible Christic significance of the golden scales also contributes to Milton's depiction of the futility of warfare. The scales that God hangs in the sky not only symbolize the angels' and humankind's dependence on the

[18] Sterry, *The Commings Forth of Christ in the Power of His Death* (London, 1649), F4v.
[19] Henry Lawrence, *Of Our Communion and Warre with Angels: Being, Certaine Meditations on That Subject* (London, 1646), *4r. Milton refers to Lawrence as "virtuous" in Sonnet 20, written to Lawrence's eldest son, Edward, a friend and possibly a student of Milton's. In *Pro Populo Anglicano Defensio Secunda* (1654), Milton also refers to Henry Lawrence (and Edward Montague) as "men of supreme genius, cultivated in the liberal arts" (*CPW* IV: 677).
[20] Revard, *The War in Heaven*, p. 116.
[21] Eugene R. Cunnar, "God's 'Golden Scales': Mercy and Justice in *Paradise Lost*," *English Language Notes* 21.4 (1984): 13–21 (pp. 18, 16).

Son as intercessor but also represent Gabriel and Satan being stuck in a "condition of equilibrium or indecision," as in the phrase "equal scale."[22] Just as the war in heaven had "long time in even scale /. . . hung" (VI.245–46), so Gabriel and Satan are poised in a similarly uneasy balance of power. As Gabriel evenly puts it, "Satan, I know thy strength, and thou know'st mine" (IV.1006). The ambiguous details about the two sides' relative strength enhance the sense of a stalemate. Satan appears as immovable as the mountains of Teneriffe or Atlas, yet the "celestial scale" shows "how light" and "weak" he is (IV.1011–12); and weighed against the threat that Gabriel's squadron poses is, as we have seen, the simile of the field of grain that may hint at the good angels' fear and vulnerability.

God's intervention with his golden balance also puns on the false sense of "scale" created by Satan's self-important swelling. That Milton specifically refers to God as "Th' Eternal" (IV.996) emphasizes the Creator's limitlessness and dwarfs the temporarily dilated Satan. The arch-fiend's "stature" may have "reached the sky" (IV.988), Milton suggests, but God still tops him, appearing "in Heav'n," high above the angelic fray (IV.997). The effect is almost cinematic: as if panning back to frame the scene in an extreme long shot, Milton introduces God's celestial scales to remind the angels – and his readers – of the necessary context for measuring military might, whether angelic or human. Like the epic's opening book, in which Milton presents Satan's heroic speeches before fully revealing the fallen angel's degrading posture – "With head uplift," "Chained on the burning lake" (I.193, 210) – here, too, Milton dramatically unveils the larger, cosmic scale on which we ought to weigh the devil's threat and presumably all such possible military conflicts. When Gabriel tells Satan, "how light, how weak, / If thou resist" (IV.1012–13), he is warning Satan about attempting to resist not only the squadron of angels but also divine justice as symbolized by the golden scales. The only strength that Satan and the angels possess, Gabriel explains, has been given to them: "what folly then / To boast what arms can do, since thine no more / Than Heav'n permits, nor mine" (IV.1007–09).

In *De Doctrina Christiana*, Milton similarly observes that "we should not trust in the strength of our forces, but in God alone" (*CPW* VI.802). While Milton in this treatise notes that the good angels in the Bible are "Sometimes . . . ministers of divine vengeance" and, "As a result they often appeared looking like soldiers," he emphasizes that these angels are cut off from God's thoughts and that the Son has nothing to do with angelic

---

[22] *OED*, s. v. "scale," def. 4.b.

"forces . . . drawn up in battle array" (*CPW* VI: 346–47). In like manner in *Paradise Lost*, Gabriel and the other good angels dress like soldiers, but Milton more often describes Satan and his followers in terms of earthly armies, as if to highlight the perversity of warfare.[23] When Satan first rebels, God may order Michael and Gabriel to "lead forth to battle these my sons / Invincible, lead forth my armèd Saints / By thousands and by millions ranged for fight" (VI.46–48). But God then puts so many restrictions on the battle that, as Samuel Johnson first complained, the war is marked by an overarching sense of "incongruity."[24] God limits the relative power of each side, ordains that the war last only three days, protects heaven from extensive damage, and on the third day sends forth his Son to end the war. To this list I would add God's action during the subsequent standoff between Gabriel and Satan: God, perhaps through his Son, is helping to prevent the two sides from resuming the fight.

The Arminian controversy

The image of God's golden scales does not, however, represent a straightforward correction of satanic error with divine will. God apparently intercedes to forestall the angelic conflict, and yet Milton, I wish to show, does not depict divine foreknowledge as irresistible. On the contrary, Milton takes pains to illustrate that the Creator's intervention is not the sufficient cause of Gabriel's and Satan's decisions. The crux of the passage rests in part with the ambiguity of "prevent": when the poet announces, "Th' Eternal to prevent such horrid fray / Hung forth in Heav'n his golden scales" (IV.996–97), "prevent" can mean to "frustrate" or "hinder," which would suggest divine intervention and thus introduce predestinationism – that is, God hinders Gabriel's defeat of Satan so that the devil will go on to cause the Fall. But "prevent" also can mean simply to "anticipate" or "precede," which would allow for the possibility that God's gesture of hanging forth his scales does not interfere with the angels' free will – that is, God merely reveals the image of the scales because he anticipates where the military standoff might lead.[25]

---

[23] James A. Freeman, *Milton and the Martial Muse* (Princeton: Princeton University Press, 1980), has reached a similar conclusion; he refers to *Paradise Lost* as a "skillful indictment of mankind's most vulgar error" (p. 62). But I would not go so far as other critics who find a commitment to quietism in Milton's late poetic works. See, for example, Andrew Milner, *John Milton and the English Revolution: A Study in the Sociology of Literature* (Totowa, NJ: Barnes and Noble, 1981), pp. 147, 175.

[24] Samuel Johnson, *Lives of the English Poets*, ed. George Birkbeck Hill, 3 vols. (New York: Octagon, 1967), I: 185.

[25] *OED*, s. v. "prevent," defs. II.8, II.10; I.1.b, I.3.

In *Naturam non pati senium* ("That Nature Is Not Subject to Old Age"), by comparison, Milton describes how God "has fixed the scales of fate [*fatorum lances*] with sure balance and commanded every individual thing in the cosmos to hold to its course forever" (lines 35–36).[26] This early Latin poem, beginning with the speaker bemoaning the error of using human practices to measure Gods' law, anticipates Gabriel and Satan's mistake in *Paradise Lost*: the two sides almost go to war because they are wrongly measuring themselves according to traditional standards of heroism instead of according to God's will.[27] But in *Naturam*, God's scales seem to operate in a determinist universe; they preserve the "righteous sequence of all things," as Milton puts it, that "shall go on perpetually, until the final fire shall destroy the world" (lines 65–67). *Paradise Lost*, in contrast, associates God's balance with acts of creation and the resolution of conflicts. When God intervenes between Gabriel and Satan, we are told that these are the same scales "Wherein all things created first he weighed, / The pendulous round Earth with balanced air / In counterpoise, now ponders all events, / Battles and realms" (IV.999–1002). This last phrase in particular, with its use of the present tense, suggests an ongoing, dynamic process as opposed to preordination. If God's scales in *Paradise Lost* illustrate divine omniscience and symbolize how God knows everything before it occurs, they are simultaneously a mechanism that can measure infinite fluctuations and thus a symbol of human and angelic contingency.

The tension between foreknowledge and contingency that Milton introduces in resolving the standoff between Satan and Gabriel may once again allude to Britain's recent civil wars. It is a striking coincidence that Milton suggests the possibility of predestination to forestall a military conflict when this very theological question contributed to the political breakdown that led to war.[28] The dispute over predestination that emerged during the 1630s stemmed from efforts by Charles I and Archbishop William Laud to restore the elaborate rituals that characterized religious

---

[26] For the English, I am working from the translation in *Complete Poems and Major Prose*, ed. Merritt Y. Hughes (New York: Macmillan, 1957), pp. 33–35.

[27] As various commentators have noted, Milton seems to have based the opening of *Naturam* on Isaiah 55:8, "For my thoughts *are* not your thoughts, neither *are* your ways my ways, saith the Lord."

[28] Nicholas Tyacke first discussed the controversy surrounding predestination as a leading cause of the civil wars. See Tyacke, *Anti-Calvinists: The Rise of English Arminianism, c. 1590–1640* (Oxford: Oxford University Press, 1987). Among the historians who support Tyacke's thesis are Conrad Russell, *Parliaments and English Politics, 1621–1629* (Oxford: Clarendon, 1979), and Patrick Collinson, *The Religion of Protestants: The Church in English Society, 1559–1625* (Oxford: Clarendon, 1984). Some historians, however, have challenged Tyacke's thesis: see, for example, Christopher Haigh, review of Tyacke's *Anti-Calvinists*, in *The English Historical Review* 103.407 (1988): 425–27; and Kevin Sharpe, *The Personal Rule of Charles I* (New Haven: Yale University Press, 1992), pp. 284–92, 298.

practices before the Reformation.[29] Underlying Laud's insistence on the "Beauty of Holiness" were two anti-Calvinist premises: that external worship is intimately connected to inner faith, and that the human will, through the sacraments, can affect salvation.

Laud accordingly appears to have denied predestination and to have promoted instead an Arminian interpretation of the articles of religion. Whereas Calvinism posited that divine foreknowledge is based on divine decrees and thus God from eternity predestines all humans to either salvation or damnation, the essence of Arminian theology was a belief in universal grace and conditional election – that is, the idea that Christ died for all humans (not just the elect) and that God saves anyone "who, through the grace of the Holy Ghost, shall believe on this his Son Jesus, and shall persevere in this faith and obedience of faith, through this grace."[30] Admittedly, the significance of the Arminian controversy for the civil wars might seem slight, given that few Calvinist ministers were formally charged during the early 1630s for violating the king's proclamations forbidding debate over predestination, and Laud himself, at his trial in 1644, denied that he was an Arminian – "I have nothing to do to defend [myself from] *Arminianism*," he said.[31]

Yet, that Charles I issued three royal statements trying to silence ministers who espoused supralapsarianism (the belief that God predestined all of humankind from eternity as either saved or damned) suggests the political threat that Calvinists represented to both the king's ecclesiastical program and his broader efforts to impose order and harmony across all three kingdoms. If Laud did not see himself as a doctrinal Arminian, he nevertheless defended the theology at his trial; he argued that Arminianism should not be treated as controversial because it largely agreed with Luther's beliefs: "I do heartily wish these [theological] Differences were not pursued with such Heat and Animosity, in regard that all the *Lutheran Protestants* are of the very same Opinions, or with very little difference from those which are now called *Arminianism*."[32] And, regardless of Laud's testimony at trial, he adamantly supported some Arminian principles, writing separately, for example, that "my very soul abominates" the Calvinist idea of reprobation and that the complementary notion of a

---

[29] See William Laud, *The History of the Troubles and Tryal of the Most Reverend Father in God and Blessed Martyr, William Laud* (London, 1695). In the introduction I discuss the church's emphasis under Laud on visual imagery.

[30] "The Five Arminian Articles," in *The Creeds of Christendom*, ed. Philip Schaff, 4th edn., 3 vols. (Grand Rapids: Baker, 1977), III: 545–49 (p. 545).

[31] Laud, *The History of the Troubles and Tryal*, Zz1v.

[32] Laud, *The History of the Troubles and Tryal*, Zz1v–Zz2r.

special elect "teareth up the very foundations of religion, induceth all manner of profanness into the world, and is expressly contrary to the whole current of the Scripture."[33] Historians who have downplayed the Arminian controversy in the events leading up to the civil wars also overlook that Laud and other members of Charles' administration resorted to a systematic – albeit quiet – method of intimidation to enforce compliance to Arminianism. Instead of relying on formal trials, Laud and his associates, as David Como has shown, used informal hearings along with threats of imprisonment and suspension to bully Calvinist ministers into at least remaining silent on the question of predestination versus free will.[34]

But whereas Laud's opponents objected to his Arminian theology in the 1630s and early 1640s because, they felt, his emphasis of external worship smacked of popery, a second controversy over predestination and free will emerged during the succeeding decades as Arminian thinking permanently supplanted the Calvinist theology that dominated the church during the reigns of Elizabeth and James. This "Arminianism of the left" – or "new Arminianism," as it is sometimes named[35] – shared with Laudian theology its rejection of supralapsarianism, but instead of turning to high-church rituals as the means of salvation, the so-called new Arminianists believed that Christians had the privilege and obligation to think for themselves and to interpret the Bible by following their conscience. Even as the Westminster Confession of Faith formally established a Calvinist creed for the English Church in 1647, the second controversy over predestination continued in print: arguments for and against Arminianism appeared throughout the succeeding decades, often, as in the works of the Calvinist theologian Andreas Rivetus, asserting that not only men but also angels were predestinated.[36] The roughly one hundred works about predestination published during the late 1640s and 1650s – frequently in multiple editions – point to the intellectual vigor associated with this theological issue during the period when Milton began working on *Paradise Lost*. Writing in 1675, Richard Baxter summed up the "stir and

[33] *The Works of the Most Reverend Father in God, William Laud, Sometime Lord Archbishop of Canterbury*, ed. William Scott and James Bliss, 7 vols. (Oxford: J. H. Parker, 1847–60), VI: 132–33.

[34] David R. Como, "Predestination and Political Conflict in Laud's London," *The Historical Journal* 46.2 (2003): 263–94 (p. 283).

[35] The former phrase comes from Christopher Hill, *Milton and the English Revolution* (London: Faber and Faber, 1977), p. 272; the latter term occurs in, for example, Ellen More, "John Goodwin and the Origins of the New Arminianism," *Journal of British Studies* 22.1 (1982): 50–70 (p. 51).

[36] Andreas Rivetus, "Disputatio III, Thesis I, 4," *Operum Theologicorum*, II: 1158 as cited in *CPW* VI: 163. For an excellent overview of the principal writers who participated in this controversy, see Dennis Richard Danielson, *Milton's Good God: A Study in Literary Theodicy* (Cambridge: Cambridge University Press, 1982), pp. 75–82.

confusion" of the period's theological debates as the "controversie between the defenders of *Necessary Predetermination*, and of *Free-will*; that is, . . . *Whether ever in Angels or Innocent man there was such a thing, as a will that can and ever did determine it self to a Volition or Nolition* in specie morali, *without the predetermining efficient necessitating premotion of God as the first Cause.*"[37]

Critics generally agree that Milton was Arminian, but we don't know exactly when he adopted this theology. As late as 1644, in the second edition of *The Doctrine and Discipline of Divorce*, he identifies himself as a Calvinist, defending predestination from "The Jesuits, and that sect among us which is nam'd of *Arminius*," who "are wont to charge us of making God the author of sinne" (*CPW* II: 293). In the same year in *Areopagitica*, Milton continues to associate Arminians and Catholics: he writes that "many have bin corrupted by studying the comments of Jesuits" in the same way that "the acute and distinct *Arminius* was perverted meerly by the perusing of a namelesse discours writt'n in *Delf*, which at first he took in hand to confute" (*CPW* II: 519–20). While "acute" and "distinct" suggest Milton's respect for Arminius, the comparison of Arminianism with Jesuitical thinking indicates Milton's ongoing commitment to Calvinism, as does the specific choice of "perverted," a word that he later uses to describe Satan in *Paradise Lost* (XII.547).

Yet part of Milton's argument against pre-publication censorship in *Areopagitica* already implies an Arminian position. As Maurice Kelley first observed, Milton's insistence on the responsibility of individual readers challenges the fundamental assumption of high Calvinism.[38] When, for example, Milton asserts, "that which purifies us is triall, and triall is by what is contrary," he hardly sounds like a Calvinist (*CPW* II: 515). Or, to take another example, Milton criticizes the "foolish tongues" who "complain of divin Providence for suffering *Adam* to transgresse"; he argues that, on the contrary, God gave Adam "freedom to choose" so that he could demonstrate his own merit: "If every action which is good, or evill in man . . . were to be under . . . prescription, and compulsion, what were vertue but a name, what praise could be then due to well-doing" (*CPW* II: 527).

I would suggest that even Milton's Sonnet 7 "How soon hath Time," probably composed around 1633, intimates a burgeoning Arminian

---

[37] Richard Baxter, *Catholick Theologie: Plain, Pure, Peaceable, for Pacification of the Dogmatical Word-Warriours* (London, 1675), Qqqq4v.

[38] Maurice Kelley, Introduction, *Christian Doctrine*, by John Milton, in *CPW* II: 3–99 (see p. 82). Kelley was also the first to show that Milton formulates his Arminianism by borrowing from Wollebius' *Compendium*. See Kelley, "Milton's Debt to Wolleb's *Compendium Theologiæ Christianæ*," *PMLA* 50 (1935): 156–65.

perspective. The speaker overcomes his anxiety about a lack of "inward ripeness" (line 7) by recalling that, regardless of his efforts, he will receive "that same lot, however mean or high, / Toward which Time leads me, and the will of Heaven" (lines 11–12). Milton concludes the sonnet with an emphatically Calvinist spondee, "All is" – but he then inserts a caesura and the conditional clause, "if I have grace to use it so" (line 13), which together suggest that he accepted some responsibility for achieving his "lot" and was not relying entirely on providence. The sonnet also underscores the importance of individual will by deviating from the expected rhyme scheme in the sestet. The egregiously irregular pattern of *cde dce* demonstrates that the poet can "use" and make his own the preordained forms – the "strictest measure" (line 10) – that he inherits.

By the time Milton began compiling and composing *De Doctrina Christiana* – probably most actively in the late 1650s[39] – he clearly embraced an Arminian plan of predestination. Here Milton forcefully asserts that the "object of the divine plan was that angels and men alike should be endowed with free will" (*CPW* VI: 163), and he adduces copious examples from the Bible to argue that God's foreknowledge has no external effects:

> By virtue of his wisdom God decreed the creation of angels and men as beings gifted with reason and thus with free will. At the same time he foresaw the direction in which they would tend when they used this absolutely unimpaired freedom. What then? Shall we say that God's providence or foreknowledge imposes any necessity upon them? Certainly not: no more than if some human being possessed the same foresight. For an occurrence foreseen with absolute certainty by a human being will no less certainly take place than one foretold by God. . . . [N]othing happens because God has foreseen it, but rather he has foreseen each event because each is the result of particular causes which, by his decree, work quite freely and with which he is thoroughly familiar. So the outcome does not rest with God who foresees it, but only with the man whose action God foresees. (*CPW* VI: 164).

Although we ought not treat *De Doctrina Christiana* as a gloss on *Paradise Lost*, the idea Milton emphasizes here – that divine providence resembles human foreknowledge – is dramatized most fully in the final books of his epic as Michael teaches Adam "what shall come in future days / To thee and to thy offspring" (XI.357–58). Michael "wak'st" Adam "to foresight" (XI.368), but the angel does not possess nor bestow on Adam any authority

[39] Gordon Campbell, Thomas N. Corns, John K. Hale, and Fiona J. Tweedie, *Milton and the Manuscript of "De Doctrina Christiana"* (Oxford: Oxford University Press, 2007), p. 33.

over the events that are revealed. As Adam laments the consequence of his disobedience, he concludes that "no man [should] seek / Henceforth to be foretold what shall befall / Him or his children" because "neither [his or his children's future] his foreknowing can prevent" (XI.770–73). Adam, in other words, can control his own choices, but even with foreknowledge he cannot control the repercussions of those choices for himself or his offspring.

If the sudden introduction of God's scales in *Paradise Lost* raises the possibility that Milton continued to subscribe to some Calvinist articles, other passages in the epic dovetail with the theology of *De Doctrina* and emphasize that the celestial powers have the same freedom and limitations as Adam and Eve. God announces that he "created all th' ethereal Powers / And spirits" to be "Sufficient ... though free to fall," and he places complete responsibility for the angels' rebellion on the angels themselves: "Freely they stood who stood, and fell who fell. / Not free, what proof could they have giv'n sincere / Of true allegiance, constant faith or love" (III.99–101, 102–04). Raphael similarly explains to Adam that the rebel angels "headlong themselves ... threw / Down from the verge of Heav'n" (VI.864–65); the rebels could have preserved their happy state simply by obeying God: "firm they might have stood, / Yet fell" (VI.911–12).[40] Satan, too, grudgingly admits in a soliloquy that he can only blame himself for his fall: "Hadst thou the same free will and power to stand? / Thou hadst" (IV.66–67).

The repetition in all these passages of "stand" or "fall" as the two options available to the celestial powers corresponds to the action of God's scales in the standoff between Gabriel and Satan. Milton has chosen a mechanism that neatly captures the logic of God's justice and the choice available to all of God's creations: to fall or stand, to defy or obey. That Milton uses this same image after Adam and Eve eat the forbidden fruit further suggests that he envisioned the divine balance as depicting free will. Emphasizing humankind's culpability, God concludes his eloquent I-told-you-so by explaining to the assembled angels, "no decree of mine / Concurring to necessitate his fall, / Or touch with lightest moment of impulse / His free will, to her own inclining left / In even scale" (X.43–47). God, in other words, did not influence either Adam and Eve's or the angels' choices, as he treats the balanced scales as something separate from his person. "Lightest

---

[40] Raphael more fully explains the status of angels: "Myself and all th' angelic host that stand / In sight of God enthroned, our happy state / Hold, as you yours, while our obedience holds; / On other surety none; freely we serve, / Because we freely love, as in our will / To love or not; in this we stand or fall" (V.535–40).

moment" signifies the most gentle pressure that could be – but is not – applied to the scales' trays. According to the logic of this imagery, the scales themselves do not decree the choices made by God's creations, unless God were to tip the balance with his thumb.

My point in discussing God's scales in *Paradise Lost* in relation to Milton's evolving theology and the seventeenth-century controversy over Arminianism is not that readers should approach the scene between Gabriel and Satan as an allegory of England in the 1640s. But the temporary angelic standoff in book IV seems to dramatize on a higher spiritual plain a way to avoid military conflict – "to prevent such horrid fray" (IV.996) – that depends on both God's justice and individual will. In contrast to Royalists and Parliamentarians during the civil wars – to which, as we have seen, pamphlet writers compared God's spiritual armies – Milton's angelic combatants recognize the futility of military conflict and choose to part instead of fighting. Surely Barbara Lewalski is right to interpret Satan's proud words and quick exit at the end of book IV as another sign of his debased heroism.[41] But the scene also presents the conditions for war and depicts one of the central issues that led to Britain's recent conflicts – and then it shows a non-violent way out of the apparent impasse.

Epic scale

Any lingering concerns we may have about the Calvinist implications of God's scales in *Paradise Lost* are answered by comparing the different ways that Homer and Virgil deploy the same image. While Gregory Machacek has recently cautioned against putting too much interpretive pressure on individual "points of comparison or contrast" in Milton's and Homer's works, a brief examination of the broader epic traditions that inform the standoff between Gabriel and Satan reveals how Milton in book IV manages a delicate balance between God's justice and angelic will.[42] Repeatedly in both the *Iliad* and *Aeneid*, divine scales are strictly used in battles – and they are used much more strictly than in *Paradise Lost*. Each time Zeus consults his golden scales in the *Iliad*, for example, the gods promptly act on the results. Thus, Zeus places in his scales "two fates of

---

[41] Barbara Kiefer Lewalski, *"Paradise Lost" and the Rhetoric of Literary Forms* (Princeton: Princeton University Press, 1985), p. 60.

[42] Machacek, *Milton and Homer: "Written to Aftertimes"* (Pittsburgh: Duquesne University Press, 2011), p. 89. More generally, Machacek calls for an expanded understanding of allusions to Homer in Milton's works: they not only enrich the epic's meaning, he argues, but also helped to establish *Paradise Lost*'s canonical status.

death ... / one for the Trojan horsemen, one for Argives." When "down went Achaea's day of doom, Achaea's fate /. . . / as the fate of Troy went lifting toward the sky," Zeus immediately begins to help the Trojans: he lets loose "a huge crash of thunder from Ida, / hurling his bolts in a flash against Achaea's armies."[43] Achilles' victory over Hector is decided in the same way: Zeus grips the beam of his "sacred golden scales," raises them in the air, and, as soon as "down went Hector's day of doom," the gods hurry to execute the scales' verdict: Apollo abandons Hector, and "Athena rushe[s] to Achilles, her bright eyes gleaming" (XXII.249, 252–55 [208–13]).

The difference between the use of the golden scales in *Paradise Lost* and the *Iliad* allows us to measure the difference between Milton's Arminian epic and classical notions of fate. Perhaps most notably, God's scales in *Paradise Lost* are not used for determining who will die in battle; God weighs the consequences of his creatures' actions, not their fates. Nor does Milton's God immediately enforce the scales' verdict and decide for Gabriel and Satan whether they should fight or part. Instead, God publishes his scales' results in the sky – "yet seen" in the stars, as Milton describes them (IV.997).

In Virgil's *Aeneid*, the gods also do not spring into action at the drop of Jupiter's scales, but here the divine balance arguably has a more far-reaching effect: "Jupiter himself / holds up two scales in equal balance, then / he adds two different fates, one on each hand: / whom this trial doom, what weight sinks down to death."[44] Whereas Zeus turned to his scales in the *Iliad* to judge battles that did not directly lead to the war's outcome, Jupiter's scales, brought forth only at the epic's climax, seem prophetic within the larger narrative. Signaling Turnus' defeat at Aeneas' hands, the scales also symbolize the Trojans' victory over the Latins, and, more broadly, the founding and flourishing of Rome.[45]

---

[43] Homer, *The Iliad*, trans. Robert Fagles (New York: Penguin, 1990), VIII.82–89 [68–77]; subsequent quotations in this chapter are also from this edition unless otherwise indicated. Louden, "Milton and the Appropriation of a Homeric Technique," proposes a subsequent but related precedent in the *Iliad* (VIII.130–33) as Homer describes "the deeds beyond remedy" that would have ensued without Zeus' intervention (p. 330).

[44] For the English verse translations, I am working from *The Aeneid of Virgil*, trans. Allen Mandelbaum (Berkeley: University of California Press, 1981), XII.961–64. The Latin reads, "*Iuppiter ipse duas aequato examine lances / sustinet et fata imponit diversa duorum, / quem damnet labor et quo vergat pondere letum.*" See Virgil, *Aeneid*, trans. H. Rushton Fairclough, rev. G. P. Goold, 2 vols. (Cambridge: Harvard University Press, 2000), XII.725–27.

[45] Merritt Y. Hughes, in his unpublished notes for the Milton Variorum, is also reminded of Trissino's similarly prophetic use of scales in *L'Italia Liberata da Gothi* (1547; book 27; 3: 178) where "the Mover of the heavens weighs the fate of the barbarians against that of the Romans in 'the golden scales which are high when the nights begin to lengthen,' and all the angels witness the plunge of the scale of the Goths into the abyss."

In *Paradise Lost*, the scales' verdict may similarly refer to more than the outcome of a single battle. When Milton says that God weighs "the sequel" of Gabriel's and Satan's decisions (IV.1003), the general term "sequel" leaves open the possibility that the verdict extends beyond the immediate consequence of their not going to war. Also, as various critics have noted, the passage's possible allusion to stellar constellations – Libra, Virgo, and Scorpio – allegorically foretells Satan's temptation of Eve.[46] As Clay Daniel explains, "just as Libra separates the scorpion from the virgin, so Gabriel seconded by the divine scales, interposes between Satan and Eve."[47]

But if the answers in *Paradise Lost* are written in the stars, it is only because we – and not God – read them there. This distinction is significant: whereas in both the *Iliad* and *Aeneid* the deity consults his scales to answer a particular question, in *Paradise Lost* first Gabriel and then Satan look up for answers and then make their own decisions by interpreting God's sign.[48] In like manner, Raphael instructs Adam before the Fall to approach heaven "as the book of God before thee set, / Wherein to read his wondrous works, and learn" (VIII.67–68); and after Adam and Eve have eaten the forbidden fruit, Adam begins to read the "mute signs" that appear in nature: the sky grows dark, an eagle chases a bird, and a lion chases a dog and hart (XI.182–94). Adam, like Gabriel and Satan, can try to interpret these images, but the signs in themselves do not exert any control over Adam or his choices. And while God's scales deliver a decisive verdict for Gabriel and Satan – the "sequel" of fighting "quick up flew, and kicked the beam" (IV.1003–04) – the ambivalent language in the surrounding passage demonstrates the difference between divine foreknowledge and the limited understanding of God's creatures. Words such as "seemed" and "doubting" (IV.990, 983) reflect the reader's own uncertainty. In contrast to the scales' definitive answer, we read that heaven's cope "perhaps" had been disturbed (IV.992–93) and various "dreadful deeds / Might have ensued" (IV.990–91).

Milton includes Gabriel and Satan within the passage's interpretive uncertainty, for both ultimately misread the scales' meaning. According to epic precedent, the heavier weight should indicate imminent defeat – as with both Achaea's armies and Hector in the *Iliad*, and with Turnus in the

---

[46] See in particular Clay Daniel, "Astrea, the Golden Scales, and the Scorpion: Milton's Heavenly Reflection of the Scene in Eden," *Milton Quarterly* 20 (1986): 92–98; and Frank Harper Moore, "Astrea, the Scorpion, and the Heavenly Scales," *English Literary History* 38 (1971): 350–57.

[47] Daniel, "Astrea, the Golden Scales, and the Scorpion," p. 92.

[48] As Francis C. Blessington observes about Virgil's diction, the "subjunctive of an indirect question tells us that Jupiter is seeking an answer." See Blessington, *"Paradise Lost" and the Classical Epic* (Boston: Routledge and Kegan Paul, 1979), p. 43.

Aeneid – while the lighter weight ought to reveal imminent victory – as with, respectively, the Trojan horsemen, Achilles, and Aeneas. John Dryden first suggested that Milton in *Paradise Lost* was confused about the epic precedent. Claiming that he "dare not condemn so great a genius as Milton," Dryden nevertheless interrupts his "Dedication of the Æneis" to point out that Milton "makes the good angel's scale descend, and the Devil's mount, quite contrary to Virgil."[49]

While I, in turn, would not dare condemn so great a genius as Dryden, the apparent error he detects here may not be Milton's. Certainly we could defend such a reversal as a deliberate gesture on Milton's part to indicate a new, Christian scale for measuring heroic fortitude. Just as God corrects Satan's dilated sense of scale as he stands like the mountains Teneriffe or Atlas, so God could be correcting the angels' misplaced reliance on military might by turning things upside down. A survey of Christian art from the ninth to the sixteenth century also reveals that representations of the Last Judgment usually depict the scale of good deeds as the heavier of the two pans.[50]

And yet the passage in question reads that God put in his golden scales "two weights / The sequel each of parting and of fight; / The latter quick up flew, and kicked the beam" (IV.1002–04). In other words, God never weighs Satan against Gabriel's squadron; the scales' two sides do not correspond to the two combatants, as in the classical tradition, but instead signify the repercussions of Satan's choice. In this context, that the sequel of parting proves heavier than the sequel of fighting still adheres to the logic of Homer's and Virgil's scales, for Satan's departure is still a defeat: it signals death for humankind as well as for himself. Leaving so that he can seduce God's newest creations, Satan will achieve only a pyrrhic victory and will ultimately suffer a "fatal bruise" as he is "tread at last under our feet" (X.190–91). Milton thus aptly allies Satan in his departure at the end of book IV with the description of the defeated Turnus at the end of *Aeneid*. Just as Turnus dies "with a moan / his life, resentful, fled to Shades below" (XII.1270–71 [951–52]), so Satan "fled / Murmuring, and with him fled the shades of night" (IV.1014–15).

It is Gabriel and Satan – and not Milton – who arguably are confused. Instead of realizing that God is weighing the consequences of their choices,

[49] John Dryden, "Dedication of the Æneis," in *Essays of John Dryden*, ed. W. P. Ker, 2 vols. (Oxford: Clarendon, 1926), II: 212–13.

[50] Mary Phillips Perry, "On the Psychostasis in Christian Art, Parts I and II," *Burlington Magazine* 22 (1912–13): 94–105, 208–18 (p. 216). Perry notes, by comparison, that in representations of the weighing that accompanies Michael's battle with the dragon, the scale of good deeds is usually the higher: "it is raised in order to set it out of the reach of the embodiment of evil."

Gabriel tells Satan to "read thy lot in yon celestial sign / Where thou are weigh'd, and shown how light, how weak, / If thou resist" (IV.1011–13). Either Gabriel uses language that will appeal to Satan, as Alastair Fowler suggests, or Gabriel himself misunderstands God's sign.[51] In this latter case, Gabriel's misapprehension would arise because he reads the sign as pagan but attaches to it a Christian signified – that is, he assumes the scales weigh his and Satan's fates based on epic precedent, but he interprets the scales' results based on biblical logic and assumes that the lighter side would indicate defeat. According to the judgment of Belshazzar in the Book of Daniel, for example, "Thou art weighed in the balances, and art found wanting" (5.27).[52]

Also relevant for Gabriel's identifying of Satan with the lighter scale may be the pejorative implication of lightweight goods during the seventeenth century. Because the basic technology of balances remained mostly unchanged for millennia – namely, two pans or "scales" suspended from the ends of a beam – we cannot assume that the image of the golden scales in *Paradise Lost* was informed by Milton's contemporary culture. Paintings and sculptures that survive from ancient Egypt use balances to depict psychostasis, and images of a personified Justice holding a balance occur commonly in Christian art dating from the beginning of the Common Era and continued to appear throughout the seventeenth century.[53] Thus, the Leveller leader John Lilburne, in a striking mixed metaphor, argued for his release from custody in 1654 by asserting "That the Law, and Courts of Justice, are the Scales of a Nation, and ought to be the Keyes for opening of prison doors."[54]

Yet Milton and his readers would have also been familiar with scales from everyday experience. Various types of balances that resemble the image in book IV had been in common use in England since medieval times – by, among others, apothecaries, assayers, bankers, drapers, farmers, grocers, jewelers, miners, spicers, and traders. Even candles and silk, for example, were purchased according to their weight throughout the early modern period, and at least one seventeenth-century balance survives made of gilded

---

[51] Fowler, p. 280. More recently, Angelica Duran has argued that Gabriel embodies the "English Scientific Revolution" as he "correctly" interprets God's scales. However, Duran overlooks the implications of the classical scales that also inform Milton's image. See Duran, *The Age of Milton and the Scientific Revolution* (Pittsburgh: Duquesne University Press, 2007), p. 88.

[52] See also Isaiah 40:15 and Job 31:6.

[53] Bruno Kisch, *Scales and Weights: A Historical Outline* (New Haven and London: Yale University Press, 1965), pp. 76–77.

[54] John Lilburne, *A Declaration to the Free-born People of England*, 2nd edn. (London, 1654), A3v–A4r.

silver that resembles God's golden scales in *Paradise Lost*.[55] Each large port in England, moreover, was required by royal statute to have a "king's beam," a balance whose use was compulsory for all imported and exported goods sold in bulk.[56] In *The Merchants Map of Commerce* (1671), Lewes Roberts describes the Kings Beam in London as a mechanism that, like the one in *Paradise Lost*, helped "to decide Differences and Controversies arising by Weights and Weighing." A *"sworn Weigher,"* according to Roberts, kept a detailed register of "all ponderous Commodities bought or sold" to help resolve disputes among merchants and customers: anything brought to the Kings Beam that proved too light was considered counterfeit.[57] Thus, when Gabriel says that Satan has been "weigh'd, and shown how light, how weak, / If thou resist," he suggests that if Satan attempts to resist God's authority, he will expose himself as a phony.

In this context, that Milton at the end of book IV never refers to God's hand raising his golden scales may be significant. Traditional Christian iconography as well as the works of Homer and Virgil consistently depict auncel balances – that is, hand-held instruments which had to be lifted by users to determine the equality or difference between the things being weighed. In the earliest Christian art, the hand of God holds the balance from heaven, whereas later art more often associates the instrument with the angel Michael's hand.[58] Similarly, as we have seen in the *Iliad*, Zeus "lifted up his golden scales" (καὶ τότε δὴ χρύσεια πατὴρ ἐτίταινε τάλαντα), and in the *Aeneid* Jupiter "himself / holds up two scales in even balance" (*Iuppiter ipse duas aequato examine lances / sustinet*).[59] In *Paradise Lost*, by comparison, we read, "Th' Eternal . . . / Hung forth in Heav'n his golden scales" (IV.996–97), which suggests that Milton might have been envisioning the more modern type of hanging or free-standing instrument used in seventeenth-century England. Parliament had begun to outlaw auncel balances in 1353 because of both their inexactness and their susceptibility to fraudulent weighing: such hand-held devices could easily be tipped to one side or the other when lifted by the user.[60] Milton's image of a more

[55] Kisch, *Scales and Weights*, pp. 52–55, 47.

[56] More precisely, each port had two such balances – a "great beam" for weighing heavy merchandise such as wool, and a "small beam" for weighing luxury goods such as silk. See Ronald Edward Zupko, *British Weights and Measures: A History from Antiquity to the Seventeenth Century* (Madison: University of Wisconsin Press, 1977), p. 25.

[57] Lewes Roberts, *The Merchants Map of Commerce*, 2nd edn. (London, 1671), C2v.

[58] Perry, "On the Psychostasis in Christian Art," pp. 102–04.

[59] Homer, *Iliad*, trans. A. T. Murray, rev. William F. Wyatt, 2 vols. (Cambridge: Harvard University Press, 1999), XXII.209; and Virgil, *Aeneid*, trans. H. Rushton Fairclough, rev. G. P. Goold, 2 vols. (Cambridge: Harvard University Press, 2000), XII.725–26.

[60] Kisch, *Scales and Weights*, p. 29; Zupko, *British Weights and Measures*, pp. 24–25.

modern balance accordingly emphasizes divine impartiality. Later, as we have seen, God will tell the angels that he did not predestine Adam and Eve to sin: "no decree of mine / Concurring to necessitate his fall, / Or touch with lightest moment of impulse / His free will, to her own inclining left / In even scale" (X.43–47). So, at the end of book IV Milton implies through the image of the scales that God does not in the least interfere with angelic free will and does not in any way influence the sequel of Satan and Gabriel's choices.

More specifically, Satan's being found too light by God's golden balance could have alluded to the contemporary practice of weighing coins to determine counterfeits – typically produced, according to one seventeenth-century tract, by clipping, filing, washing, or scaling – which could be detected by weighing the suspect denominations against their respective standards.[61] False coins would fly up and kick the beam, as does the pan in *Paradise Lost* holding "The sequel . . . of fight," because, when compared to royal standards, counterfeit money typically lacked the required amount of gold or silver – an especially significant problem after the Restoration, as Charles II's government found itself without sufficient funds in part because of the circulation of so much counterfeit currency.[62] Francis Quarles, in his *Emblemes* (1635), playfully connects biblical and contemporary imagery as he glosses Psalm 62:9. Quarles describes how the "counterfeit desire" of a worldly life cannot outweigh the treasure of a life with God: "Imposture," he laments, has "cheated man" with its "false weights and measure, / Proclaiming Bad for Good; and gilding death with pleasure" (see figure 2.1).[63]

Of course, neither Milton nor his readers may have had such mercantile associations in mind as Gabriel attempts to interpret Satan's place in God's scales. But that Satan is "weighed, and shown how light" also recalls the preceding epic simile in which the "careful plowman doubting stands / Lest on the threshing floor his hopeful sheaves / Prove chaff" (IV.983–85). A farmer or plowman during the early modern period could readily winnow the chaff from the grain after raking away the straw: chaff always weighs less. Tossed or poured into an air current, it could then be blown aloft, like Satan as he departs Paradise and flies away. We can

---

[61] William Badcock, *A Touch-stone for Gold and Silver Wares* (London, 1677), H6r–H8v.

[62] See, for example, Charles II, *A Proclamation, against Exportation, and Buying and Selling of Gold and Silver at Higher Rates Then in Our Mint: As Also against Culling, Washing, or Otherwise Diminishing Our Current Moneys* (London, 1661).

[63] Francis Quarles, *Emblemes*, 2nd edn. (London, 1635), B4v–B6r. The text of Psalm 62:9 reads, "Surely men of low degree *are* vanity, / *and* men of high degree *are* a lie: / to be laid in the balance, / they *are* together *lighter* than vanity."

16   EMBLEMES,   Book 1.

IV.

Quis leuior? cui Iesus ponderis addit amor.

Will: Marshall: sculpsit.

Figure 2.1 Francis Quarles, *Emblemes* (London, 1635), B4v.

accordingly amplify Stanley Fish's interpretation of the confrontation between Gabriel and Satan as an indication of Satan's debased heroism and empty rhetoric; in the context of this simile, Milton specifically allies Satan with waste.[64]

---

[64] Stanley Fish, *Surprised by Sin: The Reader in "Paradise Lost,"* 2nd edn. (Cambridge: Harvard University Press, 1997), pp. 175–76.

Nor should we be surprised to witness Satan flying away at the end of book IV if he thinks that the lighter weight represents his lot. Whereas Satan threatened Gabriel that "Far heavier load thyself expect to feel / From my prevailing arm" (IV.972–73), Satan sees God's scales above him and presumably remembers that the last time he challenged the omnipotent Creator in a military conflict his efforts proved "light" and "weak" (IV.1012). Satan sees that he is outnumbered, accepts Gabriel's interpretation of the scales, and flees. But he might still mistakenly believe that he can win another day and wishfully identify with the "mounted scale aloft" (IV.1014), which, according to pagan precedent, would signify victory. As Satan dilates himself during the standoff with the good angels, he figuratively becomes "mounted" – that is, elevated like a mountain.[65] Also, "aloft" could mean to be positioned at a high rank or with high estimation, which would describe Satan's various vain attempts to climb a different type of scale in *Paradise Lost*, the "scale of nature," introduced by Raphael as he tells Adam and Eve that their bodies may be "Improved by tract of time, and winged ascend / Ethereal" (V.509, 498–99).[66]

But Satan in *Paradise Lost* has a terrible sense of direction. Not only does he have to stop and ask for help – first from Chaos (II.968–87), then from Uriel (III.654–80) – but he also travels uncertainly, "Through the calm firmament; but up or down / By center, or eccentric, hard to tell" (III.574–75). This ambiguous description may be Milton's coy excuse for not committing to a specific astronomical model for the epic's universe, but it also may indicate Satan's ignorance and directionless flight. When in hell Satan climbs "High on a throne of royal state" (II.1), he once again confuses his further downfall for his ascent. He remains painfully unaware that to be "by merit raised / To that bad eminence" (II.5–6) means that, on the scale of nature, he continues to put himself at the bottom, the farthest away from God.

As Satan chooses to flee in the final lines of book IV, he ultimately fails to understand the image that God provides. Regardless of why Satan identifies with the lighter scale, he and Gabriel still seem to assume, according to classical precedent, that the scales weigh Satan's victory (or defeat) against the defeat (or victory) of Gabriel's squadron. More

---

[65] *OED*, s. v. "mounted," def. 1. *Mounted* could also mean "the state of being armed" (def. 5), which would recall Satan's use of cannons and gunpowder during the war in heaven.

[66] *OED*, s. v. "aloft," def. 11. Contrary to Satan's false expectations, his fallen nature and material debasement would recommend that his scale fall, not ascend toward heaven. For a discussion of Satan and the bad angels' material hardening, see chaps. 4 and 5.

important, Satan never realizes that he has other options besides the either-or of parting or fighting. As the narrator explains early on, all of Satan's "malice served but to bring forth / Infinite goodness, grace and mercy shown / On man by him seduced, but on himself / Treble confusion, wrath and vengeance poured" (I.217–20). In other words, whether Satan flees or fights, he will continue to promote God's glory and to make things worse for himself. Milton in *Paradise Lost* does not subscribe to the theory of a fortunate fall – God, for example, says about Adam that "Happier, had if sufficed him to have known / Good by itself, and evil not all" (XI.88–89) – but, if we take the long view, the ultimate "sequel" of Satan's departure includes both his doom and the Son's sacrifice and salvation, while Satan's choice of fighting the good angels would have also proven disastrous for Satan, resulting in a "horrid fray" in which Gabriel threatens to "trample" Satan "as mire" (IV.996, 1010).[67] Simply put, Satan in book IV cannot win – not because God has predestined Satan to lose, but because the fiend keeps asking the wrong question. The scales convey a clear answer – war is ruinous – but the question is whether to obey or defy God, not whether to fight or fly. If Satan and Gabriel rightly choose to avoid a battle, Satan should then part from his wicked ways, drop to his knees, and beg for God's mercy.

The ending of book IV re-enacts the conclusion that Satan has already reached in the book's opening soliloquy. Just as he acknowledges his culpability but then bids hope "farewell" and decides that "Evil be thou my good" (IV.108, 110), so he flies away from the possible insight that God's golden scales momentarily offer. At the end of book IV, Satan, following Gabriel's interpretation, "looked up and knew / His mounted scale aloft; nor more; but fled" (IV.1013–14). The sudden interruption of "nor more" emphasizes the limitation of Satan's knowledge. God's scales appear in the sky, but, we might say, the scales do not drop from Satan's eyes. More generally, Milton in this episode measures the dissonance between divine and angelic knowledge. Even when God gives us such a telling image, even when the readers are celestial creatures, still we must choose for ourselves, and the choice is not easy.

---

[67] On the improbability of Milton accepting a fortunate fall, see Danielson, *Milton's Good God*, pp. 202–27.

CHAPTER 3

Heaven's gates

That thou mayest rightly obey power, her bounds know;
Those past, her nature and name is changed.

– John Donne, Satire 3[1]

Whereas God's scales appear in the sky only fleetingly as Satan and Gabriel prepare for battle, other images associated with the divine in *Paradise Lost* have considerably more staying power. In particular, Milton refers repeatedly to various aspects of heaven's architecture – "many a towered structure high" (I.733). In some places, he seems to envision heaven as a garden or pastoral landscape so that, for example, the angels sit in "blissful bow'rs" (XI.77), and the tall blooms of the "Immortal amarant" give shade to "the fount of life, / And where the river of bliss through midst of Heav'n / Rolls o'er Elysian flow'rs her amber stream" (III.353, 357–59). But other details in the epic suggest that Milton also thought of heaven as an enclosed urban space, with a paved road, a wall, and gates. While discussions of architecture in *Paradise Lost* typically focus on fallen and satanic forms – most notably Pandemonium and the bridge that Sin and Death build over chaos[2] – I wish to show in this chapter that heaven's architectural features, some of the most specific visual images that Milton offers of the "eternal regions" (III.349), deserve scrutiny for the way that they express the epic's theology.

In *The Faerie Queene*, by comparison, Spenser's Red Crosse Knight gazes with wonder at "Hierusalem," the city "that God has built / For those to dwell in, that are chosen his," but Spenser includes few details beyond the city's "stately building" and "bright Angles towre" which were "builded high and strong / Of perle and precious stone, that earthly tong[ue] /

---

[1] John Donne, Satire 3, in *John Donne*, ed. John Carey (Oxford: Oxford University Press, 1990), pp. 29–31 (lines 100–01).
[2] See, for example, Steven Blakemore, "Pandemonium and Babel: Architectural Hierarchy in *Paradise Lost*," *Milton Quarterly* 20.4 (1986): 142–45; and Jeffrey S. Theis, "Milton's Principles of Architecture," *English Literary Renaissance* 35.1 (2005): 102–22.

Cannot describe."[3] Similarly, in *The Pilgrim's Progress*, John Bunyan depicts the City of God, but offers little information about its appearance. Christian must pass through a "Wicket-gate" and follow the "narrow way" to arrive at the walled "Cœlestial City."[4] Aside from the gate's gold inscription – "*Blessed are they that do his commandments, that they may have right to the Tree of Life; and may enter in through the Gates into the City*" – we learn only that "the City shone like the Sun, the Streets also were paved with Gold, and in them walked many men, with Crowns on their heads, Palms in their hands, and golden Harps to sing praises withall."[5]

While Milton's account of heaven in *Paradise Lost* is hardly thorough or cohesive, the few tantalizing visual details that are included about the divine realm suggest a much more specific physical space. Heaven in *Paradise Lost* has "opal tow'rs" (II.1049), battlements of "living sapphire" (II.1050), and gates "thick with sparkling orient gems" (III.507) that turn on "golden hinges" (VII.207) and bear "frontispieces of diamond and gold" (III.506). Clearly, in these passages Milton, like Spenser and Bunyan, was working from the account of the bejeweled "great city, the holy Jerusalem, descending out of heaven from God," as described in the Book of Revelation (21:10). The association of heaven with precious stones might originate with the earth-bound experience of gazing at a starry night sky, and a more precise connection between celestial bodies and gems, which purportedly reflected planetary virtues, was a long-standing tradition reaching back to ancient Babylonian lapidaries.[6] But Milton's specific language echoes Revelation in combining the image of jewels with urban structures:

> And the building of the wall of it was *of* jasper: and the city *was* pure gold, like unto clear glass. And the foundations of the wall of the city *were* garnished with all manner of precious stones. The first foundation *was* jasper; the second, sapphire; the third, a chalcedony; the fourth, an emerald; The fifth, sardonyx; the sixth, sardius; the seventh, chrysolite; the eighth, beryl; the ninth, a topaz; the tenth, a chrysoprasus; the eleventh, a jacinth; the twelfth, an amethyst. And the twelve gates *were* twelve pearls; every several gate was of one pearl; and the street of the city *was* pure gold, as it were transparent glass. (21:18–21)

---

[3] Edmund Spenser, *The Faerie Queene*, ed. A. C. Hamilton (Harlow, Eng.: Longman, 2001), I.X.57, 56, 58, 55. All subsequent references to Spenser's poem in this chapter are taken from this edition and cited parenthetically.

[4] John Bunyan, *The Pilgrim's Progress from This World to That Which Is to Come*, ed. James Blanton Wharey, rev. Roger Sharrock, 2nd edn. (Oxford: Clarendon, 1960), pp. 10, 27, 88.

[5] Bunyan, *The Pilgrim's Progress*, pp. 161, 162.

[6] See Joan Evans, *Magical Jewels of the Middle Ages and Renaissance* (Oxford: Clarendon, 1922), p. 24.

Although we might doubt the ability of readers, then or now, to visualize all of the gemstones that the author of Revelation mentions here – Thomas Browne, for example, complained that "St. John's description by emeralds, chrysolites, and precious stones is too weak to express the material Heaven we behold"[7] – Milton in imagining heaven in *Paradise Lost* may have been consciously or unconsciously assuming that readers could supplement the details he provides with the Bible's fuller (although still incomplete) account of the New Jerusalem. He might even have expected that some of his poem's fit audience would be familiar with the properties of gems explained in the lapidaries of the Middle Ages and Renaissance and thus would know, along with Robert Burton, for example, that sapphire "frees the minde, mends manners," while chalcedony "preserves the vigour and good estate of the whole body."[8] But in terms of the epic's visual imagery, Milton also suggests that a partial description of the city of God is the best that one can attain. In keeping with God's unknowableness and invisibility, Milton emphasizes that a comprehensive image of heaven is impossible. Despite his poetic efforts, the "sparkling orient gems" that adorn the doors to the celestial realm remain "inimitable on Earth / By model, or by shading pencil drawn" (III.507–09).

In this chapter, I focus less on the gems that decorate heaven's wall and gates in *Paradise Lost*, and examine more generally Milton's image of heaven as an enclosed citadel. Just as various critics have proposed that the depiction of Pandemonium might draw on his familiarity with specific contemporary buildings – St. Peter's in Rome, Saint Paul's in London, or the Tempietto by Donnato Bramante in Rome[9] – I wish to suggest that the details of heaven as a citadel might have been influenced by the architecture that Milton would have encountered both in London and during his visit to the Continent. The poem's divine wall and gates, as I show, mark boundaries but not strictly enforced limits. Instead, they appear to separate and distinguish, but not to prevent ingress and egress. Like God's golden scales, these imposing but permeable structures manifest physically the epic's central, apparently paradoxical premise of free will and absolute divine authority.

---

[7] Thomas Browne, *Religio Medici*, ed. James Winny (Cambridge: Cambridge University Press, 1963), p. 59 (part I, sec. 49).

[8] Robert Burton, *The Anatomy of Melancholy*, 5 vols., ed. Nicolas K. Kiessling, Thomas C. Faulkner, and Rhonda L. Blair (Oxford: Clarendon, 1989–90), II: 220 (part 2, sec. 4, memb. 1, subs. 4).

[9] For these three possible models for Pandemonium, see Blakemore, "Pandemonium and Babel," pp. 142–45; Joseph Lyle, "Architecture and Idolatry in *Paradise Lost*," *Studies in English Literature* 40.1 (2000): 139–55; and Roland Mushat Frye, *Milton's Imagery and the Visual Arts* (Princeton: Princeton University Press, 1978), p. 138.

A marriage of heaven and hell

On one level, as commentators have long observed, the buildings that Milton describes in the divine realm resemble but contrast with the epic's diabolic structures so as to highlight God's glory and the rebels' degrading sinfulness. Just as Milton treats Adam and Eve's fallen condition as a debased but not entirely distinct form of their previous lives in Paradise, so he does not simply juxtapose the divine and satanic realms in *Paradise Lost* but depicts hell as a cracked reflection of heaven.[10] Thus, most obviously, "The riches of Heav'n's pavement, trodden gold" (I.682), become the material out of which the rebels build the roof of Pandemonium. That the good angels walk on this precious metal suggests both the splendor of heaven and the indifference – or, perhaps, the contempt – that divine beings have for material riches. By comparison, Satan and his followers seem to covet gold, and, after escaping the burning lake, immediately turn their thoughts to building a palace, instead of seeking forgiveness. Pandemonium's golden roof, in conjunction with heaven's gold pavement, neatly symbolizes how hell inverts divine values. And whereas gold can literally be found all over the ground in heaven, Satan's followers in hell obtain it only with great effort, by having "Ransacked the center" and "with impious hands / Rifled the bowels of their mother Earth" (I.686–87) – a distinction that anticipates the hard labor imposed on Adam and Eve after the Fall and suggests in its violence the fallen angels' abject acquisitiveness.

Similarly, walls enclose both heaven and hell, but the divine structure is apparently a single, beautifully bejeweled form – the "crystal wall of Heav'n" (VI.860), as Raphael describes it – whereas hell is walled in nine times with "fire, / Outrageous to devour" (II.434–35). The gates to the two realms also express the difference between the satanic and the godly. When Satan refers to hell as a "prison strong" with "gates of burning adamant / Barred over us" (II.434–37), we might suspect him of exaggerating the difficulty of leaving the region so as to dissuade his followers from volunteering to go in search of the new world. Yet the narrator also enumerates nine flaming gates reaching to the "horrid roof" of hell (II.644) that block the rebels' passage out of the underworld: "three folds were brass, / Three iron, three of adamantine rock, / Impenetrable, impaled with circling fire, / Yet unconsumed" (II.645–48). In addition, two "formidable shape[s]" (II.649), Sin and Death, stand on each side of hell's "dismal gates"

[10] For this reading of Adam and Eve, see Dobranski, *The Cambridge Introduction to Milton* (Cambridge: Cambridge University Press, 2012), pp. 172–78.

(VIII.241). As Sin explains, ingress and egress occur only with her permission; at the time of the Fall, "this powerful key / Into my hand was giv'n, with charge to keep / These gates for ever shut, which none can pass / Without my op'ning" (II.774–77).

But if details of this image remain difficult to visualize – what, for example, would "adamantine rock" look like? How can it be "impaled with circling fire /... unconsumed"? – the subsequent description of Sin's opening of hell's gate for Satan is more pictorial:

> the huge portcullis high up drew,
> Which but herself not all the Stygian powers
> Could once have moved; then in the key-hole turns
> Th' intricate wards, and every bolt and bar
> Of massy iron or solid rock with ease
> Unfastens: on a sudden open fly
> With impetuous recoil and jarring sound
> Th' infernal doors, and on their hinges grate
> Harsh thunder, that the lowest bottom shook
> Of Erebus. She opened, but to shut
> Excelled her power; the gates wide open stood,
> That with extended wings a bannered host
> Under spread ensigns marching might pass through
> With horse and chariots ranked in loose array;
> So wide they stood, and like a furnace mouth
> Cast forth redounding smoke and ruddy flame.   (II.874–89)

Clearly, the main details of this account are allegorical. Drawing up the portcullis represents an act of Sin and thus a sinful action, whereas closing hell's gate exceeds Sin's power because doing so would be righteous, not sinful. In like manner, that the hinges "grate" and the doors make a "jarring sound" symbolizes Satan's violation and threat as he leaves the infernal realm, while "impetuous recoil" points to the punishment that Satan will heap on his own head for his rashness. And the imposing physical presence of the gates' mechanism – "intricate wards," "massy iron," and "solid rock" – presumably conveys the severity of the rebels' punishment, in contrast to the "sudden" movement as the lock unfastens, which suggests the ease of sin and the freedom to defy God's commandments.

Yet, all of the passage's symbolic elements are expressed in a burst of almost cinematic detail shots: the portcullis flying up, the key turning in the lock, and the iron bolts suddenly sliding open. The rapid succession of material images foregrounds the physical experience of leaving hell, as does the visual description that measures the space between the newly opened gates; Milton invites us to imagine how an angelic squadron "with extended wings" and "Under spread ensigns" could march through "With horse and chariots ranked in loose array." This latter image may associate the unlocking of hell's gates with traditional forms of epic heroism, but it diminishes those forms to mere pageantry. Similarly, the comparison of the open gates with the mouth of a furnace could suggest the rapacious threat that hell's new open-door policy holds for earth's inhabitants, but the simile simultaneously reduces Satan's heroic potential to smoke and ash. The strongly visual emphasis of all these lines seems to indicate hell's material debasement, which lends itself to imagery more than the poem's spiritual realm does. In terms of the spiritous versus material creations that Raphael describes with his plant metaphor (in book V), hell's form appears to be dominated by hardened substance.

The walls and gates enclosing heaven, by comparison, seem less physically present than hell's boundaries and pose no obstacle for the entrance and exit of God, the Son, and the angels. If, as Jeffery Theis has argued, fallen structures in *Paradise Lost* are characterized by their "ornamentation, rigidity, and hostility to the immediate environment,"[11] then divine architecture, while still ornate, is most notable for being pliable and in harmony with the heavenly realm and its inhabitants. When, for example, God sends forth the Son to create a new world,

> Heav'n opened wide
> Her ever-during gates, harmonious sound
> On golden hinges moving, to let forth
> The King of Glory in his powerful Word
> And Spirit coming to create more worlds.   (VII.205–09)

In keeping with God's creative motive in these lines versus Satan's destructive mission at the gates of hell, so the individual details in the two scenes limn the differences between divine beneficence and satanic vengeance. In particular, the hinges' "harmonious sound" echoes but contrasts with the "jarring sound" and "Harsh thunder" of hell's doors, while the beauty of the mechanism's opening "golden hinges" points up the sense of restriction and degradation implied by the "bolt and bar / Of massy iron or solid rock" that lock in hell's inhabitants. Most striking, though, heaven's gates open on their own, whereas Sin must unlock hell's doors for Satan to pass through. Even if we accept, as I think we should, that the allegorical figure of Sin, like Death, does not have the ontological reality of the epic's other

---

[11] Theis, "Milton's Principles of Architecture," p. 108.

characters and, as a symbolic form, can express but not effect change, her presence still indicates that Satan himself has to open the gates of hell.[12] The difference is that the gates of heaven require no physical contact and swing open automatically.

Three other times in *Paradise Lost* the gates of heaven open on their own – when Raphael departs heaven (V.254–56), when the rebel angels are ejected (II.996–97, VI.861), and when the Son as God returns on the seventh day after creating the world (VII.565–75). Most immediately behind Milton's image may be the similarly automatic gates depicted in antiquity and scripture. As Hera returns to Olympus in the *Iliad*, for example, she "swiftly touched the horses with the whip, and of themselves groaned on their hinges the gates of heaven, which the Hours had in their keeping."[13] In like manner, after the angel releases the apostle Peter from prison, "they came unto the iron gate that leadeth unto the city; which opened to them of its own accord: and they went out" (Acts 12.10). Milton, in placing his self-opening gates at the door to the divine realm, may have been aspiring to supersede – to fly high above – both his classical and biblical sources: he borrows the idea of self-opening gates in *Paradise Lost* to express directly the mystery and power of the Christian deity.

More generally, though, we can read Milton's image of heaven's "ever-during gates" in relation to the variety of marvelous mechanisms described in ancient, medieval, and Renaissance literature. For twenty-first-century readers, accustomed to electrically automated gates and motion or pressure sensors, Milton's image of self-opening doors may seem mundane – albeit prescient – but for early modern readers the image must have sounded wondrous. Joseph Addison, for example, thought it necessary to defend Milton's fantastic self-opening gates and pointed to the Homeric prece-dent of Hephaestus' "*Tripodes*, running on Golden Wheels, which, upon Occasion, might go of themselves to the Assembly of the Gods, and, when there was no more use for them, return again after the same manner [*Iliad* XVIII.434–40]."[14] Or, we might recall the gold and silver dogs, also fashioned by Hephaestus, that guard Alcinous' palace in the *Odyssey* (VII.92–94); the "double folding doors" at the palace of the Sun in Ovid's *Metamorphoses* (II.1–7); the incredible devices invented by Daedalus – his wings, labyrinth, and wooden figures – as retold in various

[12] See Stephen M. Fallon, *Milton among the Philosophers: Poetry and Materialism in Seventeenth-Century England* (Ithaca: Cornell University Press, 1991), pp. 183–90.

[13] Homer, *Iliad*, trans. A. T. Murray, rev. William F. Wyatt, 2 vols. (Cambridge: Harvard University Press, 1999), V.745–47 (vol. I: pp. 260–61).

[14] Joseph Addison, *Criticism on Milton's "Paradise Lost,"* ed. Edward Arber (London, 1869), p. 88.

ancient texts; or the beautiful ivory statue, created by Pygmalion, that wondrously comes to life in *Metamorphoses* (X.243–97).[15]

The frequent retelling of these classical stories – in particular the legend of Pygmalion, which was not only included in Ovid's poem but also reinterpreted in the *Romance of the Rose* – helps to explain the lingering credulity for mechanical wonders during the medieval period. This ongoing interest was also no doubt fueled by the clockwork automata introduced into England from the Arab world in the twelfth and thirteenth centuries.[16] The wide array of mechanical curiosities in romances – flying horses, magnetic castle walls, magic gemstones, and guardians made of gold or other metals – suggests the special status that marvels held in the medieval imagination. Most memorable may be Chaucer's depiction of the brazen horse in *The Squire's Tale*, "rather lyk / An apparence ymaad by som magyk," but medieval craftsmen also began to construct actual mechanical marvels for court performances and lavish public pageants.[17] These intricate clockworks and automated men and animals were sometimes based on devices described in romances and sometimes, in turn, influenced the machines depicted in later medieval writings.

The theater during the Renaissance provided a new forum for displaying mechanical marvels, as technological innovation and the desire for spectacle inspired elaborate visual effects.[18] In addition to the sophisticated flying machines and wave-making devices used in Italian theaters and opera houses, contemporary theatrical records from England include references to winches, traps, pulleys, and counterweights. Philip Henslowe first refers in his diary to flying machinery in 1595, and, as John Astington has shown, the flying effects required for the staging of *deus ex machina* were used commonly in academic, public, and court theaters, especially in the early

---

[15] Ovid, *Metamorphoses*, trans. Frank Justus Miller, rev. G. P. Goold, 2 vols. (Cambridge: Harvard University Press, 1977), II.1–7 (vol. I, pp. 60–61) and X.243–97 (vol. II, pp. 80–85). We should also recall that each of the gods' palaces, although not described in detail, was built by Hephaestus "with cunning skill" (Homer, *Iliad* I.605–08 [vol. I: pp. 58–59]).

[16] See Scott Lightsey, *Manmade Marvels in Medieval Culture and Literature* (New York: Palgrave Macmillan, 2007); and Lorraine Daston and Katharine Park, *Wonders and the Order of Nature, 1150–1750* (New York: Zone, 1998). In this paragraph, I am indebted to Lightsey's discussion of medieval devices.

[17] Geoffrey Chaucer, *The Squire's Tale*, in *The Riverside Chaucer*, ed. Larry D. Benson, 3rd edn. (Oxford: Oxford University Press, 1987), pp. 169–77 (lines 217–18). In *Il Penseroso*, Milton specifically recalls Chaucer's "wondrous horse of brass" (line 114).

[18] See "The Development of Scenic Spectacle," US Institute for Theatre Technology and Appalachian State University 2007, maintained by Frank Mohler available at www1.appstate.edu/orgs/spectacle /index.html.

seventeenth century.[19] Among the works of Shakespeare, *Cymbeline* includes the intriguing stage direction, "Jupiter descends in thunder and lightning, sitting upon an eagle: he throws a thunderbolt"; while *The Tempest* calls for the use of a "quaint device" as Ariel claps his wings and Prospero's banquet vanishes.[20]

But beyond the incredible, often symbolic marvels in early modern plays and poetry – the fountain "with curious ymageree / . . . overwrought" in the Bower of Bliss, for example, or the intricate "Buskins of shell" that Hero dons in *Hero and Leander*[21] – a group of copiously illustrated "machine books" were published in England and on the Continent in the sixteenth and seventeenth centuries. These texts contain detailed descriptions of virtual Rube Goldberg inventions, multiple-firing catapults and complicated water-lifting devices, which appear to have invited contemplation and appreciation more than they provided any practical benefit.[22] Craftsmen during the Renaissance also continued to construct machines that aspired to realize ancient and medieval legends of marvelous inventions. Roy Strong refers to a "cult of the automata" that reached its apogee in the gardens and grottos of Jacobean and Caroline England.[23] These marvels – relying, alternatively, on suction, compressed air, water pressure, or winches and pulleys – were primarily objects of display, costly machines that could inspire wonder in a spectator and thus reinforce the authority or status of their owner or patron (see figures 3.1 and 3.2).

Most influential during the Renaissance seems to have been the rediscovery of Hero of Alexandria's *Pneumatics* (*c.* 10–70 CE), first republished in 1501 in a Latin translation by Lorenzo Valla (printed again in 1575, 1583, and 1680), then published in 1589 and 1595 in two Italian translations by, respectively, G. B. Aleotti and Alessandro Giorgi (reprinted in 1647 and 1693). Hero's book circulated so widely that Francis Bacon could explain in passing that, "the mechanics here understood is that treated . . . by Hero in

---

[19] *Henslowe's Diary*, ed. R. A. Foakes, 2nd edn. (Cambridge: Cambridge University Press, 2002), p. 7; and John H. Astington, "Descent Machinery in the Playhouses," *Medieval and Renaissance Drama in England* 2 (1985): 119–33.

[20] Shakespeare, *Cymbeline*, ed. J. M. Nosworthy (New York and London: Routledge, 1991), V.iv; and *The Tempest*, ed. Frank Kermode (New York and London: Routledge, 1987), III.3.

[21] Spenser, *The Faerie Queene*, II.xii.60–66; and Christopher Marlowe, *Hero and Leander*, in *The Collected Poems of Christopher Marlowe*, ed. Patrick Cheney and Brian J. Stiar (New York and Oxford: Oxford University Press, 2006), pp. 193–220 (line 31).

[22] Jonathan Sawday, "'Forms Such as Never Were in Nature': the Renaissance Cyborg," in *At the Borders of the Human: Beasts, Bodies and Natural Philosophy in the Early Modern Period*, ed. Erica Fudge, Ruth Gilbert, and Susan Wiseman (New York: St. Martin's, 1999), pp. 171–95; and Wayne Shumaker, "Accounts of Marvelous Machines in the Renaissance," *Thought: A Review of Culture and Idea* 51 (1976): 255–70.

[23] Roy Strong, *The Renaissance Garden in England* (London: Thames and Hudson, 1979), p. 76.

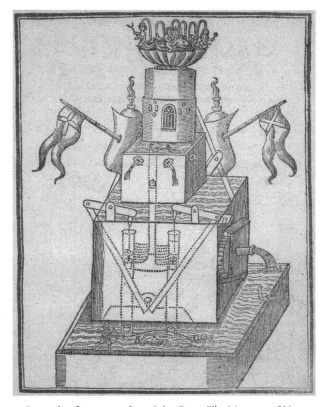

Figure 3.1 Example of automata from John Bate, *The Mysteryes of Nature, and Art*
(London, 1634).

his Pneumatics" (*Enimvero mechanicam, de qua nunc agimus ... Hero in spiritalibus*), while Robert Burton could ask, "What so intricate, and pleasing withall as to peruse and practise *Heron Alexandrinus* workes, on the air engine, the war engine, the engine that moveth itself" ("*de spiritalibus, de machinis bellicis, de machinâ se movente*").[24] Hero's book describes seventy-eight mechanical and hydraulic theorems, each one illustrated

[24] Francis Bacon, *De Augmentis Scientarum*, in *The Works of Francis Bacon, Baron of Verulam*, 10 vols. (London: J. Johnson, 1803), vol. VII: p. 199 (book III, chap. 5); and Burton, *The Anatomy of Melancholy*, II: 92–93 (part 2, sec. 2, memb. 4, subs. 1). See also Marie Boas, "Hero's *Pneumatica*: A Study of Its Transmission and Influence," *Isis* 40.1 (1949): 38–48 (p. 42). Bacon elsewhere calls Hero "an ingenious man and engineer" (*Hero, vir ingeniosus et mechanicus*); see Bacon, *The Great Instauration*, in *The Works of Francis Bacon*, vol. IX: p. 217 (chap. 6; see also p. 121).

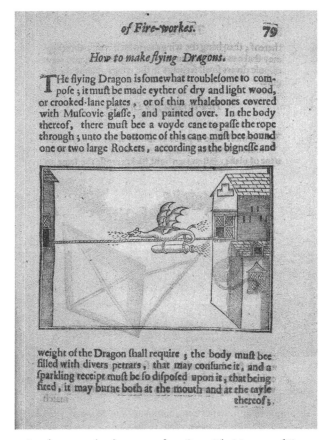

of Fire-workes. 79

How to make flying Dragons.

THe flying Dragon is somewhat troublesome to compose ; it must be made eyther of dry and light wood, or crooked-lane plates , or of thin whalebones covered with Muscovie glasse, and painted over. In the body thereof, there must bee a voyde cane to passe the rope through ; unto the bottome of this cane must bee bound one or two large Rockets , according as the bignesse and

weight of the Dragon shall require ; the body must bee filled with divers petrars , that may consume it, and a sparkling receipt must be so disposed upon it, that being fired , it may burne both at the mouth and at the tayle thereof ;

Figure 3.2 Another example of automata from Bate, *The Mysteryes of Nature, and Art.*

with a manmade machine ornamented with human or animal figures. For Milton's depiction of heaven's self-opening gates, Hero's Theorems XXXVII and XXXVIII seem especially relevant. They explain how to build a temple with an altar in front: when a fire is lit on the altar, the temple doors "shall open spontaneously" (see figure 3.3).[25]

It is Milton's "On Time" that probably engages most fully with the broader early modern culture of mechanical marvels. The poem was apparently conceived to be "set on a clock case," a phrase jotted below

[25] *The Pneumatics of Hero of Alexandria: A Facsimile of the 1851 Woodcroft Edition*, intro. Marie Boas Hall (London: MacDonald; New York: American Elsevier, 1971), p. 57.

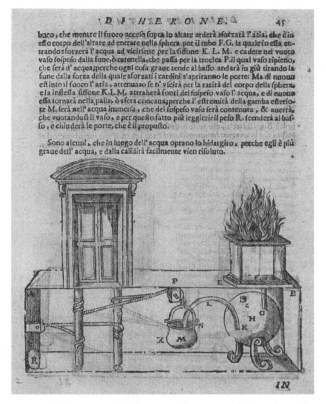

Figure 3.3 Temple doors opened by fire on an altar, Hero of Alexandria, *Gli Artificiosi, e Curiosi Moti Spiritalidi Herone*, trans. Giovanni Battista Aleotti (Bologna, 1647).

the poem's title in the Trinity College Manuscript, either as an explanatory tag or an alternative early title.[26] The description of time's "lazy leaden-stepping hours" (line 2) and "heavy plummet's pace" (line 3) suggests that Milton specifically had in mind the earliest clock made in England – the so-called "lantern" or "bracket" clock, driven by a lead weight on the short end of a cord threaded through the time piece's mechanism.[27] Just as the length of the cord's two ends would repeatedly alternate with the weight's gradual descent and subsequent repositioning, so the poem's varying line-lengths

---

[26] *Poems: Reproduced in Facsimile from the Manuscript in Trinity College, Cambridge, with a Transcript*, ed. William Aldis Wright (Menston, Eng.: Scolar, 1970).

[27] See Kenneth Ullyett, *In Quest of Clocks* (New York: Macmillan, 1951), pp. 48–62. The weight had to be moved to the new shorter end each time that the cord worked its way through the clock.

seem an attempt to measure and control temporal progression as the speaker waits expectantly for "long eternity" (line 11).

But if Milton in "On Time" ultimately contrasts the limitations expressed by such manmade constructions with "everything that is sincerely good / And perfectly divine" (lines 14–15), he more often uses mechanical devices in *Paradise Lost* to dramatize godly wonder and authority, as with heaven's self-opening gates. Similarly, when Abdiel flies from Satan's palace, we learn about a natural mechanism that modulates heaven's brightness:

> There is a cave
> Within the Mount of God, fast by his throne,
> Where light and darkness in perpetual round
> Lodge and dislodge by turns, which makes through Heav'n
> Grateful vicissitudes, like day and night;
> Light issues forth, and at the other door
> Obsequious darkness enters, till her hour
> To veil the Heav'n.   (VI.4–11)

Here Milton seems to be working from Hesiod's account of the "great bronze threshold" where night interchanges with day.[28] But Hesiod had located night and day in "murky Tartarus," whereas Milton raises their home to heaven and converts the abode of dark and light into a type of circling clockwork – "light and darkness in perpetual round / Lodge and dislodge" – a revision that underscores how he imagines the mechanical as not just natural but expressive of divine power.[29]

This co-opting of manmade marvels for the depiction of heaven dovetails with medieval and Renaissance justifications of mechanical progress. In *Paradise Lost*, Michael warns Adam about the race of Cain's descendants: "studious they appear / Of arts that polish life, inventors rare, / Unmindful of their Maker, though his spirit / Taught them, but they his gifts acknowledged none" (XI.609–12). Michael is alluding to the common criticism of manmade devices – namely, that they might encourage worldliness or, worse, idolatry. But he also implies the defense offered by some early Christian writers who treated human technology as a gift from God to supplement our fallen condition. Augustine in *De civitate Dei*, for example, emphasizes "the unspeakable boon [God] has conferred upon our rational

---

[28] Hesiod, *Theogony*, ed. and trans. Glenn W. Most (Cambridge: Harvard University Press, 2006), sec. 744–54 (pp. 62–65). Spenser in *The Faerie Queene* also seems to have had Hesiod's image in mind when describing Jove's virgin daughters, the Hours, as porters "Of heavens gate (whence all the gods issued) / Which they did dayly watch, and nightly wake / By even turns" (VII.vii.45).

[29] Hesiod, *Theogony*, sec. 721 (pp. 60–61).

nature, by giving us even the capacity of such attainment."[30] Singling out "What wonderful – one might say stupefying – advances . . . human industry made in the arts of weaving and building, of agriculture and navigation . . . pottery, painting, and sculpture" as well as "What wonderful spectacles are exhibited in the theatres," Augustine concludes that all of these "astonishing arts" reflect not sinfulness but the "goodness of God" and the "providence of the great Creator."[31] He goes on to develop the connection between God and such marvelous mechanisms by treating manmade arts (*mirabilibus*) as pale imitations of God's own wonders (*miraculi*):

> If, then, very many effects can be contrived by human art, of so surprising a kind that the uninitiated think them divine, . . . then, cannot God effect both that the bodies of the dead shall rise, and that the bodies of the damned shall be tormented in everlasting fire – God, who made the world full of countless miracles in sky, earth, air, and waters, while itself is a miracle unquestionably greater and more admirable than all the marvels it is filled with?[32]

Augustine uses the evidence of manmade marvels to argue analogously that God must be able to effect even greater miracles. But the comparison also implicitly defends humanity's mechanical achievements by allying them with the divine.

The self-opening mechanism that Milton imagines to depict heaven in *Paradise Lost* seems to indicate both divine power and divine benevolence. That he specifically refers to heaven's "*living* doors" (VII.566, emphasis added) not only implies that the doors are "not made" and are in their "native condition and site," as editors have traditionally interpreted this word, but also suggests that the doors are alive literally.[33] Here Milton may have been alluding to the psalmist's imperative, "Lift up your heads, O ye gates; / and be lifted up, ye everlasting doors; / and the King of glory shall come in," a passage in which *gates* is often glossed as a metonymy for *gate-keeper* (Psalm 24:7). Yet, Milton's individual descriptions of heaven's doors seem to personify the divine realm: "Heav'n gates / Poured out by millions her victorious band" (II.996–97), "[the] crystal wall of Heav'n, . . . opening wide, / Rolled inward" (VI.860–61), "Heav'n opened wide / Her ever-during gates" (VII.205–06), and "Heav'n, / That opened wide her blazing portals" (VII.574–75). All of these passages suggest that heaven is somehow

---

[30] Augustine, *The City of God*, trans. Marcus Dods (New York: Modern Library, 1993), p. 852 (book XXII, sec. 24).

[31] Augustine, *The City of God*, pp. 852–53 (book XXII, sec. 24).

[32] Augustine, *The City of God*, pp. 772–73 (book XXI, sec. 6).

[33] *OED*, s. v. "living, *adj.*," defs. 2d, 2a.

alive and opens herself up to her inhabitants, a provocative image of female accessibility that recalls the personification of Truth in *Areopagitica*: when Truth "gets a free and willing hand," Milton writes in that tract, she "opens her self faster, then the pace of method and discours can overtake her" (*CPW* II: 521). The emphasis in both contexts seems to be an unbounded goodness; like Truth, heaven cannot be contained and offers herself enthusiastically. The added detail of "poured" and the repetition of "wide" in the above lines from *Paradise Lost* emphasize the munificence of heaven's opening gesture.

But whereas Isaiah had promised that Jerusalem's gates will ultimately remain open – "they shall not be shut day nor night; that *men* may bring unto thee the forces of the Gentiles, and *that* their kings *may* be brought" (60:11) – Milton envisions the gates of the divine realm shutting. The music that accompanies the gates' motion indicates the mechanism's beauty and naturalness:

> the sound
> Symphonious of ten thousand harps that tuned
> Angelic harmonies: the Earth, the air
> Resounded, ...
> The heav'ns and all the constellations rung,
> The planets in their stations list'ning stood,
> While the bright pomp ascended jubilant.
> "Open, ye everlasting gates," they sung,
> "Open, ye Heav'ns, your living doors; let in
> The great Creator from his work returned
> Magnificent, his six days' work, a world." (VII.558–68)

That heaven's gates in these lines swing open in concert with the angelic choir suggests the figurative harmony of God's creation. The angels themselves do not open the doors, but they can ask heaven to open herself, and the jubilant song that they voice accompanies the movement like a celestial soundtrack.

Still, if heaven's gates need to open on such occasions, then they sometimes must be closed, an idea that the doors' hinged mechanism also implies. The image of heaven's opening gates thus enacts divine selectivity: while early modern readers could marvel that the doors open on their own, only some of God's creations are evidently allowed exit and entrance. In contrast to the gates of hell that are perilously left open after Satan passes through – an apparent symbol of the unending possibility of disobedience and punishment – heavenly exit and entrance are limited. As God explains the possibility of humanity's salvation, he accordingly uses terms of a select admission: some of his creations will "safe arrive," but He will "exclude" others who neglect his offered mercy (III.197, 202). By comparison, the speaker in the Nativity Ode, momentarily carried away by the expectation of returning to the "age of gold" (line 135), imagines how "Truth and Justice then / Will down return to men" (lines 141–42) and ultimately "Heav'n as at some festival, / Will open wide the gates of her high palace hall" (lines 147–48). Milton in fashioning the self-opening gates in *Paradise Lost* has devised an image that emphasizes God's power, wonder, and generosity. But it still conveys the crucial freedom and restriction that both angels and humankind face. The gates of heaven open easily, but they are not open to everyone.

"Within the walls of cities"

But why does Milton's heaven have a wall in the first place – to keep out the unwanted or to enclose its holy inhabitants? Even after we recognize the implications of the gates' self-opening mechanism, does the divine wall primarily restrict or protect? Understanding Milton's heaven – like hell and Paradise – as a gated community invites us to consider that Milton and his contemporary readers may have most immediately envisioned such images by drawing on their experience of both walled cities and great houses. While cultural and legal historians have discussed the early modern controversy generated by the enclosure of public grazing lands and the extinguishing of common rights, these agrarian practices entailed the hedging and fencing of meadows or pastures.[34] By comparison, cities and great houses in the seventeenth century were surrounded by walls and richly decorated gates that more closely resemble the divine fortifications that Milton's describes in *Paradise Lost*. I am not suggesting that Milton based his depiction of heaven on London or any of the other fortified cities he visited during his Grand Tour, but certainly his firsthand knowledge of enclosed cities and mansions may have influenced the way he imagined the walled spaces in his poem, and contemporary readers may have approached his account of walls and gates with some of the same preconceptions about design and architecture.

Elsewhere in his works Milton repeatedly envisions cities as walled in, so that in Prolusion VII, for example, he refers to the time when "of a sudden the Arts and Sciences breathed their divine breath into the savage breasts of men, and instilling into them the knowledge of themselves, gently drew them to dwell together within the walls of cities" (*CPW* I: 299). Here Milton allies the enclosure of urban space with civility, specifically the way

---

[34] On the enclosure of grazing lands, see Joan Thirsk, ed., *The Agrarian History of England and Wales. Vol. IV: 1500–1640* (Cambridge: Cambridge University Press, 1967), pp. 200–55.

that the arts and sciences can lead to personal insight. In contrast to an apparently natural postlapsarian savagery, the impetus to live in walled cities acts "gently" and is allied with an inspiring godliness.[35] Similarly, in *Elegia prima* Milton praises the virtues of his native London by emphasizing the city as an enclosed space:

> *Tuque urbs Dardaniis Londinum structa colonis*
> *Turrigerum late conspicienda caput*
> *Tu nimium felix intra tua moenia claudis*
> *Quicquid formosi pendulus orbis habet*   (lines 73–76)

> [And you, city of London, built by Trojan settlers, whose tower-bearing head can be seen from far around, you are too happy for enclosing within your walls whatever beauty the pendulous earth holds.]

In these verses, London's walls and tower look back to the city's storied founding. The poem depicts London as, paradoxically, both on display and sealed up, as a cynosure (its tower "can be seen from far around") and a fortress. Milton may have added playfully that the city's wall protects its "prime glory ... Britain's virgins" (line 71), but he more seriously suggests that such a structure distinguishes – and thus defines – beauty and happiness.

References to walls and gates in Milton's works are not strictly laudatory, however. As Michael instructs Adam about the consequences of the Fall, the angel lights on "Cities of men with lofty gates and tow'rs, / Concourse in arms, fierce faces threat'ning war" (XI.640–41).[36] This image associates urban structures with worldly splendor and military power, and as Michael goes on to explain the fractious debates about war from which Enoch is rescued, the angel shows Adam how "In other part the sceptered

---

[35] In *The History of Moscovia*, Milton also compliments Russia by highlighting its various fortifications, lingering, for example, on the details of Cathay's defensive structures: "in four daies they came to the Borders of *Cathay*, fenc't with a stone Wall, 15 fathom high; along the side of which, having on the other hand many pretty Towns belonging to Queen *Manchika*, they travail'd ten daies without seeing any on the Wall till they came to the Gate. Where they saw very great Ordnance lying, and 3000 men in watch. They traffick with other Nations at the Gate, and very few at once are suffered to enter" (*CPW* VIII: 507). Milton was working from two source texts in composing *Moscovia* and was accordingly constrained by the information that they offered. But his choice to dwell repeatedly, as here, on the details of the cities' walls and gates suggests the significance that he attached to the presence of such structures.

[36] In *Paradise Lost*, Milton also refers to "the destined walls / Of Cambalu" (XI.387–88), while in *Paradise Regained* walls reoccur as the newly baptized search in vain for Jesus "in Jericho / The city of palms, Aenon, and Salem old, / Machaerus and each town or city walled / On this side the broad lake Genezaret" (II.20–23). And later, after Satan takes Jesus to the top of a mountain, the large capital of Assyria, Nineveh, is said to be "of length within her wall / Several days' journey" (III.275–76). See also *Samson Agonistes*, as the Chorus recollects how Milton's protagonist bore "the gates of Azza, post, and massy bar / Up to the Hill by Hebron" (lines 147–48), and later the Messenger reports, "Occasions drew me early to this city, / And as the gates I entered with sunrise, / The morning trumpets festival proclaimed / Through each high street" (lines 1596–99).

heralds call / To council in the city gates" (XI.660–61). Both descriptions anticipate the Son's rejection of the furniture of war in *Paradise Regained*, "what numbers numberless / The city gates outpoured, light-armèd troops / In coats of mail and military pride" (III.310–12). Here, as in the postlapsarian scenes of *Paradise Lost*, Milton returns to the image of city gates not only to disparage armed conflict but also to depict a bounded strength or energy that seeks release. Thus, presenting the Son with the temptation of Rome in *Paradise Regained*, Satan specifically invites Jesus

> to the gates cast round thine eye, and see
> What conflux issuing forth, or ent'ring in,
> Praetors, proconsuls to their provinces
> Hasting or on return, in robes of state
> Lictors and rods the ensigns of their power,
> Legions and cohorts, turms of horse and wings.   (IV.61–66)

The image of bustling activity, presumably meant by Satan to demonstrate Roman vitality, already in its hecticness anticipates Jesus' disdain for worldly power. Not surprising, the Son will reject outright Rome's "conflux" and put himself high above the city's praetors, proconsuls, lictors, and legions: "Nor doth this grandeur and majestic show / Of luxury, though called magnificence, / . . . allure mine eye, / Much less my mind" (IV.110–13).

But that Milton seems to have understood urban space first and foremost as confined suggests a connection between his depiction of the city of God and contemporary assumptions about fortifications.[37]

---

[37] Milton does not always refer explicitly to a city's wall or gates. Satan approaches an unsuspecting Eve in *Paradise Lost*, for example,

> As one who long in populous city pent,
> Where houses thick and sewers annoy the air,
> Forth issuing on a summer's morn to breathe
> Among the pleasant villages and farms
> Adjoined, from each thing met conceives delight,
> The smell of grain, or tedded grass, or kine,
> Or dairy, each rural sight, each rural sound.   (IX.445–51)

Milton in this simile was surely working from the pastoral tradition and conveying an urban poet's nostalgia for the *otium* of life in the country. In particular, the associative placement of "thick" and "Forth issuing" subtly enhances the pungency of the sewers that "annoy the air," in contrast to the idealized smells of grain, grass, kine, and dairy. But the glancing image of Satan's advance also captures one of the real consequences of London's rapid expansion. As the city's walled-in population more than doubled from 200,000 to 500,000 in Milton's lifetime, London's streets were indeed "thick" with houses, and the resulting strain on the system of sewage troughs – what Ben Jonson complained was a "merd-urinous load" – became a significant health problem. See Ian Archer, "London," in *Milton in Context*, ed. Stephen B. Dobranski (Cambridge: Cambridge University Press, 2010), pp. 361–71; Christopher Hibbert, *London: The Biography of a City* (New York: Morrow, 1969), pp. 73–77; and Ben Jonson, "On the Famous Voyage," in *Ben Jonson*, ed. Ian Donaldson (Oxford and New York: Oxford University Press, 1985), pp. 276–81 (line 65).

Throughout the early modern period London remained literally walled-in, as did many of the cities that Milton visited in France and Italy in 1638 and 1639. London's wall, built of Kentish ragstone, was a strong, solid, apparently permanent, virtually impenetrable structure that had fixed the shape of the city's physical growth and continued to mold London's expansion. Up until the seventeenth century, two small posterns and seven main gates – Aldersgate, Aldgate, Bishopgate, Cripplegate, Ludgate, Moorgate, and Newgate – were the only landed entrances into the city.[38] The gates were formidable: built with thick walls, each one contained multiple rooms so heavily fortified that they sometimes served as prisons. Yet the city wall itself no longer had much practical value. The use of heavy artillery had long ago diminished any defensive advantage of such a structure, and, while some residents and visitors, as in Milton's first elegy, may have been reminded of the city's Roman heritage, most seem to have viewed the wall as an impediment, particularly to trade. Samuel Pepys in 1667, for example, laments traveling by coach "home round by London Wall, it being very dark and dirty." And one year later he complains again about having to travel "home in a coach round by the Wall, where we met so many stops by the Wa[t]ches that it cost us much time and some trouble, and more money, to every watch to them to drink."[39]

By the start of the 1600s, as various new posterns were broken through to enable the flow of increased traffic of all kinds, the areas abutting the original city gates nevertheless remained important public spaces. As the traditional landed entrance and exit for London's goods and people, the gates continued to be used not only for posting royal proclamations and exhibiting heraldic ornaments, but also for expressing judicial authority.[40] There criminals were punished and executed, and their bodies or heads conspicuously displayed. Thus, it is at the city's gates in *Measure for Measure* that the Duke stages his triumphant return and the restoration of order, a symbolic performance for which the Bible also provided ample precedent: in Hebrew scriptures, a city's gates frequently serve as the place of legal tribunals (for example, Deut. 16:18, 25:7) and

[38] In this paragraph and the next, I am drawing from C. H. Holden and W. G. Holford, *The City of London: A Record of Destruction and Survival* (London and Hertford: Shenval, 1951); and J. E. Kaufmann and H. W. Kaufmann, *The Medieval Fortress: Castles, Forts and Walled Cities of the Middle Ages* (New York: DaCapo, 2001).

[39] *The Diary of Samuel Pepys*, ed. Robert Latham and William Matthews, 11 vols. (Berkeley and Los Angeles: University of California Press, 1970–83), VIII: 451 (26 Sept. 1667), IX: 134 (26 March 1668).

[40] An additional river wall, over time a hindrance to trade, gave way to an open front for the Thames by the twelfth century.

public audiences with the king (for example, 2 Sam. 19:8, 1 Kings 22:10). Heaven's gate in *Paradise Lost* is similarly associated with justice and power, as it seems to afford an excellent vantage point for watching over creation. When the Son descends to judge Adam and Eve, we learn that he is accompanied by angels to "Heaven gate, from whence / Eden and all the coast in prospect lay" (X.88–89).

Individual castles and great houses were the other places during the early modern period that commonly had the type of walls and gates that surround heaven in Milton's epic. These residential structures, like their urban counterparts, originally had significant defensive value. As late as 1642, when the Parliamentary army occupied Windsor Castle, the surrounding walls foiled an attempt by a group of cavalry to recapture the property on behalf of the Royalists. Charles I's nephew, Prince Rupert of the Rhine, ordered his soldiers to draw up four guns from one side while another group attempted to dig trenches at the base of the walls. When parliamentary forces repeatedly thwarted this latter effort, the prince's soldiers withdrew, explaining that they "would willingly fight for Prince Rupert against men, but not against stone walls."[41]

By the middle of the seventeenth century, however, most private walls and gatehouses had, like their urban counterparts, become largely ornamental and would have deterred only "less well-equipped intruders, thieves and marauding bands."[42] In particular, owners of great houses no longer deemed necessary the added fortification that large gatehouses offered. The medieval colleges at both Cambridge and Oxford universities were still adorned with gatehouses, as was Whitehall Palace, where Milton, as Latin Secretary, lodged for two years beginning in November 1649. But, as mansions and palaces adopted a more lavish architectural style, their gatehouses became correspondingly simpler, replaced by mere gates or "great doors," and a pair of smaller porter's lodgings, sometimes connected by a modest archway.[43]

These later, Jacobean and Carolinian structures were still decorated, most often with heraldic symbols to express a family's achievement and its loyalty to the monarch, but the walls of a great house allowed for more access than did early Tudor fortifications. According to a breviate from 1605, the great doors of a nobleman's house were to be locked only at

[41] Robin Mackworth-Young, *The History and Treasures of Windsor Castle* (New York: Vendome, 1982), p. 36.

[42] Paula Henderson, *The Tudor House and Garden: Architecture and Landscape in the Sixteenth and Early Seventeenth Century* (New Haven and London: Yale University Press, 2005), p. 35.

[43] Henderson, *The Tudor House and Garden*, pp. 36, 46, 53.

certain times, at night and "before dinner, and supper, or beefore prayer," and even at these times could be opened "upon speciall occasion."[44] The primary function of a house's wall and gates was evidently to monitor – as opposed to prohibit – ingress and egress. Thus for a lord's residence, the yeoman porter

> is to looke to the gates continuallie, and that none come in, or out thereat, but such as bee in his discretion meete; and if ther bee countrie people, that woulde speake with any in the house, hee is to acquainte them withall, and those to stay eather at the gate, or in the porter's lodge, untill hee, whom they woulde speake withall, doe come to them, and soe to bee dispatchede.[45]

As this language suggests, private walls and gates, like those built around the city of London, were mostly symbolic – they designated the entrance into a different, more exclusive space. But, according to this passage from the breviate, private walls differed from a city's wall in that they enabled the porter to surveil possible visitors. That the porter is instructed to keep "countrie people" outside the grounds and to have the residents "come to them" suggests the restrictions and social distinctions that walls and gates could still enforce. Although "countrie people" had access to the resident of an estate, they remained literally and figuratively marginalized, prohibited from penetrating the house's domestic space.[46]

In this context we can appreciate Thomas Carew's high praise of John Crofts' country residence in "To Saxham." Carew compliments the estate for its easy access, having "no porter at the door / To examine or keep back the poor; / Nor locks nor bolts: thy gates have been / Made only to let strangers in; / Untaught to shut" (lines 49–53).[47] Similarly, Jonson, in "To Penshurst," uses the walls of Robert Sidney's estate to emphasize the family's nobility and benevolence. Jonson describes the house's espaliered walls as almost a part of the natural landscape:

[44] "A Breviate touching the Order and Governmente of a Nobleman's House [1605]," in *Archaeologia: or, Miscellaneous Tracts Relating to Antiquity* (London: Society of Antiquaries, 1800), Ss2r–Ddd3r (Xxɪr).

[45] "A Breviate touching the Order and Governmente," Xxɪr.

[46] Various critics have explored early modern depictions of enclosed domestic space, especially as an analogue for understanding the formation of the nation-state, either in terms of exclusion and purity or, alternatively, in terms of hybridity and acceptance of difference. See, for example, Peter Stallybrass, "Patriarchal Territories: The Body Enclosed," in *Rewriting the Renaissance: The Discourses of Sexual Difference in Early Modern Europe*, ed. Margaret W. Ferguson, Maureen Quilligan, and Nancy J. Vickers (Chicago: Chicago University Press, 1986), pp. 123–42; and Jean Howard, "Women, Foreigners, and the Regulation of Urban Space in *Westward Ho*," in *Material London, ca. 1600* (Philadelphia: University of Pennsylvania Press, 2000), pp. 150–67.

[47] Thomas Carew, "To Saxham," in *Seventeenth-Century English Poetry*, ed. John T. Shawcross and Ronald David Emma (Philadelphia and New York: J. B. Lippincott, 1969), pp. 248–49.

The blushing apricot and woolly peach
Hang on thy walls, that every child may reach.
And though thy walls be of the country stone,
They're reared with no man's ruin, no man's groan;
There's none that dwell about them wish them down,
But all come in, the farmer and the clown.[48]

Formerly an apprentice to his bricklayer step-father, Jonson must have known firsthand about the "groans" that the construction of a stone wall could elicit, yet the walls he imagines enclosing Penshurst are so benign and natural that, he claims, their origin was painless. They evoke a prelapsarian world in which work was not yet labor. Based on this account, why should anyone wish the walls down? Both Saxham's and Penshurst's walls are there and not there: in extolling the residents' virtue, Carew and Jonson assume distinctions of class and wealth, but then insist that social barriers, physically manifested in the walls, don't matter.[49] In the case of Penshurst, the Sidney family's estate not only remains accessible to everyone – "the farmer and the clown" – but its walls represent a nurturing force, providing succulent, low-hanging fruit that even children can enjoy.

In *The Faerie Queene*, the fence of "precious yuory" that encloses the Bower of Bliss similarly seems to demarcate more than to exclude or restrict. Although Spenser writes that the fence served "Aswell their entred guests to keep within, / As those unruly beasts to hold without" (II.xii.43, 44), we also learn that it is "weake and thin" and that its gate "was wrought of substaunce light, / Rather for pleasure, then for battery or fight" (II.xii.43). Moreover, the gate "ever open stood to all, / Which thether came" (II.xii.46).[50] Readers might reasonably question why Spenser would bother to fortify the Bower if he then emphasizes the structure's inefficacy. As with Saxham's and Penshurst's walls, the fence's primary value seems symbolic, underscored by its detailed artwork. The fence bears the "famous history" of Jason and Medea – "Her mighty charmes, her furious loving fitt, / . . . / His falsed fayth, and love too lightly flitt" (II.xii.44) – a narrative of excess, betrayal, and madness that

---

[48] Ben Jonson, "To Penshurst," in *Ben Jonson*, pp. 282–85 (lines 43–48).

[49] In the same vein, Jonson subsequently acknowledges that his waiter must dine separately "below" but then tries to deny such a social hierarchy by praising the lord's egalitarian generosity: "the same beer and bread and self-same wine / That is his lordship's shall be also mine" (lines 70, 63–64).

[50] Another gate of ivory appears earlier in *The Faerie Queene* as Archimago's spright travels to Morpheus' house to bring the Red Cross Knight a lustful dream. The spright encounters, "double gates he findeth locked fast, / The one faire fram'd of burnish Yvory, / The other all with silver overcast" (I.i.40). Here Spenser seems to be alluding, in turn, to the description of the two gates of sleep in Virgil's *Aeneid*, VI.893–96.

signals the danger of entering the Bower and indulging intemperately in its pleasures.[51]

The function of the permeable, bejeweled wall surrounding heaven that Milton imagines in *Paradise Lost* appears, like Carew's, Jonson's, and Spenser's structures, to be principally symbolic, an expression of the region's holiness more than a defensive obstacle. Following the logic of contemporary urban design and seventeenth-century residential architecture, heaven's wall in Milton's poem distinguishes the privileged space of God's realm from chaos and creation, but does not prohibit movement between all three regions. On the contrary, as we have seen, the gates' self-opening mechanism encourages passage into and out of God's company, also corresponding to urban and residential gates during the seventeenth century, which did not prevent entrance so much as they marked the place of proper egress and ingress and allowed for the surveillance of travelers and visitors. But just as the yeoman porter at a great house is told to keep out "countrie people" and the house's owner is to meet such visitors outside the gates, so Milton's God figuratively meets his fallen creations part way. As we saw in the preceding section, God's "offered grace / Invites" us to "safe arrive" in heaven, but not everyone can enter, only those who "pray, repent, and bring obedience due" (III.187–88, 197, 190). Satan and the other fallen angels, by comparison, have permanently closed themselves off from heaven through their sin and degradation. If only the most poorly prepared marauders were deterred by the decorative walls surrounding great houses during the seventeenth century, then Milton suggests that the bad angels are especially ill-equipped: they must remain "outcast, exiled" beyond heaven's gate unless they were to repent and the Deity were to pardon them (IV.106).[52] As Satan realizes, this is not going to happen: God is "as far / From granting . . . as I from begging peace" (IV.103–04). God sees the devil "Coasting the wall of Heav'n" but denies the fallen angel the grace to re-enter His realm (III.71).

Heaven's fortification in *Paradise Lost* ultimately seems most remarkable for being – as with Saxham's, Penhurst's and the Bower's walls – there and not there, separating but also facilitating. Like the prohibition

[51] Spenser's precedent here is the gate leading to Armida's garden in Tasso's *Gerusalem Liberata*, which apparently bears the stories of Hercules and Iole, and Antony and Cleopatra 16.2–7. For the implications and ambiguity of Spenser's *ekphrastic* description, see Page DuBois, *History, Rhetorical Description and the Epic: From Homer to Spenser* (Cambridge: D. S. Brewer, 1982), pp. 75–78.

[52] That God promises "mine eye not shut" (III.193) to all sincere appeals once again, like the description of heaven's gates, associates divine grace with the image of openness.

not to eat the fruit from the Tree of Knowledge, which paradoxically defines Adam and Eve's free will, so the wall that surrounds heaven appears to represent a restriction but instead defines the acceptance of God's grace, freely given.[53] If we are looking for a classical precedent for Milton's image of the divine wall, the structure resembles less Ilium's famous fortification than it recalls the permeable barrier in the story of Pyramus and Thisbe. A wall separates the young lovers but also enables their courtship:

> "O envious wall," they would say, "why do you stand between lovers? How small a thing 'twould be for you to permit us to embrace each other, or, if this be too much, to open for our kisses! But we are not ungrateful. We owe it to you, we admit, that a passage is allowed by which our words may go through to loving ears."[54]

Similarly, the wall of heaven that Milton envisions marks off the divine realm but its self-opening doors emphasize the region's flexible nature. Thus, when Satan and the rebel angels flee the Son on the third day of the war in heaven, the divine wall even accommodates their desire to leave and, "op'ning wide, / Roll[s] inward" (VI.860–61).

In and out

In scriptural terms, Milton was also surely drawing on the theory of sacred space in Ezekiel 40 and Revelation 21 to depict heaven's fortifications. Michael Lieb has argued that the "spatial strategies" in these two biblical texts correspond to Milton's enclosure of not only heaven but also hell and Paradise: the walls of all three regions differentiate between the sacred and profane – what Lieb calls "a fundamental propensity in religious thought" – while portraying "the proper form of penetration, on the one hand, and the perverted form, on the other."[55] Thus, when Satan enters Paradise for the first time, to take a well-known example, "Due entrance he disdained, and in contempt, / At one slight bound high over leaped all bound / Of hill or highest wall" (IV.180–82). Here "bound" punningly indicates the fiend's physical leap and literal trespass, while "slight" as an adjective could describe the devil's lack of exertion, or, as a noun, the affront of his

---

[53] For a similar conclusion about the wall of Paradise, see Karen L. Edwards, "The Natural World," in *Milton in Context*, ed. Stephen B. Dobranski (Cambridge: Cambridge University Press, 2010), pp. 406–17 (p. 416).

[54] Ovid, *Metamorphoses*, IV: 65–80 (vol. I, pp. 182–84).

[55] Michael Lieb, *Poetics of the Holy: A Reading of "Paradise Lost"* (Chapel Hill: University of North Carolina Press, 1981), pp. 139, 122.

jumping. The added detail that Satan "over leaped" suggests the arch-fiend's vaulting ambition and anticipates the seductive appeal he will use with Eve to eat the fruit and become godly. And just as we saw earlier how the architecture of hell resembles but contrasts with heaven's forms, so Satan's contempt for Paradise's "Due entrance" indicates his fallenness, whereas in subsequent descriptions the Son's easy coming and going through heaven's doors helps to dramatize the Son's merit.

In his depiction of heaven Milton frequently returns to this contrast of legitimate and illegitimate entrances and exits. When introducing the Paradise of Fools, for example, the narrator foresees how Dominicans and Franciscans will one day appear to ascend toward the divine region, "And now Saint Peter at Hea'n's wicket seems / To wait them with his keys" (III.484–85). Here the choice of *wicket* seems especially meaningful: a small door for foot-passengers placed in or alongside a large gate, St. Peter's modest entranceway momentarily holds out hope for "all who in vain things / Built their fond hopes of glory or lasting fame" (III.448–49).[56] Perhaps these misguided Christians might still "pass disguised" (III.480) into God's realm through such a loop-hole, another possible punning name for a *wicket* during the seventeenth century. But just as the fools cannot enter heaven by the main doors – that is, not by the "strait gate" and "narrow way," as described in scriptures (Matt. 7:13–14) – they are also blown past the secondary entrance "Into the devious air" by "A violent crosswind" (III.489, 487), a further indication of their souls' unworthiness.

In contrast, when Adam and Eve repent, their prayers resemble birds that fly to heaven, passing straight through the "doors" and becoming visible to God:

> To Heav'n their prayers
> Flew up, nor miss'd the way, by envious winds
> Blown vagabond or frustrate: in they passed
> Dimensionless through Heav'nly doors; then clad
> With incense, where the golden altar fumed,
> By their great Intercessor, came in sight
> Before the Father's throne.   (XI.14–20)

Here "Heav'nly doors" mark "the way" to a redolent "golden altar" and God's magisterial "throne." Instead of being "Blown vagabond or frus-trate," like the fools' souls, Adam and Eve's prayers fly directly to "their great Intercessor," an apparent symbol of the couple's newfound merit.

---

[56] *OED*, s. v. "wicket," defs. 1, 2.

But the description of Adam and Eve's prayers also suggests the frustration that some readers experience with Milton's heavenly imagery. Paradoxically, it is at the moment of visualization, when the couple's appeals somehow "came in sight," that the physical specificity of "doors," "altar," and "throne" – even the image of the couple's words like birds in flight – dissolves into the deity's fundamental invisibility. When Milton describes Adam and Eve's spoken words as "clad" with an aroma, the synesthesia of sound, sight, and smell further obscures the passage's visual imagery. And, although "Dimensionless" could modify Adam and Eve's spontaneous expressions of remorse, the syntax of "passed / Dimensionless through Heav'nly doors" also leaves open the possibility that the realm's entrance lacks a specific shape.

Despite all of the details that Milton provides about heaven's gleaming fortifications, he never in fact establishes whether heaven's wall in *Paradise Lost* is round or square. Satan beholds "Far off th' empyreal Heav'n, extended wide / In circuit, undetermined square or round, / With opal tow'rs and battlements adorned / Of living sapphire, once his native seat" (II.1047–50). Certainly these lines reflect Satan's fallen ignorance: he no longer can ascertain the shape of the realm where he once resided. But the passage also denies readers a concrete image of God's home. In Revelation, we instead read:

> And the city lieth foursquare, and the length is as large as the breadth: and he measured the city with the reed, twelve thousand furlongs. The length and the breadth and the height of it are equal. And he measured the wall thereof, a hundred *and* forty *and* four cubits, *according to* the measure of man, that is, of the angel. (21:16–17)

Milton's comparative lack of specificity in *Paradise Lost* seems purposeful. The "undetermined" shape of heaven corresponds with its "Dimensionless" doors and, as Karen Edwards has proposed, may also fit the description of heaven's "living" gate (VII.566).[57] All these details suggest that divine fortifications are not rigid barriers but responsive, malleable forms: they can roll inward, pour out, and open wide. As with heaven's self-opening gates, the divine wall thus underscores God's potency and benevolence, in contrast to material rigidity, which we will see in the next two chapters, preoccupies the fallen angels and helps to characterize their fall. Working potentially from classical and biblical images of fortifications as well as seventeenth-century ideas about the utility of walls and gates, Milton imagines an idealized, symbolic structure in heaven that must ultimately

---

57 Edwards, "The Natural World," p. 410.

be "inimitable on Earth" (III.508) so that it can express God's sanctity and accessibility but still respect his unknowableness.

The dynamic nature of heaven's wall and gates also suggests the metonymic function of divine architecture. In the epic's first description of heaven, the morning light "appears, and from the walls of Heav'n / Shoots far into the bosom of dim Night / A glimmering dawn" (II.1035–37). Here the divine wall separates not just day from night but also God from chaos, the latter of which must "retire / As from her [Nature's] outmost works a broken foe / With tumult less and with less hostile din" (II.1038–40). This martial simile evokes the formerly defensive use of such fortifications – in particular, "broken foe," "tumult," and "hostile din" – but the added reference to the "sacred influence / Of light" that "from the walls of Heav'n / Shoots" (II.1034–36) replaces the tactic of raining down arrows from a city's or castle's walls with a description of God's creative power emanating from his divine citadel. Heaven's wall in Milton's poem seems to manifest God himself in his capacity as creator.

Elsewhere in *Paradise Lost* Milton accordingly describes divine creation as an act of walling in or closing off. Raphael will later explain, for example, that God acts through the Son to form the universe by restricting chaos's boundaries: "in his hand / He took the golden compasses, prepared / In God's eternal store, to circumscribe / This universe, and all created things" (VII.224–27). The Son similarly pronounces that he will enclose "Matter unformed and void" to create humanity's world: "Thus far extend, thus far thy bounds, / This be thy just circumference, O world" (VII.233, 230–31). Interestingly, Milton in his invocations also describes his epic narrator as closed off, "In darkness, and with dangers compassed round" (VII.27), and earlier the narrator says that "everduring dark / Surrounds me" (III.45–46).[58] For Milton, marking boundaries is apparently a way of creatively harnessing what is contained within; the potency of heaven – as presumably with hell and Paradise – finds expression through being enclosed.

* * *

In contrast, the imagery associated with Satan and the other fallen angels, as we will see in the next two chapters, lacks the flexible, dynamic quality of heaven's architecture. Both divine and fallen material forms are expressive, but the latter, anticipating the fate of the fallen angels themselves, are

---

[58] Milton posits a similar but loose connection between partitioning and poetic creativity in Sonnet VIII, where he treats his verses as enhancements to "defenseless doors" (line 2) and capable of saving "th' Athenian walls from ruin bare" (line 14).

hardened. The rigidity of the objects that depict Satan and his followers may render their scenes more vividly, but this stony quality also demonstrates the devils' ongoing material debasement. C. S. Lewis referred ironically to Satan's "progress" in Milton's poem, summarizing the fiend's gradual degeneration, "From hero to general, from general to politician, from politician to secret service agent, and thence to a thing that peers in at bedroom or bathroom windows, and thence to a toad, and finally to a snake."[59] Beginning in chapter 4, I will show that, on the continuum of nature described by Raphael, Satan and his acolytes are not just falling down a social and zoological hierarchy. Adamantly opposed to God, the rebels are becoming literally closer to the mere things – the jeweled walls and gates – that Milton uses to depict heaven symbolically.

[59] C. S. Lewis, *A Preface to "Paradise Lost"* (1942; London: Oxford University Press, 1961), p. 99.

CHAPTER 4

Pondering Satan's shield

Milton charges himself so full with thought, imagination, knowledge, that his style will hardly contain them. He is too full-stored to show us in much detail one conception, one piece of knowledge; he just shows it to us in a pregnant allusive way, and then he presses on to another.
– Matthew Arnold[1]

As Satan lumbers off the burning lake in *Paradise Lost*, just before addressing the other fallen angels, readers first glimpse the arch-fiend's armament. He wears a shield and carries a spear – specifically, a "ponderous shield / Ethereal temper, massy, large and round," hanging "on his shoulders like the moon," and a "spear, to equal which the tallest pine / Hewn on Norwegian hills, to be the mast / Of some great ammiral, were but a wand" (I.284–85, 287, 292–94). Critics have long noted that Satan does not use his spear properly: here it helps "to support [his] uneasy steps" as he reaches the shore (I.295), and in heaven he again uses it as a crutch when Abdeil's blow sends him recoiling (VI.195). As Stanley Fish has observed, we do not even know how big the spear is. Readers may first think it "equal" in size to the tallest tree in Norway, until, on reaching the end of the simile, we discover the comparison's inadequacy with the words, "were but a wand."[2] Still, lest we conclude that size doesn't matter, James Freeman, with a nod to the weapon's Freudian implications, has suggested that "the longer Satan is away from Heaven, the more his 'spear' shrinks."[3]

I would add that Satan's spear also measures his material debasement: that he uses it literally as a crutch implies his misplaced dependence on external force and forecasts a larger pattern whereby Satan's hardening heart is figured in his association with hardened matter. By casting this

---

[1] Matthew Arnold, *On Translating Homer*, in *The Complete Prose Works of Matthew Arnold*, ed. R. H. Super, 11 vols. (Ann Arbor: University of Michigan Press, 1960–1977), 1: 145.
[2] Stanley Fish, *Surprised by Sin: the Reader in "Paradise Lost,"* 2nd edn. (Cambridge: Harvard University Press, 1999), p. 25.
[3] James R. Freeman, *Milton and the Martial Muse: "Paradise Lost" and European Traditions of War* (Princeton: Princeton University Press, 1980), p. 132.

emblem of Greco-Roman warfare as a crutch, Milton may also subtly suggest that such conventions have become old and lame. Later, when Ithuriel wields his own spear against Satan, the cherub needs only touch Satan "lightly" to capture him (IV.811). This simple gesture – a peaceful use for an offensive weapon – exemplifies Milton's own larger project. The poet breathes new life into ancient epic and, like Ithuriel making a prince out of a toad, he turns a pagan genre preoccupied with warfare into a meditation on "the better fortitude / Of patience and heroic martyrdom" (IX.31–32).[4]

This chapter addresses how the image of Satan's "ponderous shield" (I.284) in the same passage also advances Milton's Christian epic. Commentators have traditionally glossed the lunar metaphor that Milton uses for Satan's shield as either an allusion to Achilles' "massive shield flashing far and wide / like a full round moon," or an echo of Radigund's lunar armament as she challenges Artegall in *The Faerie Queene*.[5] I want to offer a new reading of Milton's epic simile by turning to contemporary discoveries in the natural world. When examined in the context of Renaissance warfare and, perhaps surprisingly, seventeenth-century animal histories, the image of Satan's shield symbolizes, updates, and subverts his heroic aspirations, and simultaneously it exposes his amphibious nature, creeping from lake to land, and transgressing from heaven to hell.

Defensive weaponry

To understand fully the implications of the devil's armament, we first need to return to Milton's concept of material and spiritual continuity that I discussed in the Introduction. If, as Raphael explains, the body and soul are different degrees of the same original substance, and God's creations are "more refined, more spiritous, and pure, / As nearer to him placed or nearer tending" (V.475–76), then, conversely, when Satan falls from heaven, his

---

[4] John Guillory alternatively uses Ithuriel's spear to describe the "poetic principle" in Milton's epic whereby the author introduces similes that he then reveals to be literally true – what Guillory calls the "literal drift of Milton's tropes" – as Milton attempts to accommodate biblical truths by exposing the process of representation. See Guillory, *Poetic Authority: Spenser, Milton, and Literary History* (New York: Columbia University Press, 1983), pp. 147–51.

[5] Homer, *The Iliad*, trans. Robert Fagles (New York: Penguin, 1990), XIX.442–43 [375–80]; and Edmund Spenser, *The Faerie Queene*, ed. A. C. Hamilton (Harlow, Eng.: Longman, 2001), V.V.3. All subsequent references to the *Iliad* are taken from Fagles' translation and cited parenthetically; the line numbers of the Greek text appear in brackets according to the Loeb edition of the *Iliad*, trans. A. T. Murray, rev. William F. Wyatt, 2 vols. (Cambridge: Harvard University Press, 1999). For the history of connecting Satan's and Radigund's armor, see *The Works of Edmund Spenser: A Variorum Edition*, ed. Edwin Greenlaw, Charles Grosvenor Osgood, Frederick Morgan Padelford, et al., 10 vols. (Baltimore: Johns Hopkins University Press, 1932–1949), V: 200.

fall is not only moral but also material (and spatial and temporal). That is, when Satan turns away from God, Satan's spirit becomes less rarified, and he literally begins to harden (I.572), until in the temptation of Eve he is "mixed with bestial slime" and mysteriously becomes "incarnate and imbrute" with the serpent (IX.165–66).[6]

As I discuss more fully in the next chapter, Satan and the other fallen angels never entirely lose their spiritual nature within the narrative. Thus, even as Satan enters the snake and is "constrained / Into a beast," he sounds spiritous, "wrapped in mist / Of midnight vapor" (IX.164–65, 158–59). Yet, Satan's dependence on material weapons suggests the start of his ontological decline while pointing up his destructive narcissism. The devil is attracted to things that are more material than spiritual.[7] Instead of returning to God and seeking forgiveness, he again and again puts his faith in these physical objects – whether a sword, shield, or apple.

Satan's armament in particular illustrates the folly of his rebellion. Unlike the spiritual armor that St. Paul described in his letter to the Ephesians (Eph. 6.11–17), Satan's shield actually exists but it fails to protect him, first from Abdiel (VI.192–93), then from Michael (VI.323–28), until finally the rebels drop their shields while fleeing the Son:

> they astonished all resistance lost,
> All courage; down their idle weapons dropped;
> O'er shields and helms, and helmèd heads he rode
> Of Thrones and mighty Seraphim prostrate.   (VI.838–41)

That the Son rides roughshod over the rebels' weapons symbolizes both his imminent victory over Satan and the ascendance of a new type of heroism that will obviate traditional emblems of war. While this image of discarded armament is hardly original to Milton, the specific term "astonished" punningly suggests the link between the rebels' material arms and their own material debasement: the rebels may drop their weapons, but their shapes, like their hearts, are already starting to become "stony."[8] Later,

---

[6] As Stephen M. Fallon observes, "Satan's literal hardening is the monist complement of the figurative scriptural trope of the hardened heart." See Fallon, *Milton among the Philosophers* (Ithaca: Cornell University Press, 1991), p. 208.

[7] Here I largely agree with N. K. Sugimura, who emphasizes Satan's association with "mist" in book IX to support that the devils' dependence on physical weaponry does not mean that they are "*purely*" material (emphasis added). As I show in the next chapter, the substance of the fallen angels is neither purely material nor purely spirit. See Sugimura, *"Matter of Glorious Trial": Spiritual and Material Substance in "Paradise Lost"* (New Haven and London: Yale University Press, 2009), p. 188.

[8] Milton uses this same pun in "On Shakespeare," as he describes how the dramatist "Dost make us marble" when we read his works: "Thou in our wonder and astonishment / Hast built thyself a

Milton will repeat this image when Satan, returning to hell, expects to hear his cohorts' "high applause" but is instead confronted with "A dismal universal hiss" as God changes the rebels into serpents (X.505, 508). Once again, the devils' moral and material fall is figured in their hardening forms and falling weapons: "down their arms, / Down fell both spear and shield, down they as fast" (X.541–42).[9] Milton invokes, too, Dante's concept of *contrapasso* as Satan and the rebels are "punished in the shape he sinned" (X.516). They not only take the shape of snakes, but also, having taken up material arms in a war against God, they fittingly will come to resemble their own lost shields, fallen and hardened.

Arguably, the rebels' shields prove most effective when bearing Satan's body from the field on the first day of the war (VI.337–38).[10] Just as Satan misuses his spear as a crutch, so Milton associates these shields not with military feats of heroism, but with Satan's first experience of pain, presumably a result of his hardening shape and ontological descent. Even the good angels during the war in heaven fail to use defensive weapons to their advantage. Assaulted with Satan's canon fire, they fall "The sooner for their arms, unarmed they might / Have easily as spirits evaded" the rebels' "devilish glut" (VI.595–96, 589). Stella Revard has suggested that Milton's God wanted to teach the loyal angels a lesson: their dependence on traditional weapons leaves them "prey not only to discomfiture and defeat, but also to the laughter of their enemies."[11] But if, as Revard argues, "the loyal angels must learn how vain is their trust in material arms and the glory of material warfare," the angels' subsequent tactic of hurling "seated hills with all their load" (VI.644) suggests that they do not immediately abandon a material war.[12] Milton seems to use this scene to emphasize the

live-long monument" (lines 14, 7–8). See Dobranski, "Milton and Textual Studies: Teaching 'On Shakespeare' as a Work in Progress," in *Approaches to Teaching Milton's Shorter Poetry and Prose*, ed. Peter Herman (New York: Modern Language Association, 2007), pp. 54–61. Classical instances of discarded weapons include *Iliad* XII.22–27 [20–26] and Virgil, *Aeneid*, trans. H. Rushton Fairclough, rev. G. P. Goold, 2 vols. (Cambridge: Harvard University Press, 2000), VIII.538–40.

9 Readers may be reminded as well of Adam, listening to Eve's glozing lies and standing "Astonied" while "From his slack hand the garland wreathed for Eve / Down dropped" (IX.890, 892–93).

10 This use of shields to carry the wounded and dead from the field was no mere classical convention. Compare, for example, the hasty bearing away of Patroklos' body on a bier (*Iliad*, XVIII.267–73 [231–36]).

11 Stella Purce Revard, *The War in Heaven: "Paradise Lost" and the Tradition of Satan's Rebellion* (Ithaca: Cornell University Press, 1980), p. 190.

12 Revard, *The War in Heaven*, p. 190. See also Revard, "Milton's Critique of Heroic Warfare in *Paradise Lost* V and VI," *Studies in English Literature* 7 (1967): 119–39, especially pp. 133–34; and James A. Winn, "Milton on Heroic Warfare," *The Yale Review* 66 (1976): 70–86. Like Revard, Winn notes that the good angels are implicated in the rebels' uncreative acts: the angels' "failure to restore order raises questions about the efficacy of arms," and "the 'deformed rout' and 'foul disorder' with which the day ends demean both sides" (p. 80).

destructiveness of defensive weapons. Whereas Satan and his consorts "Stood scoffing" at the failure of the good angels' armament, they are now "Under the weight of mountains buried deep" and discover that their own "armor helped their harm, crushed in and bruised / Into their substance pent" (VI.629, 652, 656–57). And Satan seems an especially slow learner: "Chained on the burning lake" after falling to hell (I.210), he continues to carry a large, massy shield that must have accelerated his drop and now must weigh him down, increasing his torment.

That the warring angels in *Paradise Lost* even carry shields identifies them as classical rather than contemporary soldiers. Milton makes this point explicitly, describing the assembled fallen angels as "a horrid front / . . . in guise / Of warriors old" (I.563–65). But, since the poet combines elements of classical, medieval, and modern battles, the epic's fighting scenes transcend Greco-Roman warfare. Milton's "defiance of archæological consistency" and "large unity of impression," as James Holly Hanford first suggested, give readers license to evaluate the poem's battles within multiple military contexts.[13]

In the particular case of Satan's shield, we should note that such defensive weapons had only recently fallen out of favor during the civil wars. While some seventeenth-century soldiers worried that metal fragments from armor could aggravate gunshot wounds, the decline of defensive weapons primarily stemmed from their inconvenience and clumsiness.[14] As soldiers strove to develop new fighting strategies, the demand increased, as one historian puts it, for "troops that could be moved like pieces on a board."[15] Both infantry and cavalry gained greater speed and mobility during the 1650s by abandoning the use of defensive weapons.[16] The musketeer, for example, wore no armor, and sometime during the civil wars – although historians have not pinpointed the exact transition – the armor for the dragoon and pikeman had either significantly declined or completely disappeared.[17] Thus, Lucy Hutchinson records that

---

[13] James Holly Hanford, "Milton and the Art of War," in *John Milton, Poet and Humanist* (Cleveland: Western Reserve University Press, 1966), pp. 185–223 (p. 215).

[14] Charles Carlton, *Going to the Wars: The Experience of the British Civil Wars 1638–1651* (London and New York: Routledge, 1992), p. 100; Guy Francis Laking, *A Record of European Armour and Arms through Seven Centuries*, 5 vols. (London: G. Bell, 1920–1922), II: 242, 244, V: 45; and Julian Corbett, "Firearms and Armour," *Longman's Magazine* 34 (June 1899): 159–70, especially p. 168.

[15] Corbet, "Firearms and Armour," p. 165.

[16] C. H. Firth, *Cromwell's Army*, 4th edn. (California: Presidio; London: Greenhill Books, 1992), pp. 72, 121.

[17] David Blackmore, *Arms and Armour of the English Civil Wars* (London: Royal Armouries, 1990), pp. 14, 63; Firth, *Cromwell's Army*, p. 124. Blackmore notes that the pikeman wore "a helmet, gorget [throat protector], backplate, breastplate and tassets." Or at least that's what military manuals describe: "during the period of the civil wars the wearing of pikeman's armour declined and there is

her husband, at the assault of Shelford House in 1645, "put off a very good suite of armor . . . which . . . was so heavie that it heated him," and "after their first experience in battle most of Colonel Hutchinson's regiment discarded their armour" as well.[18] In like manner, in July 1658, when Sir William Lockhart's regiment was sent to serve in Flanders, the men reportedly brought no weapons other than their swords.[19]

This contemporary attitude finds expression in *Paradise Regained* when Jesus specifically dismisses "that cumbersome / Luggage of war" (III.400–01). Here the language used by the Son suggests that military equipment represents not, as the devil would have him believe, a means to power; it instead has become an awkward encumbrance. Milton in *Paradise Lost* similarly indicates that Satan's shield is obsolete with the description of it as "ponderous," a term that during the early modern period meant not just "weighty" but also "clumsy" and "unwieldy."[20] In this context, the additional details that Satan's shield is "massy" and "large" would only accentuate its inconvenience.

Yet, if we briefly return to *Paradise Regained*, Jesus' additional assertion that such weaponry is an "argument / Of human weakness rather than of strength" (III.401–02) also seems to reflect new ways of thinking about military valor in seventeenth-century England. Most obviously, Jesus rejects Satan's temptation to military might as a sign of spiritual weakness, but the Son's diction also exposes a growing bias against defensive weapons that began during the civil war period. As John Cruso explains in his 1640 treatise, soldiers were reluctant to use shields and armor not just because such weapons were uncomfortable, but also because soldiers thought them a sign of cowardice. Cruso believes that soldiers could "accustome" themselves to carrying defensive weaponry, despite the fact that "they publish . . . it is want of courage to go armed, and . . . they will go in their doublets into the most dangerous places, as well as they which are armed."[21]

While Cruso ultimately looks to "a good Captain" for keeping troops combat-ready and overcoming such prejudices, the writer of *Mercurius Aulicus* observes that officers themselves sometimes disdained defensive weapons for the same reason. Colonel George Lisle, fighting at the Second

no evidence for the manufacture of it in this country after the early 1640s. It is difficult to assess the rate at which it fell into disuse" (p. 63).

[18] Lucy Hutchinson, *Memoirs of the Life of Colonel Hutchinson with the Fragment of an Autobiography of Mrs. Hutchinson*, ed. James Sutherland (London: Oxford University Press, 1973), p. 163; and Carlton, *Going to the Wars*, p. 100.

[19] Firth, *Cromwell's Army*, p. 123.

[20] *OED*, s. v. "ponderous," def. 1.

[21] John Cruso, *A Particular Treatise of Modern War*, in *The Complete Captain, Or, An Abridgement of Cesars Warres*, by Henri, Duke of Rohan, 2nd edn. (Cambridge, 1640), H2v.

Battle of Newbury (1644), for example, "had not Armour on besides his Courage ... a good Cause, and a good Holland-shirt." The newsbook's writer interprets Lisle's lack of defensive weaponry as a badge of courage and a sign of good leadership; he notes that the colonel "seldom wears defensive Arms" and speculates that "perhaps [it is] to animate his Men, that the meanest Souldier might see himself better armed than his Collonel, or because it was dark they might better discern him ... to receive both Direction and Courage."[22] The trend of not using armor became popular enough that General George Monck, writing in 1644, thought it necessary to argue for the value of "Defensive Arms." He notes that defensive weapons "are much slighted by some in these times" but insists that "men wear not Arms because they are afraid of danger."[23] Surely such stories as Philip Sidney's famous death on the battlefield, an account retold and glorified in Fulke Greville's biography prefixed to all seventeenth-century editions of the *Arcadia*, contributed to this changing perception. Fighting in the Netherlands, Sidney – who, as Greville claimed, represented the "exemplarie to all Gentlemen" – was fatally shot in the leg after racing into battle and neglecting to put on his thigh-pieces.[24]

When judged by these contemporary standards, Satan's use of a shield, "massy, large," and "ponderous," diminishes his heroic stature even as it allies him with such figures as Radigund and Achilles. Aside from the absurdity of brandishing this type of weapon against an omnipotent God, Satan's desire for the shield's protection reveals that he is not as courageous as his opening speeches suggest. Unlike the rebels who dropped "their idle weapons" when they threw themselves from heaven (VI. 839), Satan evidently refused to relinquish his.

Satan's backwardness

Milton first alerts us to the problem of Satan's shield with the specific description that it was "Behind him cast; the broad circumference / Hung

---

[22] John Rushworth, *Historical Collection of Private Passages of State, Weighty Matters in Law, Remarkable Proceedings in Five Parliaments*, 6 vols. (London, 1690–1701), V: 728 (part 3, vol. 2, sig. Rrrr3v).

[23] George Monck, *Observations upon Military and Political Affairs* (London, 1671), D4r. Monck emphasizes the value of defensive weapons: "one Army well armed with Defensive Arms, may very well expect without any great difficulty to win twenty Battels one after another of Armies equal in strength, equally conducted, and fighting upon equal advantage of ground, but not armed with Defensive Arms" (D4v).

[24] "Life and Death of Sir Philip Sidney," in Philip Sidney, *The Countess of Pembroke's Arcadia* (London, 1655), A4r–c1r (b2r).

Figure 4.1 Greek amphora depicting warriors with shield.

on his shoulders like the moon" (I.286–87). Satan has not, in other words, properly attached his shield by a strap to his left arm as a protection against an enemy's weapon, nor does he wear it slung over his left shoulder for ready use. It instead hangs behind him. Modern readers of Milton, accustomed perhaps to toting backpacks over both shoulders, might initially appreciate the practical advantage of the shield's placement. Strapping such a cumbersome weapon over both shoulders would distribute its weight more evenly and thus make it easier for Satan to bear. Yet, little in ancient epics recommends this particular placement of Satan's weapon. When, by comparison, Venus brings Aeneas his famous shield, he does not hang it on his back; instead, "Upon his shoulder he / lifts up the fame and fate of his sons' sons."[25] Virgil's use of the singular "shoulder[*umero*]," suggests that Aeneas wears his shield on one arm, and, when not in use, that it hangs by his side, two positions that correspond to the illustrations of soldiers with shields on ancient vase-paintings and monuments (see figure 4.1). As Graham Sumner explains,

[25] The Latin reads, "*attollens umero famamque et fata nepotum*" (*Aeneid*, VIII.731). For the English verse translation, I am working from *The Aeneid of Virgil*, trans. Allen Mandelbaum (Berkeley: University of California Press, 1981), VIII.954–55.

"when circular shields are attached by a leather strap and carried over the shoulder, they almost naturally tuck under the left arm."[26]

In like manner, Achilles, donning his armor before rejoining the battle in the *Iliad*, does not wear his shield over both shoulders. Homer instead describes how the warrior "grasped" or "hoisted the massive shield flashing far and wide" (XIX.442 [372–73]). The Greek verb is βάλετο, which recurs in the arming scenes of both Paris (III.334) and Patroklos (XVI.135) and describes the act of placing over the head the shield's neck-strap or telamon.[27] As with Roman shields, these Greek weapons were apparently worn over one shoulder by a strap that extended under the left arm and slanted across the back and chest like a baldric.[28]

That Milton describes Satan's shield, in contrast, as "Behind him cast" and attached to both his "shoulders" (I.286–87) means that the arch-fiend has broken with convention and his weapon hangs out of easy reach. Commentators have overlooked this important distinction: Satan wears his shield the wrong way round. Interestingly, many of *Paradise Lost*'s early illustrators, from the late seventeenth through the mid-nineteenth century, attempted to correct Satan's error. James Barry, William Blake, Richard Corbould, John Henry Fuseli, William Hogarth, John Martin, George Romney, and Richard Westall – all of these illustrators, somehow recognizing that Satan's weapon does not belong behind him, drew the devil in various poses with the shield on his left arm.[29] In "Satan Rises from the Burning Lake," for example, Corbould portrays Satan holding the shield over his head by an arm-band and hand-grip (see figure 4.2), while both Michael Burgesse in "Satan Rising from the Flood" and Thomas Stothard in "Satan Rising from the Burning Lake" have solved the problem of Satan's weapon by omitting it altogether (see figure 4.3).

I would suggest instead that Milton may have purposefully misplaced Satan's shield. Like the surprise punch of the phrase, "were but a wand"

---

[26] Graham Sumner, *Roman Army: Wars of the Empire* (London: Brassey's, 1997), p. III. See also the illustrations of ancient Roman armaments in Amédée Forestier, *The Roman Soldier* (London: A. and C. Black, 1928); for an account of European shields from the early Renaissance, see Laking, *A Record of European Armour and Arms*, II: 223–50.

[27] H. L. Lorimer, *Homer and the Monuments* (London: Macmillan, 1950), pp. 188–92. Historians believe that early Greek soldiers also carried their shields by a single, central hand-grip or used a central arm-band with a hand-grip at the rim – neither of which methods would allow Satan to wear his shield on his back.

[28] Anthony Snodgrass, *Early Greek Armour and Weapons from the End of the Bronze Age to 600 B.C.* (Edinburgh: Edinburgh University Press, 1964), pp. 37–68; and Andrew Lang, *The World of Homer* (New York: Longmans, Green, 1910), pp. 48–49.

[29] These illustrators' works are reproduced in Marcia R. Pointon, *Milton and English Art* (Toronto and Buffalo: University of Toronto Press, 1970).

Forthwith upright he rears from off the pool, / His mighty stature...

Book I.221.

Figure 4.2 Richard Corbould, "Forthwith upright he rears from off the pool, / His mighty stature...," in Milton, *Paradise Lost*, 2 vols. (London, 1796).

(I.294), which undercuts the simile that describes Satan's spear, the delayed phrase "Behind him cast" brings readers up short: we may acknowledge the classical weapons the shield alludes to and anticipates, but suddenly, we discover, Satan has things reversed. Whereas Virgil depicts Aeneas carrying his father on his shoulders out of a burning Troy (*Aeneid*, II.705–20),

Figure 4.3 Michael Burgesse, illustration opposite page 1, in Milton, *Paradise Lost*
(London, 1688).

Milton demeans Satan by having him climb off hell's burning lake carrying
on his back only this weapon – useless, obsolete, and cowardly. And, just as
using a spear as a crutch enfeebles the ancient traditions that it symbolizes,
Satan's backwards shield, in the context of Milton's Christian epic, suggests that classical modes of heroism are backwards, perhaps thoroughly
wrong, at least retrograde.

The precedent for Satan's misplaced shield is probably Homer's account of Ajax's flight from battle in the *Iliad*. Ajax turns his shield behind him for protection as he flees:

> He stood there a moment, stunned,
> then swinging his seven-ply oxhide shield behind him,
> drew back in caution, throwing a fast glance
> at his own Achaean troops like a trapped beast,
> pivoting, backpedaling, step by short step.   (XI.639–43 [544–47])[30]

By evoking this scene of retreat and combining it, as we have seen, with an allusion to contemporary military culture and Achilles' and Radigund's lunar armaments, Milton simultaneously suggests both Satan's heroism and cowardice. On the one hand, Satan in this scene is wrathful like Achilles; on the other hand, he shares Ajax's wariness and powerlessness. Milton may have also had in mind Ajax's reputation for caring too much about material weapons. That the Greek soldier ultimately kills himself because he is not awarded Achilles' armor prefigures Satan's own self-destruction, which was prompted by a similar sense of having been slighted and is similarly expressed through his association with emblems of traditional warfare. Just as Ajax did not deserve Achilles' defensive weaponry, Milton seems to imply, Satan, too, falls short of the glory that Achilles garnered.

More directly, the allusion to Ajax's flight from battle suggests God's omnipotence, for "Father Zeus on the heights *forced* Ajax to retreat" (*Iliad*, XI.638 [544], emphasis added), and it is God in *Paradise Lost* who causes Satan and his consorts to give up the fight and leap from heaven. But whereas Homer has Ajax pick on someone his own size until Zeus intervenes, Milton attempts to surpass the *Iliad* by pitting Satan against the Creator himself. And in Milton's Arminian theodicy, God does not force Satan to retreat but instead forces Satan to choose whether he will stay or go. Ultimately, Satan and the rebels "headlong themselves . . . threw / Down from the verge of Heav'n" (VI.864–65) – while Ajax fled from battle "much against his will" (XI.654 [556–57]) – which suggests once again that Satan fails to live up to his literary predecessors.

---

[30] Milton uses a similar image of armored retreat in *Samson Agonistes*. The Chorus recalls how when Samson advanced on Ascalon "In scorn of their proud arms and warlike tools," even "the bold Ascalonite / Fled," and "old warriors turned / Their plated backs under his heel" (lines 137–40).

We should not interpret Milton's allusion to Ajax's flight as a straightforward sign of Satan's cowardice, however. Although Satan retreats, he, like the Greek warrior, remains enraged and truculent. Ajax does not sprint from battle but reluctantly zigzags:

> the giant fighter would summon up his fury,
> wheeling on them again, beating off platoons
> of the stallion-breaking Trojans – and now again
> he'd swerve around in flight.   (XI.666–69 [566–68])

Whereas in *Samson Agonistes* Milton allies Ajax with the vain, boastful Harapha, whose "gorgeous arms" (line 1119) and "clattered iron" (line 1124) include a "seven-times-folded shield" like Ajax's (line 1122), in *Paradise Lost* the poet instead uses Ajax to cast Satan as sullen and only temporarily subdued. Homer develops Ajax's conflicted feelings in the above passage with a pair of epic similes comparing him to wild animals. Ajax resembles a "tawny lion" that "quails" and "slinks away" when accosted by "hounds and country field hands," but he also acts like a "stubborn ass" that continues to ravage crops even as boys beat him with sticks (XI.644–62 [548–65]).

Of turtles and telescopes

Homer's animal similes may have recommended Milton's specific depiction of how Satan carries his shield at the opening of *Paradise Lost*, for Milton, too, seems to have been thinking about the animal world as he imagined the arch-fiend's armament. Undermining Satan's heroic pretensions and his weapon's "Ethereal temper" (I.285), Milton slyly uses Satan's shield to compare him with one of Earth's newly created "creeping things" (VII.452). Wearing his shield on his back, crawling from lake to land, slowly moving with "uneasy steps" (I.295), Satan momentarily resembles – to compare great things with small – one of the amphibious tortoises described in seventeenth-century animal encyclopedias. Here we find accounts of the tortoise's "shield," a term that during the Renaissance signified not only a piece of defensive armor but also an animal's "protective covering or shelter," as in a tortoise's mottled or "spotty" shell.[31] Such a humiliating image both captures Satan's amphibious or twofold nature and anticipates his transformation into a serpent, the animal with which the tortoise was most commonly allied during the early modern period. In *A Description of the Nature of Four-Footed Beasts* (1678), for example, Joannes Jonston observes that tortoises not only make a sound "a little

---

[31] *OED*, s. v. "shield," def. II.5.

louder than a snakes hisse" but they also "fight with Serpents, senceing themselves."[32] Edward Topsell, in *The History of Four-Footed Beasts and Serpents* (1658), similarly notes that the tortoise "in the head and tail ... resembleth a Serpent" and reports that these shelled animals are, like serpents, "accounted crafty and subtle."[33]

Satan's appearance as a tortoise may evoke, too, traditional renditions of that animal being dropped from the sky by its enemies and punished by Jove with its shell. As part of the rich Roman iconography that survives in the medieval mosaic at the Basilica in Aquileia, a rooster battles a tortoise, an image thought to represent an allegory of good versus evil. According to one story, Jupiter imprisoned the tortoise in its shell for disrespecting him.[34] Although the tortoise had not attempted anything so audacious as overthrowing heaven, its punishment still recalls Satan's sentence. Just as the tortoise in the story was forced to carry its shelter on its shoulders, always at home no matter how far it traveled, so Milton's Satan cannot escape the hell of his own making: "Which way I fly is Hell; myself am Hell," he laments (IV.75). Nor should we ignore the tradition, noted by Jonston, that fresh-water tortoises were sometimes called "divells," and tortoises' hard shells were, in turn, actually used by African and Arabian soldiers to make defensive weaponry.[35]

Even Milton's earlier simile, comparing Satan to "that sea beast / Leviathan," mistaken for an island by the pilot of a Norwegian skiff (I.200–01), finds an analogue in the lore surrounding tortoises. As Karen Edwards has observed, the name "*leviathan* simply denotes a large water animal or sea monster," and scholars during the Renaissance debated what type of animal it might have been.[36] Given Satan's resemblance to a tortoise as he reaches the shore, it is pleasing to speculate whether Milton could have thought of this beast as a giant sea tortoise, an explanation which would help to account for his reference to the creature's "scaly rind" (I.206) and which finds precedent in Renaissance animal encyclopedias. Topsell, for example, records a version of the same story in which a weary traveler fell asleep on a giant tortoise that he had mistaken for land.[37]

A seventeenth-century edition of *Aesops Fables* (1650), to take one last example, also associates the tortoise with a punitive fall and presumptive

[32] Joannes Jonston, *A Description of the Nature of Four-Footed Beasts* (1678), O2v.
[33] Edward Topsell, *The History of Four-Footed Beasts and Serpents* (London, 1658), Yyy1v, Yyy2r.
[34] Topsell, *The History of Four-Footed Beasts and Serpents*, Yyy2r.
[35] Jonston, *A Description of the Nature of Four-Footed Beasts*, O3v, O2v, O4r.
[36] Karen L. Edwards, *Milton and the Natural World: Science and Poetry in "Paradise Lost"* (Cambridge: Cambridge University Press, 1999), p. 108.
[37] Topsell, *The History of Four-Footed Beasts and Serpents*, Yyy1v.

ascent.[38] The tortoise deceives an eagle into carrying her by promising to "descry / Jewells that did upon some Mountain lie." When the tortoise fails to live up to this promise, the eagle in one version devours her and in the other "scratcheth her" to death. But the moral, that "who lifts his thoughts 'bove his estate, / Falls in th' attempt, and hastens his own Fate," evokes both Satan's fall and foolish insolence.

We cannot know whether Milton had such lore in mind while composing *Paradise Lost*, and I also do not wish to suggest that all the traditions associated with tortoises were germane for Milton's depiction of the arch-fiend.[39] Yet, these popular, contemporary perceptions support the relevance of the tortoise image as Satan reaches the shore in hell, and they may have influenced seventeenth-century interpretations of Satan's outdated weaponry.

Milton at least seems to have used this passage to suggest Satan's hardening heart and physical debasement: Satan's backwards shield initiates a string of gradually ossifying animal imagery that charts his ongoing onto-logical descent. Beginning with this subtle allusion, Milton then turns to more direct animal metaphors – Satan enters Eden, for example, like a cormorant and wolf (IV.183–96) – until with the image of Satan, "Squat like a toad, close at the ear of Eve" (IV.800), readers are unsure: has he metaphorically or literally changed? When Ithuriel touches Satan with a spear, the fiend "started up in his own shape" (IV.819), but we do not know what specific form Satan had previously adopted. Certainly, his later transformations are literal; he approaches Adam and Eve first as a lion, then tiger (IV.402–08), then as a serpent, until ultimately, in book X, Satan and the rebels are imprisoned in the shape of monstrous snakes (lines 511–45). These animal comparisons seem to calcify just as Satan's original substance begins to harden the farther he moves away from God, although the overarching metamorphosis, from tortoise to the closely related serpent, would fit within the epic's larger recoiling motif. For all Satan's apparent

---

[38] *Æsops Fables* (Cambridge, 1650), G1or. Although modern readers may be familiar with Aesop's story of the "Tortoise and the Hare," Renaissance editions of Aesop's fables instead relate how a hare races, and eventually loses to, a snail. The link between snails and tortoises extends back at least to the late fourteenth century when *snail* was used to signify shell-carrying gastropods as well as tortoises and turtles. Long before 1650, however, this latter meaning for *snail* had evidently become obsolete (see *OED*, s. v. "snail," defs. 1.a and 1.b.). Nevertheless, the description *"Of the Snail"* in Wolfgang Franz, *The History of Brutes* (London, 1670), attributes to snails qualities and anecdotes traditionally associated with tortoises (R1v–R3r).

[39] The tragic poet Aeschylus, for example, purportedly died when an eagle dropped a hard-shelled tortoise on his head. On other sixteenth- and seventeenth-century depictions of tortoises in poetry, paintings, and natural histories, see Diane Kelsey McColley, *Poetry and Ecology in the Age of Milton and Marvell* (Aldershot, Eng.; Burlington, VT: Ashgate, 2007), pp. 145–48.

motions, in other words, he ends where he began, forced backwards into a semblance of his former shape.

The image of a tortoise suggested by Satan's shield may also help to explain Milton's subsequent lunar image – what Cleanth Brooks once called "perhaps the most famous simile of them all."[40] Satan's shield hangs

> on his shoulders like the moon, whose orb
> Through optic glass the Tuscan artist views
> At evening from the top of Fesole,
> Or in Valdarno, to descry new lands,
> Rivers or mountains in her spotty globe.   (I.287–91)

Whereas some critics have seen Milton's allusion to Galileo ("the Tuscan artist") as an odd digression, I would suggest that the glimpse of Satan as a tortoise quietly prepares us for this comparison.[41] Milton has rooted Satan firmly in the material world, whether through the image of a tortoise with a spotty shield, or this description of the moon and the Florentine landscape. For Milton to turn from one branch of natural philosophy to another, to blend the old science of animal encyclopedias with the new, observational science of Galileo's astronomy, constitutes less of a leap than juxtaposing classical warfare and Galileo's telescope, especially since Galileo's own arguments challenged ontological distinctions (in his case, between the stars and the Earth).[42]

Still, such a juxtaposition – alluding to both Ajax and Galileo to describe Satan's shield – further chips away at Satan's heroic posturing. Following J. B. Broadbent, some critics have interpreted Galileo as an "admirable figure to displace Satan,"[43] while others, following Joan Webber, have thought the link between Galileo and Satan to be a repudiation of the astronomer's enterprise.[44] But this reference to Galileo, like the allusion to a tortoise, also refracts Satan's resemblance to his epic precursors and

[40] Cleanth Brooks, "Milton and the New Criticism," *The Sewanee Review* 59 (1951): 1–22 (p. 18).

[41] For example, T. S. Eliot, if we briefly stay with the New Critics, singled out this simile's "sudden transitions" as "inspired *frivolity*, an enjoyment by the author in the exercise of his own virtuosity, which is a mark of the first rank of genius." Eliot, "Milton," *The Sewanee Review* 56 (1948): 185–209 (p. 204).

[42] On the relationship between Galileo's discoveries and Milton's monism, see Donald Friedman, "Galileo and the Art of Seeing," in *Milton in Italy: Contexts, Images, Contradictions*, ed. Mario A. Di Cesare (Binghamton, NY: Medieval and Renaissance Texts and Studies, 1991), pp. 159–74.

[43] J. B. Broadbent, *Some Graver Subject: An Essay on "Paradise Lost"* (New York: Barnes and Noble, 1960), p. 72; and Freeman, *Milton and the Martial Muse*, p. 130.

[44] Joan Webber, *Milton and His Epic Tradition* (Seattle: University of Washington Press, 1979), pp. 142–43; see also Roy Flannagan, "Arts, Artists, Galileo and Concordances," *Milton Quarterly* 23 (1986): 103–05; and Neil Harris, "Galileo as Symbol: The 'Tuscan Artist' in *Paradise Lost*," *Annali dell'Istituto e Museo di Storia della Scienza di Firenze* 10 (1985): 3–29.

reflects his newly fallen state. Whereas in heaven Satan's shield resembles a sun (VI.305), in hell its luster has faded so that it looks like a "spotty globe" that can only be appreciated "Through optic glass" (I.291, 288). This pair of astronomical metaphors measures Satan's diminished radiance and heavenly estrangement.

Moreover, the necessary perspective of Galileo's telescope prompts a series of reversals that, like the backwards shield, reinforce Satan's paradoxical status as a fallen angel and "superior fiend" (I.283). Readers initially learn that Satan's shield "Hung on his shoulders like the moon" (I.287) until, upon reaching the end of the simile, we discover that the shield more precisely resembles the moon as magnified through Galileo's optic glass (I.288–91). Viewed first without, then with the telescope, Satan's shield is rendered both small and large – just as his spear in this same passage resembles both a "wand" and "mast" (I.293, 294), just as his shield is both "ethereal" and earthy, and just as the lunar metaphor takes us from Florence to hell, and from the "top of Fesole" to the valley of the Arno (I. 285, 289).[45] Through the lens of both the old and new sciences Milton focuses readers' attention on the failure of the inflated heroic ideals that Satan's shield symbolizes: like the animal encyclopedias that expose Satan's tortoise-like qualities, Galileo's telescope reveals that, upon closer inspection, the devil's weaponry is blotchy.

Milton encourages this bifocal perspective throughout *Paradise Lost*: not only that readers must again and again confront Satan's amphibious nature – simultaneously courageous and cowardly, heroic and heinous – but also that readers must work hard to interpret the poet's overlapping allusions and subtle imagery. Objects in the epic, we discover, may be larger, or more significant, than they initially appear. Whereas Stanley Fish has compared *Paradise Lost*'s uninformed reader with the pilot of the Norwegian skiff who, in mistaking the leviathan for land, does not see below the surface, I would suggest that the Tuscan astronomer represents Milton's informed reader, peering intently into the text to descry new allusions and previously ignored contexts and ideas.[46]

Among the various ideas embedded within Milton's description of Satan's shield we also should consider the image's potentially personal significance. Responding in *Pro Populo Anglicano Defensio Secunda* (1654) to a libelous attack, Milton expresses his sense of national responsibility in terms of classical armament:

[45] Lienhard Bergel, "Milton's *Paradise Lost*, I, 284–295," *Explicator* 10 (1951): item 3, observes that hell's desolation is heightened by "the poetic intensity of the passage" and "the luxuriant atmosphere of Italy which is evoked by the place names."
[46] Fish, *Surprised by Sin*, p. 36.

I should like to be Ulysses – should like, that is, to have deserved as well as possible of my country – yet I do not covet the arms of Achilles. I do not seek to bear before me heaven painted on a shield, for others, not myself to see in battle, while I carry on my shoulders a burden, not painted, but real, for myself, and not for others to perceive. (*CPW* IV: 595–96)

Here Milton aspires to become a sage counselor like Ulysses rather than a soldier like Ajax or Achilles. But this passage from the second *Defensio* also reveals, by comparison, Satan's selfishness and vanity at the opening of *Paradise Lost*. While the burden that Milton shouldered suggests once again that Satan's similarly positioned shield represents not an aid but an encumbrance, Milton emphasizes that his own burden has nothing to do with protecting himself nor impressing others. Armed with his faith in God, he has no use for a shield that, like Satan's weapon, merely resembles the heavens; the poet instead carries the real responsibility of serving heaven and his country. He rejects a soldier's material armor for the divine "shield of faith" which, as St. Paul describes, will help him "stand against the wiles of the devil" (Eph. 6.11, 16).

When viewed within its contemporary context, Satan's shield in *Paradise Lost* ultimately recalls Chaucer's knight, whose rust-stained tunic raises questions about the currency of his chivalric code and the truthfulness of his purported achievements on the battlefield. Within this brief passage Milton has forged for Satan a defensive weapon as well as an ornamental impresa, a visual device worn by both sides during the civil wars. Instead of wearing the family's coat of arms, soldiers often preferred these personal, sometimes witty devices, specifically designed for battle – what Milton alludes to elsewhere as he describes the warring angels' "shields / Various, with boastful argument portrayed" (VI.83–84).[47] In practical terms, such visual devices helped soldiers on both sides of the civil wars to distinguish between their opponents and allies, a common problem on the battlefield. Appropriately for a character whose slippery speech and heroic qualities continue to win readers' sympathies, Satan's spotty shield helps to identify his moral and material deterioration even as he appears his most resolute.

---

[47] The angels in heaven carry similar devices commemorating their great "acts of zeal and love" (V.593). For a discussion of seventeenth-century heraldry, see Dobranski, "William Cecil and the Heart of Milton's *Pro Populo Anglicano Defensio*," *Milton Quarterly* 34 (May 2000): 33–48 (especially pp. 38–39); see also the description of Renaissance pageant shields in Laking, *A Record of European Armour and Arms*, IV: 218–59.

CHAPTER 5

What do bad angels look like?

I charge thee to returne, and chaunge thy shape,
Thou art too ugly to attend on me.

– Christopher Marlowe, Doctor Faustus[1]

Some of the most arresting visual images in *Paradise Lost* describe the fallen angels in hell, as they suffer on the burning lake, "rolling in the flood / With scattered arms and ensigns" (I.324–25), and then take flight and flock to hear Satan:

> All in a moment through the gloom were seen
> Ten thousand banners rise into the air
> With orient colors waving: with them rose
> A forest huge of spears: and thronging helms
> Appeared, and serried shields in thick array
> Of depth immeasurable. (I.544–49)

Here, as if in an extreme long shot, Milton captures the excitement and anonymity of a crowd by occluding the "bad angels" themselves (I.344) and focusing on their raised banners and armament. While hell in *Paradise Lost* is memorably ablaze with scorching flames that provide "No light, but rather darkness visible" (I.63) – a paradox that underscores the rebels' permanent remove "from God and light of Heav'n" (I.73) – Milton spotlights dramatic visual details that suddenly burst into view, such as the above image of the angels' zealous militarism, or the description of an encumbered Satan crawling from lake to land, as discussed in the preceding chapter. In fact, our first glimpse of Satan as he awakens on the burning lake and "round ... throws his baleful eyes" (I.56), initiates and imitates Milton's visual technique in the epic's opening books. The poet's searching gaze temporarily lights on specific scenes and details, their abrupt introduction enhancing the violence that they sometimes portray. Thus, when Satan calls for a council, another remarkable visual image expresses

---

[1] *Marlowe's "Doctor Faustus," 1604–1616*, ed. W. W. Greg (Oxford: Clarendon, 1968), p. 177 (I.iii.251–52).

the fallen angels' misguided violence: "out flew / Millions of flaming swords, drawn from the thighs / Of mighty Cherubim; the sudden blaze / Far round illumined Hell" (I.663–66).

More often, though, images of the fallen angels occur in the midst of elaborate epic similes that draw on a combination of poetic and biblical traditions as well as objects and experiences from Milton's contemporary culture. Just in the opening book, the angels are described as "autumnal leaves" (I.302); "scattered sedge" (I.304); "floating carcasses / And broken chariot wheels" (I.310–11); "men wont to watch / On duty, sleeping found" (I.332–33); a "pitchy cloud / Of locusts" (I.340–41); "forest oaks or mountain pines" whose tops have been "scathed" and "singéd" by lightning (I.613–14); "bands / Of pioneers with spade and pickax armed" who "Forerun the royal camp, to trench a field, / Or cast a rampart" (I.675–78); "bees / In springtime" that "Pour forth their populous youth about the hive / In clusters" (I.768–69, 770–71); and "Earth's giant sons," the "smallest dwarfs," the "pygmean race," and reveling "faerie elves" (I.778–81).[2]

These comparisons have attracted considerable attention over the past three centuries in part because the similes are so vivid and surprising, almost self-contained lyric poems. James Whaler's New Critical studies of the 1930s remain especially valuable for charting the similes' visual function. Examining how the comparisons enable readers to "picture Satan, his infernal host, his punishment, his revenge," Whaler also demonstrates that some of the most evocative metaphors separate themselves from the larger narrative: "In the midst of a scene of strife, pain, or crisis the poet may use for illustration an image that carries suggestions of tranquility."[3] In this latter regard, Milton's similes advance his apparent strategy of expanding the boundaries of epic and reevaluating his literary predecessors. As John Dennis observed in 1704, *Paradise Lost*, "by vertue of its extraordinary Subject, cannot so properly be said to be against the Rules, as it may be

---

[2] Not all of Milton's similes are imagistic so that he also compares the fallen angels to invading Vandals, Huns, and Goths: "A multitude, like which the populous north / Poured never from her frozen loins" (I.351–52). And he later describes the angels somewhat vaguely as "a horrid front / Of dreadful length and dazzling arms, in guise / Of warriors old with ordered spear and shield" (I.563–65).

[3] James Whaler, "The Miltonic Simile," *PMLA* 46 (1931): 1034–74 (pp. 1034, 1036). See also Whaler's other, related essays: "Grammatical *Nexus* of the Miltonic Simile," *Journal of English and Germanic Philology* (1931): 327–34; "Compounding and Distribution of Similes in *Paradise Lost*," *Modern Philology* (1931): 313–27; and "Animal Similes in *Paradise Lost*," *PMLA* 47 (1932): 534–53. Geoffrey Hartman, "Milton's Counterplot," *English Literary History* 25 (1958): 1–12, has similarly highlighted a "counterplot" in Milton's epic – that is, "moments of relief or distancing" (p. 1), largely realized through epic similes, "to bring the terrible sublime home to the reader's imagination" (p. 4).

affirmed to be above them all."[4] Milton thus critiques and makes various epic conventions his own, including the use of extended comparisons. While no doubt indebted to Homer's sometimes disjunctive similes, Milton also allows himself considerable latitude in the way that his similes work.[5] Their "subtly relevant" details, as Christopher Ricks has observed, sometimes effect an "ironic disparity" between vehicle and tenor, and sometimes create a close correspondence between the interpolated image or object and the thing being described.[6]

Yet the abundance of visual imagery associated with the fallen angels serves another important function that has gone mostly unappreciated. In this chapter, I examine how Milton uses these often metaphorical passages to depict the rebel angels' unprecedented moral and ontological position. Whereas Peter Herman has posited a general "poetics of incertitude" in *Paradise Lost*, beginning with what Herman deems to be "troublesome metaphors" that "regularly create a Gordian knot of contrary resonances" (itself a troublesome metaphor), I wish to argue that the epic's diabolic imagery, often presented in similes, conveys the rebels' uncertain status, not Milton's uncertainty.[7] Beginning with other seventeenth-century portrayals of fallen angels, I show how Milton's rendering is uniquely equivocal as he attempts to reconcile his philosophy of matter with the poem's narrative and imagery. While in the other chapters I focus on the material things that Milton uses to help depict his epic's realms and characters, here it is the rebels themselves who are becoming mere objects, "cursèd things" (I.389) and "bestial gods" (I.435).

Falling into materiality

Milton at the start of *Paradise Lost* emphasizes that angels – even fallen ones – remain essentially fluid. Anticipating how after the Fall Adam and Eve's descendants will come to worship Satan's followers in various forms, the narrator explains,

[4] John Dennis, *The Grounds of Criticism in Poetry* (London, 1704), sig. b3r.

[5] Neil Forsyth, *The Satanic Epic* (Princeton and Oxford: Princeton University Press, 2003), echoes earlier commentators in identifying a Homeric quality in the "double nature" of Milton's similes – that is, in the way that many of them "contrast or clash in interesting ways with the narrative context" (p. 103).

[6] Christopher Ricks, *Milton's Grand Style* (Oxford: Oxford University Press, 1963), pp. 123, 127; and see Walter Raleigh, *Milton* (London: Edward Arnold, 1900), p. 213. Forsyth, in *The Satanic Epic*, similarly writes that the language in some of Milton's metaphors "disturbs the clarity of vision generally associated with similes, and therefore the authority of the voice that uses the similes" (p. 103).

[7] Peter C. Herman, *Destabilizing Milton: "Paradise Lost" and the Poetics of Incertitude* (New York: Palgrave Macmillan, 2005), pp. 25, 42.

> For spirits when they please
> Can either sex assume, or both; so soft
> And uncompounded is their essence pure,
> Nor tied or manacled with joint or limb,
> Nor founded on the brittle strength of bones,
> Like cumbrous flesh; but in what shape they choose
> Dilated or condensed, bright or obscure,
> Can execute their airy purposes,
> And works of love or enmity fulfill.   (I.423–31)

In these lines, the freedom of the rebels' forms seems to correspond to and extend their free will: the fallen angels can choose not only their "purposes" and "works" but also their physical "shape" – light or dark, expanded or compact. That they have no bodies – "Nor tied or manacled with joint or limb, / Nor founded on the brittle strength of bones" – suggests an inherent natural freedom that transcends the potential of even Adam and Eve's prelapsarian lives: the fallen angels can emulate Adam or Eve ("either sex assume") or somehow combine the couple's two forms ("or both").

The rebels' ongoing malleability appears to be connected to their residual goodness. Although fallen and in hell, they retain some of their former nature, "for neither do the spirits damned / Lose all their virtue," as the narrator explains (II.482–83). This pronouncement comes on the heels of the rebels' righteous acclamation for Satan's volunteering to go to earth, but the choice of "virtue" also points to the fallen angels' ongoing resemblance to one of the celestial orders that attends God – "Thrones, Dominations, Princedoms, *Virtues*, Powers" (V.601, emphasis added). Satan, of course, famously insists on his constancy in opposing God: "What matter where, if I be still the same, / And what I should be, all but less than he / Whom thunder hath made greater?" (I.256–58). The arch-fiend is bragging that even in hell he steadfastly defies divine authority because he remains lower than the exalted Son. But Satan in such passages also ironically hints at his vestigial glory as one of God's creations. Despite the devil's full-throated apostasy, he continues to exhibit some signs of virtue, both at the epic council when he bravely (albeit selfishly) offers to travel through the "dark unbottomed infinite abyss" (II.405) and in the garden as Eve's angelic form entirely disarms him. In the latter scene, Eve is no doubt powerful, but Satan presumably could not be "abstracted . . . / From his own evil" and, even for a moment, rendered "Stupidly good" if he did not retain some degree of his former nature (IX.463–65). As the narrator observes early on, Satan's form, though fallen,

> had yet not lost
> All her original brightness, nor appeared
> Less than Archangel ruined, and th' excess
> Of glory obscured: as when the sun new ris'n
> Looks through the horizontal misty air
> Shorn of his beams.   (I.591–96)

Ultimately, as we saw in chapter 3, God announces that the devils will never find grace, but the language in this solar metaphor raises the possibility that Satan still possesses his original illumination (if "yet" means "nevertheless") and that his diminished status is temporary, as passing as a dawn mist.

The emphasis in the enjambed phrase "had yet not lost / All," however, clearly implies that Satan has already relinquished some of his heavenly splendor, and, if "yet" instead means "thus far," the description anticipates the arch-fiend's final defeat and total degeneration: he will one day apparently lose his remaining brightness. Confirming this reading is Satan's earlier admission that since disobeying God he has "changed in outward luster" (I.97), and when in an unguarded moment the fiend alights on earth, Uriel quickly discerns Satan's "looks / Alien from Heav'n, with passions foul obscured" (IV.570–71). The narrator underscores such a physical change: he observes that Satan in his rebellion has been "disfigured, more than could befall / Spirit of happy sort" (IV.127–28), and adds more specifically that in hell the devil's "face / Deep scars of thunder had intrenched, and care / Sat on his faded cheek" (I.600–02). Encountering Satan at Eve's ear, the angel Zephon accordingly does not know "Which of those rebel spirits" he is confronting (IV.823). The cherub suggests that the appearance of all the rebels has changed with their fall:

> Think not, revolted Spirit, thy shape the same,
> Or undiminished brightness, to be known
> As when thou stood'st in Heav'n upright and pure;
> That glory then, when thou no more wast good,
> Departed from thee, and thou resembles now
> Thy sin and place of doom obscure and foul.   (IV.835–40)

Zephon emphasizes both a loss of illumination and a change in shape as a result of rebellion ("when thou no more wast good"). Although Zephon does not describe exactly how Satan now looks, the words "obscure" and "foul" indicate, respectively, a darkening and sullying, while the notion of "glory . . . / Departed" signifies, as Patrick Hume first noted in explaining the rebels' collective transformation, "the loss of that Angelick Beauty, which like a Glory attended on their Innocency, which by their foul

Rebellion they had forfeited, covered now with Shame and black Confusion."[8]

Milton highlights this physical aspect of the rebels' punishment in the epic's opening books. While the "heads and leaders" of the squadrons still possess "godlike shapes and forms / Excelling humans" (I.357–59), all of the fallen angels seem to have experienced some type of disfigurement if Satan, awakening on the burning lake, cannot confidently recognize even Beelzebub:

> If thou beest he; but O how fall'n! How changed
> From him, who in the happy realms of light
> Clothed with transcendent brightness didst outshine
> Myriads though bright: if he whom mutual league,
> United thoughts and counsels, equal hope
> And hazard in the glorious enterprise,
> Joined with me once, now misery hath joined
> In equal ruin.   (I.84–91)

We may attribute some of Satan's confusion to the rebels' nine-day fall from heaven and the subsequent nine days that they spend face-down, consumed by hellfire. But clearly the fallen angel who will become known as Beelzebub among Adam and Eve's descendants has changed in hell and has at least become less bright.[9] As Satan prepares to address the assembled host, he admits that the rebels were "Far other once beheld in bliss" (I.607), a provocative phrase that includes among its various meanings the idea of the rebels' changed appearance; in bliss, Satan could have beheld his followers as "Far other" because they have physically changed. When Satan then asks for volunteers to find the new world, Milton describes how the fallen angels can read each other's faces: "all sat mute, / Pondering the danger with deep thoughts; and each / In other's count'nance read his own dismay / Astonished" (II.420–23). This language also hints at the rebels' physical transformation. As we saw in the previous chapter, "Astonished," a possible pun on turned to stone, suggests the link between the rebels' moral and ontological debasement: their faces can now be read because their shapes are starting to decline, like their already hardened hearts.

Milton pursues the correlation between the fallen angels' physical shape and moral status when Satan gazes out at the assembly and feels remorse.

---

[8] Patrick Hume, *Annotations on Milton's "Paradise Lost,"* in *The Poetical Works of Mr. John Milton*, ed. Hume (London, 1695), D2r (note for book I, line 141).

[9] See N. K. Sugimura, *"Matter of Glorious Trial": Spiritual and Material Substance in "Paradise Lost"* (New Haven and London: Yale University Press, 2009), who emphasizes Satan's divesture of light in his fall (p. 188).

Whereas Satan's acknowledgment that he has "changed in outward luster" (I.97) seems an attempt to understate his fallen condition, reducing it to a merely superficial difference, the description of his crying – "Tears such as angels weep burst forth" (I.620) – raises the possibility of a more profound transformation. The clause could mean that the fiend remains essentially angelic in nature and that Milton is striving to describe an angelic activity in human terms: Satan thus weeps as would any one of God's heavenly attendants – that is, differently than we humans cry. But the clause also suggests that Satan has changed fundamentally with his fall and, since he is no longer a denizen of heaven, his tears are now merely *as* or *like* those of an angel.[10] Similarly, when Satan first awakens in hell, "At once as far *as* angels ken he views / The dismal situation waste and wild" (I.59–60, emphasis added). While this comparative description might be another accommo-dative linguistic strategy for overcoming the difficulty of representing angels, it also could mean that Satan now only resembles an angel; instead of angelic cognizance, his perceptive powers are merely like those of a divine attendant.[11]

Given Satan and his followers' moral, physical, and – as the last example suggests – epistemological diminishment, it is apt that the one mythical figure whom Milton includes in hell is Medusa. The rebels briefly encoun-ter her as they explore hell's rivers and lastly discover Lethe: "At certain revolutions all the damned / Are brought" (II.597–98) over "the river of oblivion" (II.583) as they "wish and struggle ... to reach / The tempting stream" and "lose / In sweet forgetfulness all pain and woe " (II.606–08). The shift in these lines to present tense – "are brought" – combined with the broadly inclusive "all the damned" and the temporal expansiveness of "At certain revolutions" suggests that Milton is anticipating when hell will become populated not just by fallen angels, but also Adam and Eve's reprobate daughters and sons. Evidently, because of Medusa, neither

---

[10] When thinking about the rebel angels in *Paradise Lost*, we should not completely conflate Satan with the fallen host. The text frequently treats the fallen angels as a group that includes Satan – for example, the angels are called "companions of his fall" (I.76) – but Milton also takes pains to describe a hierarchy. That we first encounter Satan's companions as "all *his* host / Of rebel angels," for example, indicates the rebels' subservient status (I.37–38, emphasis added). We also read that Satan "with his horrid crew / Lay vanquished, rolling in the fiery gulf / Confounded though immortal: but his doom / Reserved him to more wrath; for now the thought / Both of lost happiness and lasting pain / Torments him" (I.51–56). This latter description suggests the difference between Satan and the other rebels: his anger is fiercer, his resentment deeper, and his punishment consequently more severe. Thus, as Satan gazes on the assembled rebels, he acknowledges to himself that they are not "fellows of his crime" but "the followers rather" (I.606).

[11] For a discussion of angelic apprehension as different from human eyesight, see Joad Raymond, *Milton's Angels: The Early-Modern Imagination* (Oxford: Oxford University Press, 2010), pp. 291–99.

group will ever accomplish the complete metamorphosis that Lethe taunt-
ingly promises:

> But fate withstands, and to oppose th' attempt
> Medusa with Gorgonian terror guards
> The ford, and of itself the water flies
> All taste of living wight, as once it fled
> The lip of Tantalus. (II.610–14)

Here, as both victim and villainess, Medusa embodies the rebels' status in
hell. Like the formerly resplendent angels who are punished for the Sin that
springs from Satan's head, Medusa was a beautiful maiden who incurred
the wrath of the also head-born Athena. Perhaps just as Medusa was made
hideous so that glimpsing her face would turn men to stone, the fallen
angels in their changed appearance have also become monstrous. Milton
does not more fully describe the angels' sinful shapes, but surely, as I
discuss in the chapter's final section ("Angels into idols"), the rebels will
threaten to destroy Adam and Eve's descendants who gaze on them
worshipfully. In keeping with my own culturally inclusive approach to
the possible sources for the epic's imagery, James Dougal Fleming has
proposed that Milton's reference to Medusa could be based on the classical
statuary and automata found in Italian Renaissance gardens, which Milton
could have seen during his visit to the Continent.[12] But in this passage I
instead wish to emphasize Medusa's possible literal effect: she denies the
rebels the thorough-going change that they seek, forcing them to remain in
their oxymoronic position as bad angels. That Milton also casts the rebels'
reaction to Lethe and Medusa in physical terms suggests that she might
even cause them to harden as they look for relief to the river that she
guards: "the advent'rous bands / With shudd'ring horror pale, and eyes
aghast / Viewed first their lamentable lot" (II.615–17). If Medusa can turn
mere mortals to stone, then her petrifying gaze should have a corresponding but less stony effect on inherently spiritual beings, leaving them
incorporeal but descending into materiality.

"Gross by sinning grown"

The idea that the rebel angels decline physically when they fall from heaven
was not original to Milton. Plato in the *Timaeus* had written that when a
wicked man is reborn he "shall be changed every time, according to the

---

[12] James Dougal Fleming, "Meanwhile, Medusa in *Paradise Lost*," *English Literary History* 69 (2002):
1009–28.

nature of his wickedness, into some bestial form after the similitude of his own nature," and various early modern writers later applied this theory to explain the fall of Satan and his followers.[13] Thomas Nashe in 1592, to take one example, cited Plato in asserting that the physical selves of the rebels changed when they opposed God. In heaven, the "bodies" of the prelapsarian angels were "bright and pure," but, "after their transgression" they became "obscured with a thick, ayrie matter, and ever after assigned to darknes."[14] Nashe describes in similar terms the change that Satan suffered for his sin: the archangel Lucifer was originally a "cleer bodie, compact of the purest and brightest of the aire, but after his fall he was vailed with a grosser substance, and tooke a new forme of darke and thick ayre, which he still reteineth."[15] Henry More in *An Explanation of the Grand Mystery of Godliness* (1660) also argues that the angels' rebellion affected their physical natures and "*changed their pure Æthereal Bodies into more Feculent and Terrestrial.*"[16] Like Nashe, More distinguishes among different types or "Orders of Spirits": while some angels are "purely Immaterial," others contain a mysterious mixture of spirit and matter that degenerates when they disobey, for if they did not have some "communion . . . with Matter" then "how could they ever sin or fall?"[17]

Thomas Heywood in 1635 also accepts that "uncorporeall Spirits" possess an immortal "Angel-like Substance," but he differs from Nashe and More in rejecting that angels "by their Fall / Should gaine a Substance more materiall."[18] Instead, Heywood argues, the type of body that an angel can assume on earth is somehow affected by the creature's moral status. Whereas good angels "undoubtedly . . . can / Put on all forms" but prefer to "take the shape of Man," fallen angels must "In figures more contemptible appeare," such as dogs or apes (Ccc2v). If bad spirits were to "put on human shape," he adds, then they must bear "Some strange prodigious marke . . . / In one deficient member" so that human beings can "finde them out" (Ccc3r).

The premise in all three writers' works – that angels possess a special intellectual substance – seems to have originated with Thomas Aquinas, who defined angels as "incorporeal substances . . . midway between God

---

[13] Plato, *Timaeus*, trans. R. G. Bury (Cambridge: Harvard University Press, 1952), 42b–c.

[14] Thomas Nashe, *Pierce Pennilesse, His Supplication to the Divell*, 2nd edn. (London, 1592), H1v.

[15] Nashe, *Pierce Pennilesse*, H2r.

[16] Henry More, *An Explanation of the Grand Mystery of Godliness* (London, 1660), D6v.

[17] More, *An Explanation of the Grand Mystery of Godliness*, D5v.

[18] Thomas Heywood, *The Hierarchie of the Blessed Angells*, 2nd edn. (London, 1635), S5r, S5v. All subsequent references to this edition are cited parenthetically in the text.

and corporeal things."[19] Aquinas reasoned that angelic nature is "wholly non-material" (but still composed of substance because angels are finite) and naturally incorporeal (but able to assume "bodies made of air" so as to communicate with humankind).[20] Earlier, patristic authorities had debated both points: whether angels are material and whether they have bodies. Origen and Tertullian, for example, found evidence of angels' materiality and corporeality in Genesis. They maintained that the fallen angels were the "sons of God" who "saw the daughters of men that they *were* fair; and they took them wives of all which they chose" (Gen. 6: 2).[21] As Heywood explains, these early commentators concluded

> That these no other could than *Angels* be.
> Who if they married, must have Bodies; those
> Compos'd of Forme and Matter, to dispose,
> Else how should they have Issue? And againe;
> How are bad Spirites sensible of paine,
> In Hells eternall torments, if there faile
> That Substance on the which Fire may prevaile.   (S3v-S4r)

Heywood himself goes on to reject such reasoning – he calls it a "grosse absurditie" (S4v) – and certainly more influential during the sixteenth and seventeenth centuries was the Thomist dualism of a superior, divine spirit and a gross, earthly matter. How could spiritual beings so closely associated with God's non-material essence, Aquinas argued, have bodies and be made of matter? Yet the subtlety of Aquinas' explanation and his insistence that angelic substance is beyond human comprehension permitted writers such as Nashe, More, and Heywood to offer more mysterious – or at least less cohesive – angelic descriptions, perhaps also influenced by early modern advances in natural philosophy that challenged the Aristotelian physics undergirding Aquinas' philosophy. Instead of espousing a straightforward dichotomy and upholding that angels are incorporeal and non-material, these early modern writers attributed bodies to angels and developed Aquinas' notion of angelic substance by positing what Joad Raymond has helpfully described as a "spiritualized form of matter."[22]

---

[19] Thomas Aquinas, *Summa Theologiae*, 60 vols. (Cambridge: Blackfriars; and New York: McGraw-Hill, 1964–66), IX: 7. And see Aquinas, *Treatise on Separate Substances*, trans. and ed. Francis J. Lescoe (West Hartford, CT: Saint Joseph College, 1959), especially pp. 46–49, 75–77.

[20] Aquinas, *Summa Theologiae*, IX: 11, 35, 37.

[21] For the textual development of this passage in Genesis and the interpolation of the Greek story of the Titans, see the excellent account in Neil Forsyth, *The Old Enemy: Satan and the Combat Myth* (Princeton: Princeton University Press, 1987), pp. 147–59.

[22] Raymond, *Milton's Angels*, p. 284; and Robert H. West, *Milton and the Angels* (Athens: University of Georgia Press, 1955), pp. 149, 165.

The latter concept plays an especially significant role in Milton's depiction of the fallen angels in *Paradise Lost* because, as we have seen, he imagines a universe in which material and spiritual forms emanate from the same original substance. For Milton, in other words, the physical potential of all angels appears to be realized in the rebels. As I discussed in the Introduction, Milton's concept of the continuity between matter and spirit allows for movement in two directions along a sliding scale. Thus, angels can eat, digest, and convert to energy Adam and Eve's earthly fruits – "Tasting concoct, digest, assimilate, / And corporeal to incorporeal turn" (V.412–13) – but the angels themselves, "though spirits of purest light," can also physically degenerate and fall into materiality – "now gross by sinning grown" – as when the rebels take up arms against God (VI.660–61).

Interestingly, in *De Doctrina Christiana* Milton points to the essentially spiritual nature of fallen angels to illustrate the perfection of the original first matter: "in fact matter, like the form and nature of the angels, came from God in an incorruptible state, and even since the fall it is still incorruptible, so far as its essence is concerned" (*CPW* VI: 309). Yet angels, he goes on to argue, can impair their selves because their "matter or form has gone out from God" and become their own to act on through their free will – the same explanation that Raphael offers in *Paradise Lost* when he warns that all beings come from God but will only "up to him return, / If not depraved from good" (*CPW* VI: 309; V.470–71).[23] In other words, just as angels can choose to disobey God, so, as the result of that choice, the pure intelligential substance of angels always has the potential to deteriorate:

> Moreover spirit, being the more excellent substance, virtually, as they say, and eminently contains within itself what is clearly the inferior substance; in the same way as the spiritual and rational faculty contains the corporeal, that is, the sentient and vegetative faculty. (*CPW* VI: 309)

In this passage, Milton correlates the angels' possible physical degeneration with both their moral fall and a corresponding epistemological decline. He specifically allies the "more excellent substance" with the "spiritual and rational faculty," and associates the "inferior substance" with the "sentient and vegetative faculty." Raphael in *Paradise Lost* similarly asserts that the lower substance of humankind, like our lower form of apprehension, is

---

[23] For a similar reading of these lines, as I discuss in the introduction, see Phillip J. Donnelly, *Milton's Scriptural Reasoning: Narrative and Protestant Toleration* (Cambridge: Cambridge University Press, 2009), p. 93.

contained in the higher nature and experience of heavenly creatures. The epic's angels are "more refined, more spiritous, and pure" (V.475), but they can still converse and eat with Adam and Eve because celestial beings "contain / Within them every lower faculty / Of sense" (V.409–11).

This correspondence between levels of apprehension and degrees of materiality helps to explain why Milton would have wished to describe the fallen angels' physical appearance in *Paradise Lost*. Theologians after Aquinas traditionally had little to say about the shape of good angels because, according to a dualist philosophy, the celestial orders were purely spirit and the bodies that they might adopt were mere symbols.[24] But for Milton the repeated references to how the rebels now appear would underscore that fallen angels in *Paradise Lost* are moving downward on the epic's monistic ontological scale. With the fall of the angels, their shapes are declining to the material and are thus more capable of being apprehended visually.

Demon monsters

I do not mean to suggest, however, that the good angels in *Paradise Lost* are comparatively invisible. On the contrary, we first see Uriel, "a glorious angel" wearing "a golden tiar" (III.622, 625), and, as Satan approaches, Milton describes how Uriel's "locks behind / Illustrious on his shoulders fledge with wings / Lay waving round" (III.626–28). Later, Adam and Eve more fully view Raphael's "gorgeous wings" (V.250) as the angel alights on a cliff of Paradise and

>   to his proper shape returns
> A Seraph winged; his six wings he wore, to shade
> His lineaments divine; the pair that clad
> Each shoulder broad, came mantling o'er his breast
> With regal ornament; the middle pair
> Girt like a starry zone his waist, and round
> Skirted his loins and thighs with downy gold
> And colors dipped in Heav'n; the third his feet
> Shadowed from either heel with feathered mail
> Sky-tinctured grain.   (V.276–85)

Here Milton borrows from both the account of six-winged seraphim in Isaiah 6:2 and the rich artistic tradition that grew up around Christian angels, which was indebted in part to pagan depictions of the Roman

---

[24] Raymond, *Milton's Angels*, p. 289.

goddess Nike.[25] As Raymond has shown, such images of good angels, spiritual yet finite beings, became closely associated with the accommodated language of Scripture in the sixteenth and seventeenth centuries.[26] Both angels and the Bible's language helped to explain the relationship between the spiritual and material worlds and between God and humankind. We should not be surprised, then, that Milton in *Paradise Lost* would frequently turn to good angels both before and after the Fall to articulate the poem's religious doctrines and philosophical principles. Uriel, Gabriel, Raphael, Abdiel, and Michael – all of the named heavenly attendants play key roles in communicating and enacting the epic's theology.

Yet, given Milton's philosophy of matter and his related notion of graduated epistemologies, we might initially have expected the poem's opening books to provide even more detail about the rebels' horrid appearance. Milton, as we have seen, emphasizes the physical decline that Satan and the other fallen angels experience after their rebellion, and their new, degenerated forms would seem to warrant and, arguably, require more specific or a greater quantity of images than those afforded the good angels. Certainly Milton had a rich literary tradition from which to draw: medieval and Renaissance writers and artists regularly depicted evil demons as beasts and monsters. Following a Neoplatonic theory, these early modern authors assumed that the appearance of spiritual creatures expressed outwardly their inner purity. Edmund Spenser in *Fowre Hymnes* (1596), for example, assigns degrees of illumination to angels according to their place in the hierarchy proposed by Dionysus the Areopagite. Spenser writes that Cherubim with "golden wings . . . overdight" are "farre more faire" than Dominations; "eternall burning *Seraphins*, / Which from their faces dart out fierie light" appear "fairer then they both"; and "much more bright / Be th' Angels and Archangels, which attend / On Gods owne person."[27] Based on this illuminated hierarchy, we would at least expect fallen angels to look dark or dim, although Spenser himself does not describe the rebels' relative brightness.

Instead, if we turn to *Davideis* (1656), Abraham Cowley includes an early scene in which Lucifer's "gilded *Host* of *Sprights*" has degenerated in hell

[25] For the latter point, see Roland Mushat Frye, *Milton's Imagery and the Visual Arts* (Princeton: Princeton University Press, 1978), pp. 169–70.

[26] Raymond, *Milton's Angels*, p. 171.

[27] Edmund Spenser, *Fowre Hymnes*, in *The Yale Edition of the Shorter Poems of Edmund Spenser*, ed. William A. Oram et al. (New Haven and London: Yale University Press, 1989), pp. 682–752 (*An Hymne of Heavenly Love*, lines 92–98).

into Satan's "Troop of ghastly *Fiends*."²⁸ Here Cowley contrasts "gilded" and "ghastly," the latter term signifying not only "horrible, frightful, shocking" but also "death-like, pale, wan."²⁹ Even the diminution implied by the devil's name change – from *Lucifer*, meaning "light-bearer" or "morning star," to *Satan*, meaning "adversary" – suggests the loss of incandescence that comes with the rebels' fall from heaven, an idea that Milton also suggests as Raphael metaphorically invokes "Lucifer" to explain Satan's former glory: "So call him, brighter once amidst the host / Of angels, than that star the stars among" (VII.132–33). Ultimately, Cowley in *Davideis* indicates that the fallen angels have become monstrous, although, like Milton, he offers few other specific details about their appearance. Cowley singles out only Envy, "the direfull'st" of the "dire Throng," an allegorical Medusa-figure with "black Locks . . . / Attir'd with curling *Serpents*," who anticipates Milton's Sin but hardly seems a mimetic representation of the fallen angels.³⁰

Still, Cowley's limited but monstrous depiction of Satan and his followers fits within the tradition of more richly conceived demonic portrayals from the medieval and Renaissance periods. As John Steadman has shown, the convention of the devils' disfigurement had become a "recurrent theme" in early modern art and literature by the time Milton wrote *Paradise Lost*.³¹ The point I wish to stress is the grotesque detail that authors lavished on such diabolic accounts. Working from the lurid imagery in Revelation, writers and artists seem to have relished endowing the fallen angels with horrid features. Thus, Dante, in the *Inferno* (1472), memorably depicts Satan as a hideous giant with

> three faces on his head:
> In front there was a red one; joined to this,
> Each over the midpoint of a shoulder, he had
> Two others – all three joining at the crown.
> That on the right appeared to be a shade
> Of whitish yellow; the third had such a mien
> As those who come from where the Nile descends.³²

²⁸ Abraham Cowley, *Davideis*, in *The Complete Works in Verse and Prose of Abraham Cowley*, 2 vols., ed. Alexander B. Grosart (1881; New York: AMS, 1967), vol. II: pp. 43–125 (book I, lines 93, 133).
²⁹ *OED*, s. v. "ghastly," defs. 1.a and 2.
³⁰ Cowley, *Davideis*, book I, lines 153–54.
³¹ John M. Steadman, "Archangel to Devil: The Background of Satan's Metamorphosis," *Modern Language Quarterly* 21 (1960): 321–35 (pp. 333, 321). See also Merritt Y. Hughes, "Myself Am Hell," *Modern Philology* 54.2 (1956): 80–94 (especially pp. 91–94); and Stella Purce Revard, *The War in Heaven: "Paradise Lost" and the Tradition of Satan's Rebellion* (Ithaca and London: Cornell University Press, 1980), pp. 228–31.
³² Dante, *Inferno*, trans. Robert Pinsky (New York: Farrar, Straus, and Giroux, 1994), Canto XXXIV, lines 41–47 (p. 297).

The number three and the devil's specific colors sound symbolic, but the passage primarily highlights the sensational nature of Satan's appearance. Here, at the poem's affective climax, the devil's gruesome features are a "great marvel" (*gran maraviglia*) that the narrator experiences physically: "How chilled and faint I was" (*Com' io divenni allor gelato e fioco*).[33]

Erasmo di Valvasone in the Italian epic *L'Angeleida* (1590) echoes both Revelation and the *Inferno* as he similarly dramatizes Satan's hideous, fallen countenance:

> The seven caverns of his mouths exhaled
> A cruel stench, from slimy slaver reeking;
> In fourteen eyes a deadly anger flailed,
> Beneath his bristling eyebrows fiercely speaking;
> Across his livid cheeks stray flushes trailed
> And scornful shadows, all his visage streaking,
> Within whose midst dark Sorrow had her house;
> While locks of writhing snakes enwreathed his brows.[34]

As the reference to the snaky locks of "dark Sorrow" suggests, Valvasone's imagery is also susceptible to an allegorical reading. But again the emphasis falls on the spectacle of the devils' monstrous appearance – in particular, Satan's threatening mouths and eyes, and his characteristically truculent demeanor. The primary effect is visual and visceral, not symbolic, and the use of specific numbers once again seems an attempt to define and thus rein in the devil.

Joost van den Vondel in *Lucifer, Treurspel* (1654) also reserves some of his play's most sensational, specific imagery to describe the arch-fiend's terrible countenance. In contrast to Milton's Satan who, we saw in the previous chapter, sometimes changes metaphorically into the shapes of animals, Vondel presents Satan's bestiality as a literal disfigurement:

> So all his beauty, in that dread descent,
> Changed to deformity, accurst and vile:
> The heroic visage to a brutish snout,
> His teeth to fangs, able to gnaw through steel;
> His feet and hands into four sorts of claws;
> The skin of opal to an inky hide;
> Out of his bristled back burst dragon's wings;
> In short, the Archangel, reverenced but now

---

[33] Dante, *Inferno*, Canto XXXIV, lines 37, 22 (pp. 294–97).

[34] Erasmo di Valvasone, *L'Angeleida*, in *The Celestial Cycle: The Theme of "Paradise Lost" in World Literature with Translations of the Major Analogues*, by Watson Kirkconnell (New York: Gordian, 1967), pp. 80–87 (p. 82 [Canto II]). On the likelihood that Milton knew Valvasone's work, see Revard, *War in Heaven*, p. 153.

> By all the angelic host, was changed in aspect,
> And in most gruesome fashion, as we gazed,
> He mingled seven animals in one:
> A lion, arrogant; a greedy swine;
> A slothful ass; a horn'd rhinoceros;
> An ape, shameless alike and gross in front
> And hinder parts, and lewd and hot of nature,
> An envious snake; an avaricious wolf.
> His beauty is a beast now, to be cursed
> Ever by God, by spirits, and by men.[35]

The details of Vondel's description encourage his audience to envision how ugly the fallen angels have become as a consequence of their disobedience. While we might initially expect the already visual medium of drama to include few such descriptive passages, the ambitious scope of Vondel's play requires crucial events to occur off stage that the characters subsequently summarize. Uriel, for example, recounts the good angels' victory over their former companions, "changed in form / And limbs and stature! Lo, they roar'd and bark'd; / One yelp'd, another howl'd, What scowls we saw / On Angel-faces verging upon Hell / And hellish hideousness!"[36] If Satan and his followers before the war surpassed humankind in pristine light and beauty, they have sunk after their fall to the level of brute animals.

Milton in his early works also seems to have accepted the tradition that devils were hideously disfigured. The speaker of *In quintum Novembris*, for example, characterizes the "savage, monstrous" Typhoeus as a convention-ally horrible demon (*tabifico monstrosus*, line 37): his eyes glow, he breathes out fire and sulfur, and the "adamantine array of his teeth grinds with a noise like that of arms and of spear struck by spear" (*stridetque adamantinus ordo / Dentis, ut armorum fragor, ictaque cuspide cuspis*, lines 38–39). In "On the Morning of Christ's Nativity," Milton again borrows from Revelation: he includes among the disempowered pre-Christian gods, "Th' old Dragon under ground" who, "wroth to see his kingdom fail, / Swinges the scaly horror of his folded tail" (lines 168, 171–72). Even the "foul disfigurement" (line 74) of Comus' crew in *A Mask* recalls traditional images of Satan's monstrous followers. The countenances of the travelers who drink Comus' liquor are "changed / Into some brutish form of wolf, or bear, / Or ounce, or tiger, hog, or bearded goat" (lines 69–71).

In this context, we need to ask why Milton might have chosen not to describe the fallen angels as monsters in the opening books of *Paradise Lost*.

He repeatedly suggests, as we have seen, that Satan and his followers have declined physically with their rebellion, but he does not depict the devils' grotesque features in the same way that he portrays, say, the horror of Sin, "in many a scaly fold / Voluminous and vast," with a brood of hell-hounds bursting hourly from her bowels (II.651–52). Ultimately, in book X, Satan and the other fallen angels are transformed into "a crowd / Of ugly serpents" (X.538–39), and Milton lingers on their spectacularly monstrous metamorphosis: "They felt themselves now changing; down their arms, / Down fell both spear and shield, down they as fast, / And the dire hiss renewed, and the dire form" (X.541–43). Why would Milton have withheld this detailed account of the fallen angels' hideous appearance until the poem's final books?

One explanation for the delay stems from Satan's apparent heroism. If at the start Milton were to have more fully portrayed the fallen angels as ghastly fiends, he might have undermined Satan's appeal and any sympathy we feel for the devils' resolve and loyalty. As John Ruskin first observed, Milton "succeeds" in his depiction of Satan "only because he separately describes the movements of the mind, and therefore leaves himself at liberty to make the form heroic; but that form is never distinct enough to be painted."[37] Roland Frye has added that in the epic's first two books Milton not only omits specific physical details for Satan, but "focuses our attention instead upon the more generalized outward sign of an inner and spiritual disgrace."[38] Thus, as we saw in the preceding chapter, Milton describes Satan's spear and shield in great detail, but when the arch-fiend drags himself off the burning lake, his physical self remains indistinct, viewed analogously and often from afar.

Milton, of course, might have also thought that more specific images of the fallen angels' physical decline were unnecessary. Given the preponderance of diabolic monsters in other early modern works, perhaps he expected contemporary readers to infer the fallen angels' hideousness from his general references to the angels' changed appearance. Reticence might even augment the epic's affective impact, in the same way that modern horror films can better scare audiences with mostly unseen threats as opposed to fully revealed monsters. Writing about *Paradise Lost*, Edmund Burke famously praised how Milton sets "terrible things . . . in their strongest light by the force of a judicious obscurity," and Joseph Addison complimented Milton's depiction of hell in similar terms: "The

---

[37] John Ruskin, *The Stones of Venice*, in *The Works of John Ruskin*, 39 vols., ed. E. T. Cook and Alexander Wedderburn (London: George Allen; New York: Longmans, Green, 1903–12), XI: 174.
[38] Frye, *Milton's Imagery and the Visual Arts*, p. 73.

monstrous Animals produced in that infernal World are represented by a single Line, which gives us a more horrid Idea of them, than a much longer Description would have done."[39] Hinting at the fallen angels' changed appearance without fully disclosing how Satan's followers now look might help to make the poem's opening books immediately inductive and engage readers imaginatively with the poem's theology and narrative.

Yet, regardless of the assumptions that Milton's contemporary readers brought to *Paradise Lost*, the lack of detail about the physical change that the fallen angels have undergone with their fall enhances the drama of their later horrific metamorphosis. Whereas A. J. A. Waldock once objected that the sudden reversal when Satan returns to hell in book X better suited a "comic cartoon" than the grand style of epic, subsequent critics have shown that this delayed depiction of the rebels' punishment satisfies the poem's larger narrative.[40] Stella Revard, for example, has argued that the deferral of Satan's punishing metamorphosis "avoids the pitfalls of either making Satan merely a monster as he wars in Heaven or exciting a false pathos in the loss of angelic beauty with his loss of angelic place."[41] Postponing the description of the fallen angels' disfigurement also underscores the significance of Satan's successful temptation of Eve. Satan and his followers seem to be punished more for his corruption of humankind than for their earlier rebellion.

The delay of the devils' detailed disfigurement does not mean, however, that Milton in the opening books of *Paradise Lost* eschews visual imagery in portraying the fallen angels. As we saw at the start of this chapter, he depicts Satan and his followers with a series of striking yet coy images. The poem focuses, for example, on the rebels' "forest huge of spears" and raised "banners ... / With orient colors waving" (I.545–47), but says little about the physical appearance of the rebels themselves. Or, Milton highlights the image of the rebels' armament and flags tossed on the burning lake of hell (I.324–25), but he does not tell us what the rebels look like as they also roll in the fiery waves. Even when we momentarily glimpse Azazel, "a cherub tall" (I.534), as Satan's followers rouse themselves and

---

[39] Edmund Burke, *A Philosophical Enquiry into the Origin of the Our Ideas of the Sublime and the Beautiful*, ed. J. T. Boulton (London: Routledge and Kegan Paul; New York: Columbia University Press, 1958), p. 59 (part II, sec. iii); and Joseph Addison, *Criticism on Milton's "Paradise Lost,"* ed. Edward Arber (London, 1869), p. 64. On eighteenth-century responses to Milton's Satan, see Arthur E. Barker, "... And on his Crest Sat Horror: Eighteenth-Century Interpretations of Milton's Sublimity and His Satan," *University of Toronto Quarterly* 11 (1942): 421–36.

[40] A. J. A. Waldock, *"Paradise Lost" and Its Critics* (Cambridge: Cambridge University Press, 1966), p. 91.

[41] Revard, *The War in Heaven*, p. 272. Steadman also defended Satan's literal degeneration in book X as a "final, definitive verdict on his own merits and those of his enterprise. It unmasked his heroic pretense as vicious reality" ("Archangel to Devil," p. 334).

rally around their leader, the passage does not focus on the fallen angel but zooms in on his lustrous banner:

> Who forthwith from the glittering staff unfurled
> Th' imperial ensign, which full high advanced
> Shone like a meteor streaming to the wind
> With gems and golden luster rich emblazed,
> Seraphic arms and trophies.   (I.535–39)

This style of metonymic imagery, as we saw with Satan's "ponderous shield" in the preceding chapter (I.283), hints at the fallen angels' ontological degradation. As with Satan, his followers seem to be looking downward and fixing on material things instead of gazing heavenward to God and contemplating spiritual salvation.[42] John Martin's nineteenth-century illustrations of the fallen angels effectively capture this aspect of the poem's imagistic technique. While Martin in some of his engravings creates a largely Romantic portrait of a heroic Satan, other illustrations such as "The Fiery Gulf," "Satan Summons His Legions," and "The Fallen Angels in Pandemonium" more closely approximate Milton's angelic imagery by retreating to a landscape perspective (see figures 5.1 and 5.2). Martin, like Milton, accordingly draws attention to things he associates with the devils – pillars, rocks, and candelabra – but obscures the individual features of the devils themselves.

The opening books of *Paradise Lost* also displace some of Milton's imagistic intensity on to his similes' vehicles. These metaphors describing Satan and his followers include vivid details but the visual information they provide is always deflected, analogous instead of literal. Thus, in one of the poem's best-known similes, Milton compares Satan's followers floating on hell's fiery lake to leaves and seaweed:

> angel forms, who lay entranced
> Thick as autumnal leaves that strow the brooks
> In Vallombrosa where th' Etrurian shades
> High overarched embow'r; or scattered sedge
> Afloat, when with fierce winds Orion armed
> Hath vexed the Red Sea coast, whose waves o'rethrew
> Busiris and his Memphian chivalry,
> While with perfidious hatred they pursued
> The sojourners of Goshen, who beheld
> From the safe shore their floating carcasses

---

[42] As an extreme example of material preoccupation, Mammon represents "the least erected spirit that fell / From Heav'n, for ev'n in Heav'n his looks and thoughts / Were always downward bent, admiring more / The riches of Heav'n's pavement" (I.679–82).

Figure 5.1 John Martin, illustration for book I, line 192, in *The "Paradise Lost" of Milton with Illustrations, Designed and Engraved by John Martin* (London: Septimus Prowett, 1825–1827).

> And broken chariot wheels. So thick bestrown
> Abject and lost lay these, covering the flood,
> Under amazement of their hideous change.   (I.301–13)

The extended comparison begins with the rebels' "angel forms" and concludes with their "hideous change," but the intervening description refuses to reconcile the apparent contradiction.[43] Do the rebels still look like angels, or have they become hideous? The simile concentrates instead on the way the bad angels are floating, crowded and lifeless, and reveals almost nothing about their physical attributes. The vehicle's precise details – not just leaves, but autumnal leaves, and not just floating, but floating in the "brooks / In Vallombrosa" – have led critics to question whether Milton was recollecting a specific scene he witnessed during his youthful Italian

---

[43] Critics have long admired the simile's complexity. Stanley Fish, for example, has suggested, "The compression here is so complex that it defies analysis." See *Surprised by Sin: the Reader in "Paradise Lost,"* 2nd edn. (Cambridge: Harvard University Press, 1999), p. 36.

Figure 5.2 John Martin, illustration for book I, line 314, in *The "Paradise Lost" of Milton with Illustrations, Designed and Engraved by John Martin* (London: Septimus Prowett, 1825–1827).

sojourn.[44] More important, I think, is that he so forcefully conveys these images in *Paradise Lost* that they sound as if he were writing from memory – and yet the rebels' individual shapes or forms remain ambiguous. Just as Milton bookends the simile by describing the rebels as simultaneously hideous and angelic, so the simile's vehicles evoke both death and beauty, both doom and paradise. Even though we know that these lines depict abject demons, we cannot but admire the lyric description of colorful leaves lying on shaded Tuscan streams or the quiet image of seaweed floating along the Egyptian coast after the Red Sea has violently crested. The simile's suspension of contraries does not suggest Milton's uncertainty about the fallen angels or his refusal to pass judgment on their rebellion, as some critics have proposed. Instead, the equivocation captures the fallen angels' liminal status and ongoing transformation. In hell, they are both invisible and visualized because they remain essentially incorporeal spirits, but through their sin they are falling into the material. To have depicted the fallen angels more directly and fully at the start of *Paradise Lost* would have belied their hardening but not hardened spirituality.

The final simile in book I also fittingly dramatizes the fallen angels' unsettledness. Here, Milton describes Satan's followers entering Pandemonium:

> Behold a wonder! They but now who seemed
> In bigness to surpass Earth's giant sons
> Now less than smallest dwarfs, in narrow room
> Throng numberless, like that pygmean race
> Beyond the Indian mount, or faerie elves
> Whose midnight revels, by a forest side
> Or fountain some belated peasant sees,
> Or dreams he sees, while overhead the moon
> Sits arbitress, and nearer to the earth
> Wheels her pale course, they on their mirth and dance
> Intent, with jocund music charm his ear;
> At once with joy and fear his heart rebounds.
> Thus incorporeal spirits to smallest forms
> Reduced their shapes immense, and were at large,
> Though without number still admist the hall
> Of that infernal court.   (I.777–92)

---

[44] For differing views on the relevance of Milton's personal experience in Italy, see Charles A. Huttar, "Vallombrosa Revisited," in *Milton in Italy: Contexts, Images, Contradictions*, ed. Mario A. Di Cesare (Binghamton: Medieval and Renaissance Texts and Studies, 1991), pp. 95–111; and Edward Chaney, "The Visit to Vallombrosa: A Literary Tradition," in *Milton in Italy*, pp. 113–46.

The details in this passage draw on early modern assumptions of diabolic shape-shifting and contemporary accounts of magical creatures. Folktales regularly described demons who could change their shape and who, in many instances, seemed to change the shape of their human victims.[45] Milton, as we saw in the preceding chapter, returns to this convention as Satan disguises himself in various forms while wandering through chaos, alighting on earth, and approaching Adam and Eve. But in contrast to the arch-fiend's chicanery, the changes that the fallen angels experience in the final simile occur in rapid succession and are strictly metaphorical. The initial comparison to "Earth's giant sons" alludes to classical theogonies described by, among others, Aeschylus, Ovid, and Horace. But then, almost immediately, Milton belittles the fallen angels by comparing them to dwarfs, pygmies, and faerie elves.[46] The playfully punning "at large" near the end of the simile further highlights the devils' diminishment. If at the start of these lines the fallen angels literally might be giants, they now increase their size only figuratively.

Just as we saw in the preceding chapter that Satan's spear seems both as small as a wand and as big as a mast, the concluding simile in book I thus raises doubts about the rebels' dimensions in hell. This ambiguity diverges from Dante's, Valvasone's, and Vondel's sensational demonic portrayals, which, we have seen, repeatedly enumerate even the devils' individual features. Balachandra Rajan, for one, attempted to resolve the apparent inconsistency in Milton's simile by proposing that the fallen angels "are giants in their potentiality for destruction" and "equally pygmies in the presence of righteousness."[47] I would argue instead that the jarring series of comparisons conveys the angels' instability. As Neil Forsyth has observed, these lines "move us all around so fast that we don't know exactly where we are anymore."[48] In addition to the angels' changing size, the sudden shift in scene, figure, and tone – from the horrors of hell, to an Indian mountain, then to an enchanted wood – suggests once again the bad angels' shifting status.

---

[45] See Stuart Clark, *Thinking with Demons: The Idea of Witchcraft in Early Modern Europe* (Oxford: Clarendon, 1997), pp. 184–92; and Clark, "The Scientific Status of Demonology," in *Occult and Scientific Mentalities in the Renaissance*, ed. Brian Vickers (Cambridge: Cambridge University Press, 1986), pp. 351–74 (especially pp. 360–66).

[46] The first indication of the rebels' possible diminutive size occurs as Satan proudly gazes on his battalions "for never since created man, / Met such embodied force, as named with these / Could merit more than that small infantry / Warred on by cranes: though all the giant brood / Of Phlegra with th' heroic race were joined / That fought at Thebes and Ilium, on each side / Mixed with auxiliar gods" (I.573–79).

[47] *"Paradise Lost," Books I and II*, ed. B. Rajan (Bombay: Asia Publishing, 1964), p. 54.

[48] Forsyth, *The Satanic Epic*, p. 88.

Clearly, the occult references in the final simile fit Milton's subject. As both Minor Latham and Isabel E. Rathborne have shown, fairies during the medieval and Renaissance periods were often identified with, among other things, fallen angels and the gods of the lower world.[49] Commentators of *Paradise Lost* have also teased out various implications from the simile's multi-tiered vehicle. John Broadbent noted that Roman Catholics were sometimes identified with faeries, R. C. Jebb examined the Homeric precedent of comparing armies to pygmies, and Cedric Brown entertained a possible political allusion to a diminished post-Restoration citizenry.[50] Yet, such evocations and associations may ultimately provide more heat than light. By the end of the epic's first two books, we still don't know what the fallen angels look like. As the rebels enter Pandemonium, the vignette about a peasant who sleeps, perchance to dream, not only blurs "our moral certainties," as Forsyth observes, but it also supersedes any concrete image we have of the rebels in their newly built citadel.[51]

The successive comparisons – from giants, to dwarfs, to pygmies, and to faerie elves – instead illustrate that the fallen angels remain essentially spiritual creatures and can accordingly shrink themselves to enter Pandemonium: as Milton puts it, "incorporeal spirits to smallest forms / Reduced their shapes immense" (I.789–90). But how do the devils "far within" their fortress (I.792), crowded "In close recess" (I.795) and meeting "in narrow room" (I.779), then resume "their own dimensions like themselves" (I.793)? Are we to imagine that the bad angels are naturally immense and again become giant-sized inside Pandemonium, even if such an image defies the laws of physics? As with the inconsistent information that we receive about the number of fallen angels – they are "numberless" and "without number" (I.780, 791) but also "A thousand" (I.796) and "hundreds and ... thousands" (I.760) – the details of the rebels' dimensions seem contradictory. After all, Milton only *compares* the devils to giants – "who seemed / In bigness to surpass Earth's giant sons" (I.777–78) – and immediately before this allusion he seems to cut the rebels down to size by describing them as a swarm of bees, "both on the ground

---

[49] Minor White Latham, *The Elizabethan Fairies: The Fairies of Folklore and the Fairies of Shakespeare* (New York: Columbia University Press, 1930), pp. 41–44; and Isabel E. Rathborne, *The Meaning of Spenser's Fairyland* (New York: Russell and Russell, 1965), p. 160.

[50] J. B. Broadbent, *Some Graver Subject: An Essay on "Paradise Lost"* (New York: Barnes and Noble, 1961), p. 106; R. C. Jebb, *Homer: An Introduction to the "Iliad" and the "Odyssey,"* 2nd edn. (Glasgow: James Maclehose, 1887), pp. 16–17; and Cedric C. Brown, "Great Senates and Godly Education: Politics and Cultural Renewal in Some Pre- and Post-Revolutionary Texts of Milton," in *Milton and Republicanism*, ed. David Armitage, Armand Himy, and Quentin Skinner (Cambridge: Cambridge University Press, 1995), pp. 43–60 (p. 59).

[51] Forsyth, *The Satanic Epic*, p. 104.

and in the air, / Brushed with the hiss of rustling wings" (I.767–68). Perhaps, then, if the bad angels can fit into Pandemonium, they are not naturally gigantic. The tautology of the phrase "their own dimensions like themselves" again denies us specific information about the fallen angels' appearance. As we saw at the start of this chapter with the possible metaphor in the description of Satan's tears, "like themselves" could be yet another simile. Without telling us exactly how the angels now look, Milton suggests that they merely resemble – are "like" – their former selves.

Angels into idols

Only when forecasting future events does Milton in the opening books include clearer and more literal visual details to describe the fallen angels. The hints that he offers of the rebels' physical transformation anticipate this greater ontological decline when, among the "sons of Eve" (I.364), they will be worshipped as pagan deities in "monstrous shapes" and "brutish forms" (I.479, 481). Milton in this regard was following a patristic concept popular during the early modern period: a common explanation for pre-Christian religions was that the fallen angels came to earth and were treated as gods.

But *Paradise Lost* is unique in presenting this ultimate metamorphosis as the rebels' falling even further into materiality. In the epic's opening books, Milton compares the fallen angels to "hollow rocks" (II.285) and "dusky clouds" (II.488), two oxymora that capture the rebels' liminal status: fallen angels still have airy shapes but are in the process of becoming more material. Looking back to the future, the narrator then foresees that these spiritous forms will one day be reduced to objects:

> Nor had they yet among the sons of Eve
> Got them new names, till wand'ring o'er the Earth,
> Through God's high sufferance for the trial of man,
> By falsities and lies the greatest part
> Of mankind they corrupted to forsake
> God their Creator, and th' invisible
> Glory of him that made them, to transform
> Oft to the image of a brute, adorned
> With gay religions full of pomp and gold,
> And devils to adore for deities:
> Then were they known to men by various names,
> And various idols through the heathen world. (I.364–75)

These lines sum up all of the stages of the angels' declining ontology, from "invisible / Glory," to "the image of a brute," to "devils," and then to mere "idols." While Daniel Shore has argued that Milton uses the bad angels' future forms as an instructive warning, a way of keeping the idols "on public display as a record of their past infamy," I would emphasize the specific point that the bad angels are literally on display here.[52] The subsequent catalogue includes the type of visual details that Milton withholds when describing Satan and his followers in the present time. In contrast to the bad angels at the start of the epic who remain essentially fluid and can thus, as we have seen, "either sex assume" (I.424), the utter materiality of the rebels' final idolatrous forms underscores the senselessness of the "gay religions full of pomp and gold" that they will come to embody.

Here Milton may have been alluding to contemporary concerns about material images of the divine, as I discussed in the Introduction, which opponents to ceremonialism in the English church, especially under Archbishop Laud, had characterized as idolatry. Barbara Lewalski has observed that Milton came to conceive of idolatry much more broadly than other contemporary reformers – "Milton ... insisted that anything could be made into an idol," she writes[53] – but more relevant for the devilish catalogue in book I is the specific controversy over ceremonial objects and religious images that continued to rage throughout the poet's lifetime. The description of the "idols foul" in *Paradise Lost* (I.446) recalls some of the material monuments and images, "full of pomp and gold," that adorned English churches during the sixteenth and seventeenth centuries. Parliament had tried to have "all Monuments of Superstition and Idolatry" destroyed beginning in the 1530s, but they were restored in many parishes or were never eliminated in the first place.[54] Naturally, Milton and his readers, without specific historical knowledge of pagan religious rites beyond the Old Testament, would have visualized the ornate, material forms that the bad angels later adopt by drawing on this more immediate firsthand knowledge of English ceremonialism.

Yet Milton does not depend on such an association and does not leave the bad angels' later appearance entirely for readers to imagine. On the contrary,

---

[52] Daniel Shore, "Why Milton Is Not an Iconoclast," *PMLA* 127.1 (2012): 22–37 (p. 29).

[53] Barbara K. Lewalski, "Milton and Idolatry," *Studies in English Literature* 43.1 (2003): 213–32 (p. 214). See also Shore, "Why Milton Is Not an Iconoclast," p. 33.

[54] John Morrill, "William Dowsing and the Administration of Iconoclasm in the Puritan Revolution," in *The Journal of William Dowsing: Iconoclasm in East Anglia during the English Civil War*, ed. Trevor Cooper (Woodbridge: Boydell, 2001), pp. 1–28 (p. 12). Morrill is quoting here from the Parliamentary Ordinance of 28 August 1643. See also Margaret Aston, *England's Iconoclasts: Volume I: Laws against Images* (Oxford: Clarendon, 1988).

he at last portrays the forms of the bad angels, the clearest indication of the spirits' final hardening. Just as the future names of Satan's followers imply the emergence of specific identifies and a concomitant loss of flexibility, so these more literal images of the rebels' future selves express the completion of their physical decline. Milton thus anticipates the "grim idol" Moloch in blunt, visual terms, a "horrid king besmeared with blood / Of human sacrifice, and parents' tears" (I.396, 392–93). We similarly glimpse, without intervention of metaphor, Astoreth's "crescent horns" (I.439), Thammuz's purple "wound" (I.447), and Dagon's mismatched body, "upward man / And downward fish" (I.462–63). By comparison, the poem's opening books provide no such literal images of the individual angels as they awaken on the burning lake, build their citadel, hold an epic council, and pursue various pastimes while Satan travels to Earth. Only Beelzebub's careworn but commanding countenance may approach this level of direct visual detail in present time – "deep on his front engraven / Deliberation sat and public care; / And princely counsel in his face yet shone, / Majestic though in ruin" (II.302–05). Yet even this account remains abstract and once again mostly captures the paradox of the bad angels' current status – in hell, yet shining.

In contrast, Milton more fully foresees Dagon's ultimate physical denigration when the Ark of the Covenant will be captured by the Philistines (I Sam. 5):

> Next came one
> Who mourned in earnest, when the captive ark
> Maimed his brute image, head and hands lopped off
> In his own temple, on the grunsel edge,
> Where he fell flat, and shamed his worshippers.   (I.457–61)

This direct visual image correlates Moloch's sin with his material debasement. The angel's fall from heaven has dwindled into the mundane act of an idol tipping over. Whereas Milton in the opening books of *Paradise Lost* takes pains to portray the liminal status of Satan's followers – they are works in regress, we might say – here he relinquishes the equivocal effect of his metonymic imagery. Instead, the angel himself has become a thing – a threatening thing, as James Simpson emphasizes, but a thing nonetheless.[55] Milton is looking to the time when formerly incorporeal angels will fall further and become nothing more than broken statues of false gods.

---

[55] James Simpson, *Under the Hammer: Iconoclasm in the Anglo-American Tradition* (Oxford: Oxford University Press, 2010), pp. 102–05. Simpson notes, for example, that the idols' threat is conveyed by their "scandalous proximity" to the Temple in Milton's account (p. 104).

CHAPTER 6

Transported touch

A contract of eternal bond of love,
Confirmed by mutual joinder of your hands,
Attested by the holy close of lips,
Strengthened by interchangement of your rings.

— Shakespeare, *Twelfth Night*[1]

If Milton's depiction of hell's inhabitants depends on both metonymic and metaphorical imagery that adumbrates the bad angels' final ruin, we should once again not assume that visibility in *Paradise Lost* indicates fallenness. Satan and his followers are declining into the material, and the vivid imagery in the poem's opening books accordingly expresses the rebels' ongoing physical transformation, from pure spirit to idolatrous things. But, as we have seen with the comparable visual details that Milton provides about heaven and the good angels, the epic does not sustain a straightforward imagistic code whereby the presence or absence of visual imagery correlates with a creature's moral status. On the contrary, as I explore in the next two chapters, Milton's portrayal of Adam and Eve depends on extraordinary descriptions of their physical appearance, both before and after the Fall. Whereas the imagery at the start of *Paradise Lost* captures the bad angels' liminal status, the images associated with Adam and Eve, we will see, signify their own fragile union of spirit and matter and help to illustrate how the first couple's experience is simultaneously innocent and sensual.

Central to Milton's depiction of Adam and Eve is the image of hands joined in love. The final scene of the pair, walking "hand in hand" as they leave Paradise, probably remains the most memorable instance of hand-holding in the poem (XII.648), but even earlier Milton repeatedly draws attention to the couple's hands to describe their gardening and

[1] William Shakespeare, *Twelfth Night*, ed. Roger Warren and Stanley Wells (Oxford: Oxford University Press, 1998), V.I.152–55.

partnership.[2] In book IX, for example, the narrator observes that the couple's "work outgrew / The hands' dispatch of two" (lines 202–03) and attributes the "thick-woven arborets and flow'rs / Imbordered on each bank" to the "hand of Eve" (lines 437–38). Adam and Eve also use the metonymy of hands to describe their offspring.[3] Eve looks to the day when "more hands / Aid us" (lines 207–08) and when "more hands / Help to disburden nature of her birth" (lines 623–24); Adam also anticipates when "younger hands ere long / Assist us" (lines 246–47), and he counters Eve's proposal to work separately by insisting that "joint hands / Will keep from wilderness with ease" (lines 244–45).

But aside from such figurative descriptions of prelapsarian labor, the epic also includes striking visual images of the couple's hands to convey various stages of their love and marriage. If we continue to limit ourselves to book IX, Eve separates from Adam to garden alone as she "from her husband's hand her hand / Soft ... withdrew" (385–86); later, when she returns to Adam, "From his slack hand the garland wreathed for Eve / Down dropped" (892–93); and after Adam has also partaken of the forbidden fruit, "Her hand he seized, and to a shady bank, / ... / He led her nothing loath" (1037–39). All of these descriptions of tactile experience coalesce around book IX's central act, disobeying God's commandment "not to touch the interdicted tree" (VII.46): first Eve with "rash hand in evil hour / Forth reaching to the fruit" (IX.780–81) and then, after she returns to Adam, Eve giving to "him of that fair enticing fruit / With liberal hand" (IX.996–97).

To appreciate the significance of this visual motif for Adam and Eve's marriage, both before and after the Fall, we need to begin earlier and examine the initial instance of hands touching in love in *Paradise Lost*, when God creates Eve and leads her to her husband. As Adam relates the encounter to Raphael, "seeing me, she turned; / I followed her," until "with obsequious majesty" she "approved / My pleaded reason," and "To the nuptial bow'r / I led her blushing like the morn" (VIII.507–11). Eve, however, tells a slightly different story: she recalls that she turned away, that Adam "following cried'st aloud, 'Return fair Eve'" – but she adds that his "gentle hand / Seized mine" before finally "I yielded" (IV.481, 488–89).

---

[2] The couple's hand-holding has been much noted. See, for example, Mario A. Di Cesare, "Advent'rous Song: The Texture of Milton's Epic," in *Language and Style in Milton: A Symposium in Honor of the Tercentenary of "Paradise Lost,"* ed. Ronald David Emma and John T. Shawcross (New York: Frederick Ungar, 1967), pp. 1–29 (especially pp. 20–21).

[3] Also in book IX, Adam refers to God's "creating hand" (344) and warns Eve that Satan is "somewhere nigh at hand" (256).

Critics have long noted differences between the spouses' two narratives, especially the way Adam rationalizes Eve's motive for leaving. He says she departs because of her "innocence and virgin modesty" (VIII.501); she says she found him "Less winning soft, less amiably mild" (IV.479). While some commentators have found evidence in these episodes of the couple's hierarchical relationship – Dennis Burden, for example, contrasted Adam's "reason and authority" with Eve's "capacity for error"[4] – later critics tend to see the two versions as having equal narrative authority and thus interpret the inclusion of overlapping accounts as indicative of Adam and Eve's mutuality. Diane McColley, for example, arguing against claims for Eve's vanity and Adam's superior intelligence, first suggested that Adam's explanation for Eve's departure is a "lover's idealization" of a "moment of weakness," whereas Eve describes her reason for leaving with "self-mocking" and "a note of loving banter."[5] John Leonard similarly observed that the different stories told by Adam and Eve reflect their separate points of view: Adam emphasizes his authority by recalling that he named Eve "Woman," while Eve makes a claim for her own autonomy, preferring to remember her individual name.[6]

In this chapter, instead of discussing why Eve initially turns away from Adam, I am interested in the conflicting reports of when Adam and Eve first touch in Paradise and Eve's specific assertion that Adam grabs her – as she puts it, his "gentle hand / Seized mine" (IV.488–89). Starting with other early modern depictions of hand-holding, I wish to show how Eve's version of events is crucial for understanding Milton's idea of prelapsarian desire. The image of Adam's seizing Eve's hand, emphasized through a hard enjambment and then omitted from Adam's own narrative, not only highlights the two partners' subjectivity but also, initiating the epic's motif of hand imagery, calls attention to the importance of tactile experience for their monistic love.

Hands joined in love

Even a brief survey of other early modern literary works suggests the erotic and spiritual implications of Adam and Eve's hand-holding. A kiss may still

---

[4] Dennis H. Burden, *The Logical Epic: A Study of the Argument of "Paradise Lost"* (Cambridge: Harvard University Press, 1967), p. 85.

[5] Diane Kelsey McColley, *Milton's Eve* (Urbana: University of Illinois Press, 1983), pp. 81, 87. Similarly, Catherine Belsey, *John Milton: Language, Gender, Power* (Oxford: Basil Blackwell, 1998), describes Eve's version of events as "a piece of innocent sexual teasing which places her as simultaneously knowing and naïve" (p. 61).

[6] John Leonard, *Naming in Paradise: Milton and the Language of Adam and Eve* (Oxford: Oxford University Press, 1990), pp. 41–42.

be a kiss, but taking a man or woman by the hand had greater significance in early modern England than it does today. Thus, when Romeo and Juliet meet, they begin their romance by famously bantering about the touching of their hands in both erotic and religious terms: "palm to palm is holy palmers' kiss."[7] I do not mean to imply, however, a linear narrative whereby courting rituals were innocent during the seventeenth century and have become increasingly promiscuous. If John Lennon and Paul McCartney inspired millions of teenagers in 1964 to sing the modest declaration, "I Want to Hold Your Hand," we should also remember that Thomas Carew more than three hundred years earlier in "A Rapture" imagined Celia's "bold hand" grabbing the poet by the "rudder" so that she can "steer, and guide / [His] bark into love's channel, where it shall / Dance, as the bounding waves do rise or fall."[8]

Milton's description of Adam and Eve's tactile experience in book IV of *Paradise Lost* falls somewhere between these two extremes of sensuality and innocence. Most directly, it invites comparison with two passages from another of Shakespeare's works, *Venus and Adonis*.[9] Near the start of that poem, a "trembling" Venus tries to seduce Adonis and "seizeth on" his "sweating palm" (lines 25, 27). Then, when her direct approach fails, she tries a softer touch: "Full gently now she takes him by the hand, / A lily prison'd in a gaol of snow" (lines 361–62).[10] While the use of "seizeth" and "gently" clearly allies these two passages with Eve's account of Adam's handiwork, commentators have previously overlooked these conjunctions, perhaps because Venus' attempted seduction seems so far removed from Adam and Eve's Edenic experience. In particular, the metaphor of Adonis' imprisonment and the image of a snow-covered lily suggest the limitation and destructiveness of Venus' lust.

Yet the value of comparing Shakespeare's and Milton's works lies in their difference as much as their similarity. In contrast to Venus' passionately "enrag'd" roughness (line 29) – she then "pluck[s]" Adonis from his

---

[7] Shakespeare, *Romeo and Juliet*, ed. Dympna Callaghan (Boston: St. Martin's, 2003), I.5.97.

[8] Thomas Carew, "A Rapture," in *Ben Jonson and the Cavalier Poets*, ed. Hugh Maclean (New York: Norton, 1974), pp. 166–70 (lines 87–90).

[9] Maggie Kilgour, *Milton and the Metamorphosis of Ovid* (Oxford: Oxford University Press, 2012), discusses Shakespeare's poem more generally as a possible model for Milton's Ovidianism (pp. 64–70).

[10] Shakespeare, *Venus and Adonis*, in *The Poems*, ed. F. T. Prince (London: Methuen, 1985), pp. 3–62. All references to the poem are taken from this edition and cited parenthetically by line number. Among Shakespeare's other descriptions of hands seizing hands, see, for example, *Romeo and Juliet*, "They may seize / On the white wonder of dear Juliet's hand" (III.3.35–36); or *King John*, ed. Claire McEachern (London: Penguin, 2000), "shall these hands, so lately purged of blood, / So newly join'd in love, so strong in both, / Unyoke this seizure and this kind regreet?" (III.1.239–41).

horse," pushes him to the ground, and begins to "stroke his cheek" (lines 30, 45) – Eve describes Adam's hand as both "seizing" *and* "gentle." In this context, "gentle" not only indicates that Adam's skin was smooth but also synecdochically renders him courteous and tender.[11] And, in contrast to Adonis, who repeatedly rejects Venus' overtures, blushing with "shame" and "dull disdain" (lines 36, 33), Eve immediately "yield[s]" to Adam's touch, blushing instead, according to Adam, with "virgin modesty" (VIII.501). The uniqueness of Milton's depiction derives from the simultaneity of Adam's "gentleness" and "seizure": his "gentle hand" is not, as with Venus, a new tactic, but instead helps to convey his ardor.

If we linger on Shakespeare's poem for a moment, Venus again expresses her feelings for Adonis in terms of hand-holding: "My smooth moist hand, were it with thy hand felt, / Would in thy palm dissolve, or seem to melt" (lines 143–44). Here Shakespeare seems to have had in mind Ovid's story of Pygmalion. As the Roman sculptor continues to caress his statue, "beneath his touch the flesh / Grew soft, its ivory hardness vanishing, / And yielded to his hands."[12] When Adam persuades Eve to stay, Milton may have also been thinking of this story from *Metamorphoses*. Not only do Adam's own words cast him as a Pygmalion figure – "Whom thou fli'st, of him thou art," Adam calls to Eve, "to give thee being I lent / . . . to thee . . . / Substantial life" (IV.482, 483–85) – but also, in another echo of the Pygmalion story, it is Adam's "gentle hand" that melts Eve's resolve. Like the statue that softens with Pygmalion's touch, Eve "yield[s]" to Adam's hand and is transformed: "from that time" she sees "How beauty is excelled by manly grace / And wisdom" (IV.489–91). These final lines, expressing Eve's idealized perception of Adam, also correct the latent idolatry of Ovid's story, so that a pagan myth, in Milton's hands, is reshaped according to Christian belief. In *Paradise Lost*, the emphasis shifts from the power of art that brings things to life, to the beauty and judgment that comes with holy matrimony.

Other early modern depictions of tactile experiences similarly suggest the transformative power of hand-holding. Most well-known may be John Donne's "The Ecstasy," in which the lovers' spiritual intimacy first finds expression through their sweaty palms: "Sat we two, one another's best; / Our hands were firmly cemented / With a fast balm, which thence did spring."[13] The specific choice of "fast" punningly suggests the lovers'

---

[11] *OED*, s. v. "gentle," defs. A.1.a, 3.a, 5, 8.
[12] Ovid, *Metamorphoses*, trans. A. D. Melville (Oxford: Oxford University Press, 1987), X.282–84.
[13] John Donne, "The Ecstasy," in *John Donne: The Complete English Poems*, ed. A. J. Smith (London: Penguin, 1996), pp. 53–56 (lines 4–6). All subsequent references to the poem are taken from this edition and cited parenthetically by line number.

urgency and resolve, while "balm" indicates the pair's arousal and, as a Paracelsian term for keeping the body from decay, hints at the potency of their undying love.[14] When Donne writes, "So to' intergraft our hands, as yet / Was all our means to make us one" (lines 9–10), the lovers' handclasp anticipates their sexual union and, as is characteristic of Donne, serves as a necessary means of achieving a spiritual bond: he writes, "So must pure lovers' souls descend / T' affections, and to faculties, / Which sense may reach and apprehend, / Else a great prince in prison lies" (lines 65–68). Whereas Shakespeare's Venus attempts physically to entrap Adonis, this final simile from "The Ecstasy" suggests that the lovers' interlocked hands paradoxically release their corporally imprisoned souls.

George Herbert also claims that joining two hands can effect a spiritual transformation, but in his poem "Clasping of Hands" he conflates the idea of lovers holding hands with the image of hands folded in prayer. "[T]hou art mine, and I am thine," the speaker begins, and, when read in conjunction with the title, the successive interplay of "thine" and "mine" evokes the rhetoric of a courtly lover:

> If mine I am: and thine much more,
> Than I or ought, or can be mine.
> Yet to be thine, doth me restore;
> So that again I now am mine,
> And with advantage mine the more,
> Since this being mine, brings with it thine,
> And thou with me dost thee restore.
>   If I without thee would be mine,
>   I neither should be mine nor thine.[15]

Herbert, like Donne, however, envisions the joining of hands as anticipating something greater – in this case, the speaker's heavenly union with his beloved savior. Addressing his "Lord" instead of a mistress, the poet concludes, "O be mine still! still make me thine! / Or rather make no Thine and Mine!" (lines 19–20). Using language that could apply to either a romantic or a religious transformation, Herbert reveals the divine nature of marriage, while emphasizing his loving relationship with God. By the end of the poem, the clasping of hands has become a symbol of rapturous

---

[14] Donne in a letter to Henry Goodyer alludes to the "balm" of Paracelsian medicine when he refers to "our naturall inborne preservative," which prevents the body from decaying. See Donne, "To Sir H. G.," in *Poems, By J. D.* (London, 1633), Zz2v–Zz3v (Zz3r).

[15] George Herbert, "Clasping of Hands," in *George Herbert*, ed. Louis L. Martz (Oxford: Oxford University Press, 1994), p. 138 (lines 1–10). On Herbert's appropriation of courtly rhetoric in a religious context, see Michael C. Schoenfeldt, *Prayer and Power: George Herbert and Renaissance Courtship* (Chicago: University of Chicago Press, 1991).

dissolution as the speaker urgently strives for a complete identification with his beloved God.

George Wither, to take one final example, also includes an image of two clasped hands in his *Collection of Emblemes, Ancient and Moderne* (see figure 6.1). Wither was working within a rich emblematic tradition: beginning with Andrea Alciato's early sixteenth-century publications, emblem books commonly contain images of clasped hands to express peace and fidelity.[16] In the case of Wither's emblem, two disembodied hands emerge from opposing clouds and are coded by their cuffs as male and female. The hands clasp each other just beneath the image of a death's head and above an illustration of a flaming heart sitting on an altar. If the enflamed heart symbolizes the intensity and possible destructiveness of earthly passion, the emblem's motto describes a less volatile, spiritual love: "Death, *is unable to divide / Their Hearts, whose Hands* True-love *hath tyde.*"[17] In the accompanying verse, Wither develops this causal relationship between hand-holding and a permanent romantic attachment. The neat fit of hand in hand not only signifies but also once again enables a spiritual binding. As Wither puts it, "both *Hand* and *Heart*" are "firmely, ev'ry way ... ty'd" (lines 9, 14).

Vows, rings, and matrimony

All of these poets' claims for the spiritual significance of hand-holding no doubt reflect and would have reinforced the use of hands in the early modern marriage ceremony. Traditionally, clasped hands were a sign of amity: an extended, open palm could hold no weapon. Thus, when Adam first seizes Eve's hand, it signifies in part a peaceful, albeit enthusiastic greeting. But, as the altar in Wither's emblem indicates, a handclasp during the Renaissance also specifically symbolized marital accord. Beginning in 1549, *The Book of Common Prayer* describes how the bride and groom would three times take each other by the hand while reciting their vows. First, the minister "shal cause the man to take the woman by the right hande, and so either to geve theyr troth to other."[18] After the man pronounces, "I. N. take thee .N. to my wedded wife, to have and to hold

---

[16] Roy Strong, *Artists of the Tudor Court: The Portrait Miniature Rediscovered, 1520–1620* (London: Victoria and Albert Museum, 1983), p. 97.

[17] George Wither, *A Collection of Emblemes, Ancient and Moderne* (London, 1635), P3r.

[18] F. E. Brightman, *The English Rite Being a Synopsis of the Sources and Revisions of the Book of Common Prayer*, 2 vols. (London: Revingtons, 1915), II: 804–06. All subsequent references to the text are taken from this edition.

Death, *is unable to divide*
Their Hearts, whose Hands True-love *hath tyde.*

99

ILLVSTR. XXXVII.   *Book.* 2

Pon an *Altar*, in this *Emblem*, stands
A *Burning-heart* ; and, therewithall, you see
Beneath *Deaths-head*, a paire of *Loving-hands*,
Which, close, and fast-united, seeme to be.
These moderne *Hieroglyphickes* (vulgarly
Thus bundled up together) may afford
Good-meanings, with as much *Propriety*,
As best, with common *Iudgements*, will accord.
  It may imply, that, when both *Hand* and *Heart*,
By sympathizing dearenesse are invited,
To meet each others nat'rall *Counterpart*,
And, are by sacred *Ordinance* united :
They then have entred that strict *Obligation*,
By which they, firmely, ev'ry way are ty'd ;
And, without meanes (or thought of separation)
Should in that *Vnion*, till their *Deaths*, abide ;
  This, therefore, minde thou, whatsoere thou be
(Whose *Marriage-ring*, this *Covenant*, hath sealed)
For, though, thy Faith's infringement, none can see,
Thy secret fault, shall one day, be revealed.
And, thou that art at liberty, take heed,
Lest thou (as over great a number doe)
Of thine owne person, make a *Privy-deed*,
And, afterwards, deny thy doing so.
For, though there be, nor *Church*, nor *Chappell*, nigh thee
(Nor outward witnesses of what is done)
A *Power-invisible* doth alwayes eye thee ;
And, thy pretended *Love*, so lookes upon,
  That, if thou be not, till thy *dying*, true ;
  Thy *Falshood*, till thy *dying*, thou shalt rue.

False

Figure 6.1 George Wither, *A Collection of Emblemes, Ancient and Moderne*
(London, 1635), P3r.

from thys daye forwarde, for better, for wurse," the couple would "looce theyr handes," and the woman, "taking agayne the man by the right hande," would similarly state, "I. N. take thee .N. to my wedded husbande, to have and to holde from this day forwarde." The couple would "agyne looce theyr handes," and, after the man put a ring on the woman's left hand, the priest would join the couple's right hands for a final time so as to "pronounce that they be man and wyfe together." Not simply a speech act, marriage was performed by these symbolic gestures. Joining hands demonstrated that the groom and bride were freely choosing each other; the final handclasp, as done by the priest, symbolized that the church sanctioned the couple's union.

When in 1653 the new civil forms of marriage eliminated the giving of the ring and the receiving of communion, holding hands remained a central part of the marital service, as stipulated in the Directory of Public Worship.[19] Surviving marriage certificates from the second half of the seventeenth century accordingly emphasize the handclasp as a means of unifying the bride and groom. As one typical certificate reads, "the Said Phillip and Anne this present day came before me, and taking each other by the hand did plainly and distinctly pronounce the words in the said Acte."[20] Depositions from matrimonial enforcement suits also regularly cite hand-holding as a means of confirming a marriage. In both church weddings and marriages by contract outside the church, hand-holding served either as the principal evidence of consent or, more often, as a significant gesture to confirm the spoken vows. The detailed testimony that witnesses provided in enforcement suits – explaining, for example, whether the man first gave his hand, whether the woman offered her own hand, whether the bride's hand was taken before or after her vow, whether the couple continued to hold hands after their vows, and so on – indicates the importance attached to handclasps as opposed to, say, kissing or exchanging love tokens, neither of which is similarly emphasized in the depositions.[21] Nor was hand-holding reserved for marriage. Even earlier in the courting process, spouses-to-be might participate in a formal betrothal ceremony, an oral promise to marry sometimes called a "handfast"

---

[19] The 1653 act remained in force, with a modification in 1656, during the seven years preceding the fall of the Commonwealth. And, as a few recently wedded colleagues remind me, hand-holding still today plays a significant role in the Protestant marriage service.

[20] George Elliott Howard, *A History of Matrimonial Institutions*, 3 vols. (Chicago: University of Chicago Press, 1904), I: 431.

[21] Loreen L. Giese, *Courtship, Marriage Customs, and Shakespeare's Comedies* (New York: Palgrave Macmillan, 2006), pp. 128–30.

presumably because of the importance of hand-holding in publicly declaring an engagement.[22]

We can also measure the cultural currency of hands joined in love by the frequent use of handclasps in the design of betrothal and espousal rings. Often called *fede* rings – from the phrase *mani in fede* (hands clasped in faith) – these love-rings remained popular in England and on the Continent throughout the early modern period.[23] When, for example, James VI married Anne of Denmark in 1589, he reportedly presented her with "ane great ring of gold enameled sett with five diamondis with hand in hand in the middis callit the espousall ring of Denmark."[24] The tradition of wearing such love-rings on the fourth finger of the left hand arose because of an additional, allegedly physiological connection between hands and heart. Early modern poets could posit an emotional bond in the joining of lovers' hands in part because, as Henry Swinburne explains in 1686, it was the "received opinion of the learned . . . in Ripping up and atomizing men's Bodies, [that] there is a vein of Blood which passeth from that fourth finger unto the Heart, called Vena Amoris, Love's Vein."[25]

And while Genesis provides no specific description of Adam and Eve's hand-holding, John Speed's "Genealogies of the Holy Spirit," incorporated in 1611 at the start of the King James Bible, offers another possible precedent for Milton's imagery. In this series of engravings that trace Christ's lineage, the rundles often comprise, as the preface puts it, the "sculpture of an hand in hand."[26] Thus, at the start, Adam and Eve's names are joined by an image of two hands, symbolizing both their marriage and the union from which all future generations derive (see figure 6.2).

[22] Lawrence Stone, *The Family, Sex and Marriage in England 1500–1800* (New York: Harper and Row, 1977), p. 31.

[23] We do not know when exactly the plainer style wedding ring of a single hoop was introduced, perhaps during the Commonwealth period as another manifestation of objections to the more ornate style that characterized Laud's church. But, at least as late as the sixteenth century, wedding rings were set with gems. See O. M. Dalton, *Franks Bequest: Catalogue of the Finger Rings*. (London: British Museum, 1912), p. xlviii.

[24] Dale B. J. Randall, "The Rank and Earthy Background of Certain Physical Symbols in *The Duchess of Malfi*," *Renaissance Quarterly* 18 (1987): 171–203 (pp. 175–77); and Thomas Thomson *A Collection of Inventories and Other Records of the Royal Wardrobe and Jewelhouse* (Edinburgh: General Register House, 1815), p. 329.

[25] Dalton, *Franks Bequest*, pp. xlviii–ix. Dalton also notes that the belief is mentioned by both Aulus Gellius and Macrobius (xlviii). John Whitgift, in his *Answer to the Admonition* (1572), also refers to this vein in explaining the wedding ring's significance: "The putting of the ring upon the fourth finger of the woman's left hand, to which, as it is said there cometh a sinew or string from the heart, doth signify that the heart of the wife ought to be united to her husband" (qtd. in Howard, *A History of Matrimonial Institutions*, I: 411).

[26] John Speed's "Genealogies of the Holy Spirit," in *The Holy Bible* (London, 1611), A1v.

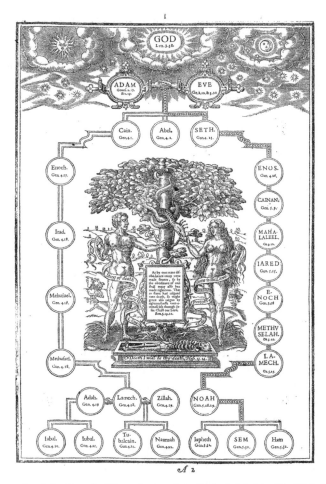

Figure 6.2 John Speed's "Genealogies of the Holy Spirit," in *The Holy Bible* (London, 1611), A1v.

It is within this context, I would suggest, that we should read Dalila's final plea to Samson in *Samson Agonistes*: "Let me approach at least, and touch thy hand" (line 951). Dalila does not just attempt to awaken Samson's physical desire, as commentators often assert; she also wants to remind him of their marriage.[27] The brutality of Samson's response – "Not for thy life, lest fierce remembrance wake / My sudden rage to tear thee joint by joint" (lines 952–53) – also suggests the implied intimacy of Dalila's desire to join hands. Threatening to dismember her, Samson offers the violent opposite of her requested contact, undoing her proffered symbol of love and destroying permanently the chance for her future bond with anyone.

This type of tactile experience must have been especially meaningful for a blind poet such as Milton who came to depend on his sense of touch in his later years. But even earlier, as Theodore Banks has argued, Milton's writings emphasized tactile perception, a feature that Banks tentatively traces to Milton's oratorical training and the importance assigned to gestures.[28] In *A Mask Presented at Ludlow Castle*, for example, Milton attributes miraculous potency to hand contact. Sabrina need only "touch with chaste palms moist and cold" the Lady's "marble venomed seat" to release her from the "gums of glutinous heat" (lines 916–18), while in *Epitaphium Damonis*, Milton laments the loss of his dear friend Charles Diodati and wishes he could "have been permitted to touch his hand at the end," a quietly personal means of bidding fair peace to his boyhood companion (lines 121, 123).

In *Paradise Lost*, by comparison, Eve's description of Adam's seizing her hand represents the first in a series of handclasps that indicates the couple's intimacy. In fact, we first spy Adam and Eve, "hand in hand ... the loveliest pair / That ever since in love's embraces met" (IV.321–22). This image suggests a temporal progression, from hand-holding, to "love's embraces," to (in the next lines) the couple's offspring: "Adam the goodliest man of men since borne / His sons, the fairest of her daughters Eve" (IV.323–24). Here the use of chiasmus enacts the couple's hand-holding, while, in comparing Adam and Eve with their sons and daughters, Milton also associates their clasped hands with the joining of their other bodily parts. Whereas Edward Le Comte has referred to Adam and Eve's handholding as the behavior of "pre-Freudian children," the gesture seems much more adult.[29] Through the joining of hands, Adam and Eve are,

[27] E. M. W. Tillyard, for example, suggests that Dalila wants "to arouse physical passion"; Douglas Bush calls it "a direct appeal to Samson's senses"; and Marcia K. Landy similarly thinks Dalila "is subtly seeking ... to revive his physical memories of her. She is hoping to lure him by sexual means." See Tillyard, *Milton*, 2nd edn. (New York: Barnes and Noble, 1967), p. 290; Bush, "John Milton," in *Major British Writers*, rev. edn., 2 vols., ed. G. B. Harrison (New York: Harcourt, Brace, 1959), I: 513; and Landy, "Character Portrayal in *Samson Agonistes*," *Texas Studies in Language and Literature* 7 (1965): 239–53 (p. 245).

[28] Theodore Howard Banks, *Milton's Imagery* (New York: Columbia University Press, 1950), p. 43.

[29] Edward Le Comte, *Milton and Sex* (New York: Columbia University Press, 1978), p. 89.

literally and figuratively, "linked in happy nuptial league" (IV.339). The couple thus approaches their bower, the site of their prelapsarian love-making, "talking hand in hand alone" (IV.689), and later we also read, "into their inmost bow'r / Handed they went" (IV.738–39). In *Paradise Lost*, the handclasp, embodying Milton's monistic concept of creation, at once joins Adam and Eve both physically and spiritually.

If we return to Eve's account of her creation in book IV, we should not be surprised, then, that Adam's action, more than his words, convinces her to stay. As she recalls, the moment "thy gentle hand / Seized mine, I yielded" (IV.488–89). The suddenness of Adam's gesture matches Eve's abrupt change of heart, while the half-rhyme of "seized" and "yield" implies both their difference and compatibility. And, as in Donne's "The Ecstasy," Adam and Eve's hands in this first encounter prefigure their amorous play. Immediately after Eve describes how their hands met, their bodies reiterate this gesture, but now Eve, not Adam, initiates the contact. She "half embracing leaned / On our first father, half her swelling breast / Naked met his" (IV.494–96).

Evoking the Renaissance marriage ceremony, the image of Adam's seizing Eve's hand also suggests that the couple freely takes each other as husband and wife. Here Milton may have been in part responding to Luther, who had argued, on the contrary, that "Adam does not snatch Eve of his own will after she has been created, but he waits for God to bring her to him."[30] While Milton, in keeping with Genesis 2:22, has both Eve and Adam recollect that Eve was "invisibly . . . led" to Adam by "her Heav'nly Maker" (IV.476, VIII.485), Milton also emphasizes the couple's free will by staging a second part to their initial meeting. After Eve decides to turn away, Adam freely chooses her, and Eve freely acquiesces.[31]

Seizures and free will

Yet, that Adam's hand specifically "seized" Eve may remind us of Venus' lusty grabbing in *Venus and Adonis* and threaten to undo the couple's Edenic reciprocity. Certainly Raphael will later admonish Adam about the danger of over-emphasizing physical contact. When Adam tells the angel about the "passion" and "Commotion strange" of his and Eve's

[30] Martin Luther, *Lectures on Genesis, Chapters 1–5*, in *Luther's Works*, trans. Jaroslav Pelikan, vol. 1. (St. Louis: Concordia, 1958), p. 134.
[31] Cheryl H. Fresch discusses the exegesis surrounding Genesis 2:22 and Milton's depiction of marriage as divinely sanctioned. See Fresch, "'And Brought Her Unto the Man': The Wedding in *Paradise Lost*," *Milton Studies* 16 (1982): 21–33.

"Transported touch" (VIII.530–31), Raphael urges Adam not to confuse these feelings for love:

> if the sense of touch whereby mankind
> Is propagated seem such dear delight
> Beyond all other, think the same vouchsafed
> To cattle and each beast; which would not be
> To them made common and divulged, if aught
> Therein enjoyed were worthy to subdue
> The soul of man, or passion in him move.
> What higher in her society thou find'st
> Attractive, human, rational, love still;
> In loving thou dost well, in passion not,
> Wherein true love consists not; love refines
> The thoughts, and heart enlarges, hath his seat
> In reason, and is judicious, is the scale
> By which to Heav'nly love thou may'st ascend,
> Not sunk in carnal pleasure, for which cause
> Among the beasts no mate for thee was found.   (VIII.579–94)

Raphael's warning, though, relates less to the innocent (albeit sensual) pleasure of joining hands in love and more clearly pertains to the over-valuing of sexual intimacy – "carnal pleasure," as the angel puts it, and "the sense of touch whereby mankind / Is propagated." Raphael does not discourage all tactile joys, but cautions Adam not to put "such dear delight / Beyond all other." The ideal that *Paradise Lost* seems to imply could be described as a monistic concept of love, one that combines both "heart" and "thoughts," both body and mind. Adam himself understands this balance, as he describes his union with Eve as "one flesh, one heart, one soul" (VIII.499), a dramatic expansion of the simple reference in Genesis to "one flesh" (2:24) and an apparent attempt to stress the simultaneously physical and spiritual nature of the couple's companionate marriage.

Milton pursues a similar ideal in a postlapsarian context in *The Doctrine and Discipline of Divorce*. Even as he defines marriage as "the apt and cheerfull conversation of man with woman" and thus downplays the possible significance of sexual contact (*CPW* II: 235), he acknowledges that the "benevolent and intimate communion of body" is an important part of matrimony (*CPW* II: 263). Only when a couple lacks spiritual and intellectual compatibility – when "their thoughts and spirits flie asunder as farre as heaven from hell" – does physical intimacy become hateful (*CPW* II: 263). *The Doctrine and Discipline of Divorce* accordingly describes a bad marriage with imagery that parodies the physical and spiritual connection that a handclasp embodies. Milton writes, for example, that a couple lacking a "correspondence ... of the minde" must forever "grind in the mill of an undelighted and servil copulation" and will be "two carkasses chain'd unnaturally together ..., a living soule bound to a dead corps" (*CPW* II: 326, 258).

It is Eve's use of "seized" that initially raises the possibility that Eve and Adam might have a bad marriage. Her diction ominously seems to anticipate Adam's use of "Transported" and suggests that at their first meeting she felt both enraptured and overpowered.[32] Richard Corum, for example, has argued that Adam in the moment of seizing Eve's hand "translates" her from an "independent, curious, imaginative person into the background, and depersonalizing states (in both senses) of 'wedded' wife, androgyne, and subject."[33] Adam's speech as Eve flees also sounds troubling in its possessiveness. He calls her "My other half" (IV.488) and twice casts her not as an equal but as quantitatively diminished. "Part of my soul," he says, and "of him ... / His flesh, his bone" (IV.487, 482–83). Concluding this appeal with a firmly declarative "I seek thee, and thee claim / My other half" (IV.488–89), Adam then seizes Eve's hand, as if to demonstrate his ownership, the boldness of his gesture underscored by the use of enjambment and the disruption in this line of the poem's iambic rhythm.

That "to seize" during the early modern period commonly meant "to take possession of," as in the confiscation of a subject's property by a sovereign or feudal lord, further suggests Adam's imperiousness.[34] The verb could also mean "to take prisoner," to take possession "by force," or "to take hold of suddenly or eagerly" with the "hands, claws, teeth."[35] In two other instances in book IV, "seize" carries these more violent connotations: first, as Satan, spying Adam and Eve, is compared to a tiger "who chose his ground / Whence rushing he might surest seize them both / Gripped in each paw" (lines 406–08); and, also in book IV, Gabriel informs Ithuriel and Zephon that Satan has escaped from hell and is heading to the garden: the warlike angel instructs the cherubim, "Such where ye find, seize fast, and hither bring" (line 796). Here we may recall Christopher Ricks' observation that Milton sometimes deliberately uses

---

[32] In this context, "transported" could mean "excited beyond self-control" (*OED*, def. 2).

[33] Richard Corum, "In White Ink: *Paradise Lost* and Milton's Ideas of Women," in *Milton and the Idea of Woman*, ed. Julia M. Walker (Urbana: University of Illinois Press, 1988), pp. 120–47 (p. 125).

[34] *OED*, s. v. "seize," def. II.5.a.

[35] *OED*, s. v. "seize," defs. II.6.b, II.6.a, II.7.a. Writing about English Renaissance drama, Frank Whigham has accordingly used *seizure* to describe moments of sometimes violent self-construction within the shaping forces of social order, gender, and family. See Whigham, *Seizures of the Will in Early Modern English Drama* (Cambridge: Cambridge University Press, 1996).

corrupted words to depict prelapsarian innocence.[36] "Seized" fits with other ambivalent signifiers in book IV – words such as "luxuriant" (line 260), "error" (line 239), and, as I discuss in the next chapter, "wanton" (line 306) – which measure Eden's integrity by anticipating its ruin. As Ricks explains, Milton at such instances is "reaching back to an earlier purity – which we are to contrast with what has happened to the word, and the world, since."[37]

Milton highlights this contrast by repeating "seize" after Adam and Eve eat from the Tree of Knowledge. As we saw at the start of this chapter, "Her hand he seized, and to a shady bank, / Thick overhead with verdant roof embow'red / He led her nothing loath" (IX.1037–39). Gone in this post-lapsarian image are both the qualifying "gentle hand" from Eve's account of their earlier meeting and the description of Eve "blushing like the morn" from Adam's version (VIII.511). That Milton uses "seize" to depict both pre- and postlapsarian desire complicates a simple dichotomy of innocence versus lust; he encourages us to see the similarity as well as the difference between the two gestures. As James Grantham Turner observes, "Fallen sexuality for Milton is not an entirely new experience . . . It is a version of Adam and Eve's established pattern, a cracked and hectic transcription of familiar music."[38] Thus, before the Fall, Adam and Eve begin and end their days bowing lowly "to praise / Their Maker, in fit strains pronounced or sung / Unmeditated" (V.147–49). Their prelapsarian prayer is entirely innocent – a spontaneous, unanimous expression of gratitude, unaccompanied by any formal ceremonies. After the Fall, Adam and Eve also pray, but now they plaintively ask for God's forgiveness, "with tears / Watering the ground, and with . . . sighs the air / Frequenting" (X.1089–91). In like manner, Milton emphasizes that before the Fall Adam and Eve enjoy an innocent, sexual relationship, free of lust and "Founded in reason, loyal, just, and pure, / Relations dear" (IV.755–56). Only after the Fall does Adam's erotic seizure of Eve's hand become tainted as the pair feel "Carnal desire" and burn "in lust" (IX.1013, 1015). Adam and Eve now look at each other with "lascivious eyes" (IX.1014), and, instead of finding their "amorous play" refreshing, they feel guilty and tired afterwards (IX.1045).

---

[36] Christopher Ricks, *Milton's Grand Style* (Oxford: Oxford University Press, 1963), p. 111.

[37] Ricks, *Milton's Grand Style*, p. 111. Arnold Stein makes a similar argument for Milton's use of "error" in *Paradise Lost*. Arthur Sherbo, though, offers a cautionary note about reading too much into Milton's ambivalent diction. See Stein, *Answerable Style: Essays on "Paradise Lost"* (Minneapolis: University of Minneapolis Press, 1953), pp. 66–67; and Sherbo, "'Mazie Error': *Paradise Lost* IV.239," *Modern Language Review* 67 (1972): 745–51.

[38] James Grantham Turner, *One Flesh: Paradisal Marriage and Sexual Relations in the Age of Milton* (Oxford: Clarendon, 1987), p. 303.

To appreciate the separate implications of "seized" in the description of prelapsarian and postlapsarian love, we can compare the various other uses of this word in *Paradise Lost*. Outside of book IV, "seize" most often describes an emotion or state that suddenly overtakes someone. If we proceed in order, "astonishment" (I.317), "deep silence and demur" (II.431), "Strange horror" (II.703), "amazement" (II.758; VI.198), "Admiration" (III.271), "wonder" (III.552), "envy" (III.553), "terror" (VI.647), and "gentle sleep / ... with soft oppression" (VIII.287–88) are all said to seize one or more character in Milton's poem. In this context, the reference to Adam's seizing Eve by the hand could imply that both of them were overcome by emotion, which would maintain the couple's reciprocity. Just as the pivotal moment occurs when Adam seizes Eve's hand in her account of their first meeting, the emphasis in Adam's version falls on how Eve's beauty overwhelms him: "her looks ... from that time infused / Sweetness into my heart, unfelt before" (VIII.474–75).

But, that in *Paradise Lost*'s final two books Milton stresses that "seize" can mean a wresting of control once again raises the possibility that Adam at Eve's birth momentarily inhibits her free will. First, as Michael goes to meet Adam, he leaves "his powers to seize / Possession of the garden" (XI.221–22). Then, the angel describes how a throng of men would have "seized" Enoch "with violent hands" (XI.669); how the Israelite priests, having grown factious, will "seize / The scepter, and regard not David's sons" (XII.356–57); and, ultimately, how God's Son, "coming in the flesh" will be "Seized on by force, judged, and to death condemned" (XII.405, 412). The repetition of this one verb implies a connection between all these events, as if they proceed from the chronologically first instance of a seizure in *Paradise Lost*, when Sin emerges from Satan's head and "amazement seized / All th' host of Heav'n" (II.758–59).

Yet, in Milton's Arminian theodicy, the events that Michael narrates do not grow inevitably from Adam's gentle hand seizing Eve's at their first meeting. If "seized" sounds proprietary or forceful, we should remember the early modern convention that a groom carry the bride over the threshold. As explained in seventeenth-century conduct guides, brides "enter, being carried over, that they may signifie that they lose their sollicited Virginity, not voluntarily, but in a manner by compulsion."[39] Women were also warned not to use their hands too loosely: according to one conduct guide, "the overmuch motion of the hands ... cannot be done without disgrace," and is "always joined with vanity and a great

[39] Francesco Barbaro, *Directions for Love and Marriage* (London, 1677), E4r.

signification of levity."[40] In reminding Adam of their first meeting, Eve could appreciate the rhetorical significance of mentioning that he seized her hand: she wishes to emphasize that she behaved modestly but still chose him freely. By comparison, Adam could selectively omit this detail from his conversation with Raphael, lest he appear to overvalue what the angel somewhat dismissively calls "every lower faculty / Of sense" (V.410–11).

More important, Eve's oxymoronic recollection, that Adam's "gentle hand / Seized mine" (IV.488–89), fits with other paradoxical descriptions of her and his prelapsarian experience, phrases such as "hand in hand alone" (IV.689), "obsequious majesty" (VIII.509), and, as I explore in the next chapter, "coy submission" (IV.310) and "modest pride" (IV.310).[41] These oxymora reveal the paradoxical nature of their relationship, simultaneously egalitarian and hierarchical, gentle and urgent. The handclasp initiated at their first encounter – at once physical and spiritual – not only brings together Adam and Eve but also symbolizes the reconciliation of these apparent contradictions.

If we return to the final glimpse that Milton provides of Adam and Eve, they are once again joined, as "They hand in hand with wand'ring steps and slow, / Through Eden took their solitary way" (XII.648–49). Here their handedness offers us hope; most notably, the image remedies the moment of separation leading up to the Fall when, as we have seen, Eve "from her husband's hand her hand / Soft she withdrew" (IX.385–86). This gesture of withdrawal again demonstrates Eve's free will and seems to enact her argument that she and Adam work apart, while the use of enjambment dramatizes their physical separation. But, after the Fall, for Adam and Eve again to join hands, they must first "prostrate fall / Before him reverent, and there confess / Humbly our faults, and pardon beg" (X.1087–89). If we recall Herbert's poem, this other type of hand-holding – hands clasped in prayer – is contained in Adam and Eve's first contact, providing the means, practically and symbolically, for them to discover, as Eve puts it, that they must "yield" to each other and to God. Only then, if we paraphrase further Eve's recollection of first meeting Adam, can the couple together learn that the beauty of paradise, now lost, can be excelled by grace and wisdom.

---

[40] Barbaro, *Directions for Love and Marriage*, F8r.

[41] Interestingly, Andrew Marvell, in his poem "On *Paradise Lost*," seems to recognize the significance of this tension for Milton's epic. Marvell writes of the reader's experience, "At once delight and horror on us *seize*" (line 35, emphasis added). See Marvell, "On *Paradise Lost*," in Fowler, pp. 53–54.

CHAPTER 7

Clustering and curling locks

There seems a love in hair, though it be dead.
It is the gentlest, yet the strongest thread
   Of our frail plant.

– Leigh Hunt[1]

When in book IV of *Paradise Lost* Adam and Eve are finally introduced –
even before we learn about their hands' touching at their first meeting –
Milton lingers on the couple's physical appearance. But instead of
following the blazon tradition and presenting a detailed catalogue of Adam
and Eve's various physical attributes, Milton primarily depicts their hair:

> His fair large front and eye sublime declared
> Absolute rule; and hyacinthine locks
> Round from his parted forelock manly hung
> Clust'ring, but not beneath his shoulders broad:
> She as a veil down to the slender waist
> Her unadornèd golden tresses wore
> Disheveled, but in wanton ringlets waved
> As the vine curls her tendrils, which implied
> Subjection, but required with gentle sway,
> And by her yielded, by him best received,
> Yielded with coy submission, modest pride,
> And sweet reluctant amorous delay.   (IV.300–11)

Here Milton conveys gender difference by combining traditional biological markers (such as "shoulders broad" and "slender waist") with culturally
constructed notions of a man and woman's appropriate hair length.[2] While

---

[1] Leigh Hunt, "It lies before me there, and my own breath," in *The Poetical Works of Leigh Hunt*, ed. H.
S. Milford (London: Oxford University Press, 1923), p. 247 (lines 9–11).

[2] John Guillory observes that Milton relies on this culturally determined difference instead of a genital
distinction. The couple's hair, Guillory adds, "foreshadows the crucial function of clothing as the
virtually universal semiotic of gender difference." See Guillory, "From the Superfluous to the
Supernumerary: Reading Gender into *Paradise Lost*," in *Soliciting Interpretation: Literary Theory
and Seventeenth-Century English Poetry*, ed. Elizabeth D. Harvey and Katharine Eisaman Maus
(Chicago: University of Chicago Press, 1990), pp. 68–88 (p. 87).

the lines immediately preceding this description enforce a hierarchical relationship – "For contemplation he and valour formed, / For softness she and sweet attractive grace, / He for God only, she for God in him" (IV.297–99) – the image of the couple's hair, we will see, emphasizes Adam and Eve's mutuality and complicates the difference in their status. Even if, as John Rogers has observed, the length of a woman's hair traditionally signified her subjection, the contrasting length of Adam and Eve's hair constitutes "exceedingly fragile evidence" to support a hierarchy of the sexes.[3]

Admittedly, hair in the popular imagination during the seventeenth century was more often associated with war, not love. Royalists beginning in the early 1640s derided members of the parliamentary party as "Roundheads" because of their unfashionably short hair, while Parliamentarians considered the courtly fashion of long hair "unnaturall, womanish, irreligious, and unmanly."[4] At the court of Charles I, men and, later, women specifically favored the French "lovelock" (also known as a *cadenette*), a single, stylish lock of hair that fell below the wearer's shoulder and was sometimes adorned with a bow or other ornament. Charles I in his triple portrait by Anthony Van Dyck wears a prominent lovelock draped over his left shoulder (see figure 7.1), and another portrait by Van Dyck of Prince Charles at age seven depicts the beginning of a lovelock in imitation of his father's. Typically, a lovelock was worn on the left side so that it extended to the wearer's heart as a sign of affection.[5] Robin Bryer speculates that the fashion evolved from the symbolic "favour" worn by a medieval knight to show his dedication to a beautiful woman: instead of adorning his attire with a glove or other love token, a man announced his devotion to his beloved by allowing a lock of his hair to remain unshorn.[6]

Parliamentarians, by comparison, presumably cut their hair short as a symbolic rejection of courtly luxury and worldliness. Most directly, this preference derived from St. Paul's admonition in 1 Corinthians: "Doth not even nature itself teach you, that, if a man have long hair, it is a shame unto him? But if a woman have long hair, it is a glory to her: for *her* hair is given her for a covering" (11:14–15). William Prynne in *Histrio-Mastix* (1633) accordingly bemoans the "shame" and "sinne" of women who "clip or cut" their hair, and he mocks men who wear long hair as "effeminate hairy

[3] John Rogers, "Transported Touch: The Fruit of Marriage in *Paradise Lost*," in *Milton and Gender*, ed. Catherine Gimelli Martin (Cambridge: Cambridge University Press, 2004), pp. 115–32 (p. 124).
[4] William Prynne, *Histrio-Mastix* (London, 1633), Bb3v.
[5] James Hall, *The Sinister Side: How Left-Right Symbolism Shaped Western Art* (Oxford: Oxford University Press, 2008), p. 278.
[6] Robin Bryer, *The History of Hair* (London: Philip Wilson, 2000), p. 51.

Figure 7.1 Anthony Van Dyck, *Charles I, King of England, from Three Angels*, 1636. Oil on canvas. Royal Collection, Windsor Castle, Berkshire.

men-monsters."[7] In *The Unlovelinesse, of Lovelockes* (1628), Prynne condemns the lovelock as ungodly by tracing its origin to the hairstyle worn by Native Americans. Lovelocks, he writes, *"had their generation, birth, and pedigree from the Heathenish, and Idolatrous Virginians, who tooke their pattern from their Devill Ockeus,"* one of the two principal gods of the Powhatan people.[8]

In this chapter, I wish to examine Milton's images of Adam and Eve's hair in *Paradise Lost* in the context of hair's cultural and spiritual value in early modern England. While the distinction between Parliamentarian and Royalist haircuts might ultimately seem negligble – after all, contemporary portraits of the Parliamentarians Oliver Cromwell, Thomas Fairfax, and Henry Ireton depict men with hair that falls loosely to their collars – the strident tone of some seventeenth-century pamphlets nevertheless

[7] Prynne, *Histrio-Mastix*, Cc4v, Dd1v.
[8] Prynne, *The Unlovelinesse, of Lovelockes* (London, 1628), B2v.

suggests the potential significance of hair in the Renaissance imagination.[9]
Still today, hair remains invested in various economies of meaning, signifying differences in gender, ethnicity, race, religion, and status. How
people wear their hair expresses individual identity and constructs the
wearers' relationship to specific cultural ideas and beliefs. During
Milton's time, the pressure put on the possible meanings of hair seems to
have been particularly acute: various hair-related artifacts from the early
modern period indicate that hair was thought to have a sacred, almost
talismanic quality. Early modern jewelry such as lockets and mourning
rings often incorporated a loved one's tresses as a sign of devotion or
bereavement, and hair-bracelets remained popular long after the
Restoration.[10] A loved one's locks might also be preserved in needlepoint
work; commemorative medallions of Charles I's execution, for example,
contain a tiny portrait of the king apparently stitched with his own hair.[11]

   Certainly, in Milton's poetry hair plays a conspicuous part, most notably Lycidas' "oozy locks" (line 175), Eve's "wanton ringlets" (IV.306), and
Samson's "Robustious" tresses (line 569); even one of Milton's earliest
poetic works, his translation of Horace's Fifth Ode, refers to Pyrrha's
golden, wreathed hair, while in Il Penseroso he imagines "bright-haired
Vesta" as Melancholy's mother (line 23). Leigh Hunt first discussed this
interest of Milton's in an 1833 essay. Hunt infers from Circe's amorous
attraction to Bacchus' "clust'ring locks" in A Mask (line 54) that Milton
"must have been more delighted than most poets at the compliments paid
to beautiful tresses by his brethren, particularly by his favourite Greeks."[12]

   With this chapter I am attempting to build on Hunt's observation and
examine the potency of hair in Paradise Lost as another part of the imagistic
depiction of prelapsarian desire. Milton's decision to introduce Adam and
Eve by focusing on images of their hair – as opposed to their eyes, mouths,
or other features – is significant. But whereas Alastair Fowler has asserted
that Milton had a "special sexual interest in hair," I would argue that

---

[9] See, for example, John Taylor, Heads of all Fashions (1642); and The Soundheads Description of the
   Roundhead (1642).
[10] See O. M. Dalton, Frank's Bequest: Catalogue of the Finger Rings, Early Christian, Byzantine,
   Teutonic, Mediaeval and Later Bequeathed by Sir Augustus Wollaston Franks (London: Longmans,
   1912), pp. li–lii, 207–08.
[11] See Margaret Sleeman, "Medieval Hair Tokens," Forum for Modern Languages 17.4 (1981): 322–36.
[12] Leigh Hunt, "The Wishing-Cap. No. 1," Tait's Edinburgh Magazine, 2 (Jan. 1833): 435–42 (p. 440).
   Hunt himself, it seems, delighted in such compliments: he went on to write three sonnets about a
   lock of Milton's hair. He pledges in one poem to wear Milton's lock "About me, while I breathe this
   strenuous air, / That nursed his Apollonian tresses free," and, in another, he wonders whether
   Milton touched this same lock while composing Paradise Lost. See The Poetical Works of Leigh Hunt,
   pp. 246, 247.

Milton's interest was not strictly sexual, nor even special to him.[13] Examining the historical context of Milton's epic reveals various cultural and poetic traditions that inform his depiction of Adam and Eve's tresses. More specifically, my goal is to show how the couple's hair in *Paradise Lost* – like their hand-holding – expresses prelapsarian love, both conveying an amorous reciprocity and signifying the paradoxical strength and fragility of their Edenic marriage.

"Oozy locks he laves"

Much of the rhetoric surrounding hair length during the seventeenth century can be traced to classical, scriptural, and folkloric sources. According to these works, long hair indicated a person's vitality while the lack or loss of a person's hair signified deficiency or illness. Thus, in ancient times, to take one example, King Nisus and his city of Megara remained unconquerable so long as he bore an unshorn purple lock of hair; he died when his daughter Scylla cut off the lock in an attempt to deliver Megara to her beloved, Minos.[14] In the *Iliad*, Homer describes Zeus and Poseidon as long-haired; and Achilles, Agamemnon, Hector, and Paris all have thick, long locks, in contrast to Thersites, "the ugliest man who ever came to Troy," whose "clumps of scraggly, woolly hair" point up his ill-temper and abusiveness.[15] Also influencing Milton's image of Adam and Eve's vibrant locks may be ancient depictions of such figures as Dionysus or Apollo. Dionysus' long, luxuriant hair apparently symbolized his status as a kind of fertility deity, while the powers of the sun-god Apollo were commonly associated with his beautiful long tresses, sometimes represented as the sun's life-giving beams. When Apollo pronounces in *Metamorphoses*, "my head is ever young and my locks unshorn" (*meum intonsis caput est iuvenale capillis*), he implies an almost causal link between his divine status and flowing tresses.[16]

In the Bible, the story of Samson most obviously reflects this same tradition; not only did Samson's hair resemble Apollo's, but both figures

---

[13] Fowler, p. 239.

[14] See Ovid, *Metamorphoses*, trans. Frank Justus Miller, rev. G. P. Goold, 3rd edn. (Cambridge: Harvard University Press, 1977), VIII.1–151. Similarly, in *Orlando Furioso*, the life of Orillo, the magician of Egypt, depends on a single hair of his head. See Lodovico Ariosto, *Orlando Furioso*, trans. John Harrington, ed. Graham Hough (Carbondale: Southern Illinois University Press, 1962), p. 170 (XI.59–68).

[15] Homer, *Iliad*, trans. Robert Fagles (New York: Penguin, 1992), II.250, 255 (Gr. II.217–19). On hair in Homer's works, see M. Eleanor Irwin, "Odysseus' 'Hyacinthine Hair' in Odyssey 6.231," *Phoenix* 44.3 (1990): 205–18 (especially pp. 210–12).

[16] Ovid, *Metamorphoses*, I.564. Lewis Richard Farnell, *The Cults of the Greek States*, 5 vols. (New Rochelle, NY: Caratzas Brothers, 1977), discusses Apollo's long hair in Greek art (IV: 329–55).

were also identified with the sun: throughout the patristic period, as F. Michael Krouse has observed, the accepted etymology of Samson's name was *sol ipsorum* ("their sun").[17] The earliest biblical commentators interpreted Samson's confession to Delilah – "if I be shaven, then my strength will go from me" (Judg. 16:17) – to mean that Samson's strength actually resided in his hair. Milton in *Eikonoklastes* seems to agree, referring to "the strength of that *Nazarites* lock" (*CPW* III: 545–46), and in *Samson Agonistes* he implies that Samson's unshorn hair may have been the source of his power: Samson laments that "God, when he gave me strength, to show withal / How slight the gift was, hung it in my hair" (lines 58–59).[18] While elsewhere in the poem Milton suggests that Samson's unshorn hair merely symbolized his adherence to his Nazaritic vows – Samson tells Harapha that his strength is "diffused / No less through all my sinews, joints and bones, / Than thine, while I preserved these locks unshorn" (lines 1141–43) – the more general connection between hair and Samson-like strength became a rhetorical trope during the seventeenth century.[19] Henry Robinson in *A Moderate Answer* (1645), for example, emphasizes the tenacity of an Episcopal church government by describing the threat of the bishops' renewed power in terms of their regrowing hair: "if [Parliament] should cut the Bishops Locks, a little regulate them, their hair would soon grow again, and pull down the house of the Common-wealth about us all."[20]

   The relationship between a person's life and locks that seems to underlie Milton's depiction of Adam and Eve also had its origin in folktales and popular legends. Most often, women's shimmering hair in these narratives denoted magical power. Elisabeth Gitter cites, for example, the thirteenth-century Old Norse *Edda*, where gold is referred to as *Sifjar haddr* – literally, "Sif's hair" – because Loki plays a prank on Sif by cutting off her yellow hair and replacing it with gold hair forged by gnomes.[21] In other folk

[17]   F. Michael Krouse, *Milton's Samson and the Christian Tradition* (Princeton: Princeton University Press, 1949), traces this idea as far back as Jerome (p. 42). For the beauty of long hair in Hebrew Scriptures, see also the description of Absalom's thick locks in 2 Sam. 14:25–26.

[18]   Samson also later refers to the "consecrated gift / Of strength, again returning with my hair" (lines 1354–55).

[19]   The vitality attributed to hair during the Renaissance included beards, which were specifically equated with manhood and sexual potency, as when Beatrice in *Much Ado About Nothing* pronounces, "he that hath no beard is less than a man." Thus the insult of "bearding" a man – that is, plucking his beard – figuratively came to mean thwarting someone with impudence. See Shakespeare, *Much Ado About Nothing*, ed. F. H. Mares (Cambridge: Cambridge University Press, 1988), II.1.28; Richard Corson, *Fashions in Hair: The First Five Thousand Years* (London: Peter Owen, 2001), pp. 198–206; and *OED*, s. v. "beard, *v.*".

[20]   Henry Robinson, *A Moderate Answer to Mr. Prins Full Reply* (London, 1645), C1r.

[21]   Elisabeth G. Gitter, "The Power of Women's Hair in the Victorian Imagination," *PMLA* 99.5 (1984): 936–54 (p. 936).

narratives, "gold hair" served not just as a synonym for "blonde hair" but also as an indication of the hair's sacred or life-giving qualities. In one version of the story of St. Agnes, the Roman prefect Sempronius sentenced her to be chained and stripped naked in front of the multitude. But, as the soldiers ripped off her clothes, God answered her prayers and caused her hair to grow miraculously, covering her chaste body in an apparent expression of saintly virtue and divine grace.[22] More directly relevant for *Paradise Lost* may be Renaissance depictions of angels with flowing, golden tresses, a popular image that Milton borrows when, as we saw in chapter 5, he describes how Uriel's "locks behind / Illustrious on his shoulders ... / Lay waving round" (III.626–28). In Milton's epic, as in Renaissance paintings and illustrations, an angel's lively, shining tresses seem to indicate its divine authority and glorious nature.[23] Surveying such traditions and myths, Julius Heuscher has concluded that golden hair came to embody more generally a person's "spirit" and represented "a live gold" that "radiat[ed] from the human head ... to a supernatural world."[24]

For Milton personally, we know that he appreciated the symbolic significance of hair from a young age. That the earliest surviving portrait of Milton depicts a ten-year-old boy with closely cropped auburn hair suggests that he was exposed to Parliamentarian ideas as a young man; according to Milton's widow, her late husband's schoolmaster, "a puritan in Essex," had "cutt his haire short."[25] Milton's later preference to grow his hair long most likely reflected his poetic aspirations; perhaps influenced by the ancient tradition of Apollo, whose harp and lute were sometimes

---

[22] F. G. Holweck, *A Biographical Dictionary of the Saints* (1924; Detroit: Gale Research, 1969), p. 33; and Gitter, "The Power of Women's Hair in the Victorian Imagination," p. 939.

[23] See Laurence B. Kanter and Barbara Drake Boehm, *Painting and Illumination in Early Renaissance Florence, 1300–1450* (New York: Metropolitan Museum of Art, 1994).

[24] Julius E. Heuscher, *A Psychiatric Study of Myths and Fairy Tales: Their Origin, Meaning and Usefulness* (Springfield, IL: Charles C. Thomas, 1974), p. 242. Charles Berg, *The Unconscious Significance of Hair* (London: Allen and Unwin, 1951), similarly concludes that hair "is to the folk-mind an index and a representative of life itself" (p. 36).
    The other typical folkloric depiction of long hair involved the figure of a wild man. In contrast to the spiritual implications of golden hair, the long hair worn by these part-human and part-animal creatures signified magic, lust, and savagery. Prominent in medieval art and literature but also carried down during the Renaissance in, say, the character of Spenser's Sir Satyrane, the figure of the wild man seems to have derived in part from the account of Nebuchadnezzar's affliction in Daniel (Dan. 4:33). See Richard Bernheimer, *Wild Men in the Middle Ages: A Study in Art, Sentiment, and Demonology* (New York: Octagon, 1970). In Milton's writing, we glimpse this latter folk tradition in *L'Allegro* as the rustic workers tell of a goblin whose hairiness seems to signify both virility and magic: he threshes more corn in one night than ten day-laborers and afterwards "Basks at the fire his hairy strength" (line 112). See also *Paradise Lost*, as Satan attempts to enter Paradise and confronts "a steep wilderness, whose hairy sides / With thicket overgrown, grotesque and wild, / Access denied" (IV.135–37).

[25] John Aubrey, "Minutes of the Life of Mr. John Milton," in *The Early Lives of Milton*, ed. Helen Darbishire (London: Constable, 1932), pp. 1–15 (p. 2).

thought to be strung with his own tresses, Milton repeatedly conceives of the ideal poet as having long hair.[26] In *Ad Patrem*, for example, he recalls a golden age when the bard sat at the happy feast, "his flowing locks crowned with a garland of oak leaves" (*Tum de more sedens festa ad convivia vates / Aescula intonsos redimitus ab abore crines*, lines 44–45). Similarly, in *Mansus*, as the poet imagines his own death, he hopes a friend will have a marble statue of him made and describes his hair wreathed with myrtle from Paphos or laurel from Parnassus (*Nectens aut Paphia myrti aut Parnasside lauri / Fronde comas*, lines 92–93).

In *Lycidas*, Milton most fully develops this ideal. Examining the crucial role that hair plays in this earlier work helps to illustrate the symbolic significance of Adam and Eve's hair in *Paradise Lost*. At the start of *Lycidas*, Milton alludes to hair by describing three evergreen crowns – the laurel, myrtle, and ivy – which, as commentators have long observed, signify poetic triumph and immortality.[27] Later, when the swain laments the elusiveness of winning such a garland, Milton again subtly alludes to hair by blaming "the blind Fury with th' abhorrèd shears" who "slits the thin-spun life" (lines 75–76). This latter image not only evokes Samson's and King Nisus' fatal haircuts, but it also associates an untimely death with the furies and their snake-wreathed tresses rather than with the mythologically correct, scissors-bearing Atropos. More directly, when the swain entertains the possibility of abandoning his poetic vocation, Milton uses hair to describe the swain's ersatz erotic pastime: instead of contending for a crown of laurel, myrtle, or ivy, he would take pleasure in "the tangles of Neaera's hair" (line 69).[28] Weaving this hair motif into his elegy, Milton emphasizes how much is at stake for Lycidas and the speaker; the mistress' tangles can supersede the immortality that the evergreen crowns symbolize.

While Phoebus Apollo's subsequent appearance in the poem may call up the image of his laurel crown and life-giving locks, the next direct reference

[26] In *Metamorphoses*, for example, Ovid associates Apollo's hair and music: "My hair, my lyre, my quiver, shall always be entwined with thee, O laurel" (*mea! semper habebunt / te coma, te citharae, te nostrae, laure, pharetrae*), I.558–59. More directly, in Shakespeare's *Love's Labour's Lost*, Berowne refers to "bright Apollo's lute, strung with his hair." See *Love's Labour's Lost*, ed. H. R. Woudhuysen (Nashville: Thomas Nelson, 1998), IV.3.317.

[27] J. B. Trapp, "The Owl's Ivy and the Poet's Bays: An Enquiry into Poetic Garlands," *Journal of the Warburg and Courtauld Institutes* 21 (1958): 227–55, offers an excellent discussion of these garlands in ancient times and the Renaissance. I also discuss hair in *Lycidas* in Dobranski, *The Cambridge Introduction to Milton* (Cambridge: Cambridge University Press, 2012), pp. 154–55.

[28] This line in the 1638 version of *Lycidas*, "Hid in the tangles of Neaera's hair" – instead of "Or with the tangles of Neaera's hair" line (69) – conveys, as Stella Revard notes, a more sensuous experience. See Revard, *Milton and the Tangles of Neaera's Hair: The Making of the 1645 "Poems"* (Columbia: University of Missouri Press, 1997), p. 187.

to hair occurs as Saint Peter shakes his "mitred locks" to express his contempt for the corrupted clergy (line 112).[29] The saint's Episcopal head-dress not only transcends the earth-bound futility embodied by Neaera's tangles but also suggests the inadequacy of the classical, natural garlands that the swain aspires to win. Milton then unites these competing registers when the shepherd "with nectar pure his oozy locks he laves" (line 175). Here Lycidas' rebirth resembles both a pagan cleansing ritual and a Christian baptism; the line's alliteration and internal rhyme demonstrate how the swain has at last reconciled nature and antiquity with Christian belief.

The final image of Lycidas fittingly completes the poem's hair motif:

> So sinks the day-star in the ocean bed,
> And yet anon repairs his drooping head,
> And tricks his beams, and with new spangled ore,
> Flames in the forehead of the morning sky.   (lines 168–71)

In this culminating image, the "beams" emanating from the sun's "head" evoke the description of Lycidas' submerged hair and Phoebus' luxuriant locks; that the day-star's golden rays then rise and "flame" in the sky's "forehead" encapsulates the poem's redemption narrative and suggests the glorious effulgence of the resurrected Son. Critics have traditionally read the swain's ultimate gesture of rising like the sun and turning "to fresh woods, and pastures new" (line 194) as a sign of hope: the speaker seems to take comfort in Lycidas' poetic apotheosis and Christian redemption, as well as in nature's cycles, his monody's echoing repetition, and the pastoral tradition. But also comforting the speaker is the continuity he discovers in the powerful mythic symbol of locks and tresses, which helps him to connect all these things. And that this larger motif and the poem's final, inclusive image hang by a hair may itself be significant: Milton subtly suggests how fragile yet strong remains the promise of everlasting life to which Lycidas and the speaker aspire.

---

[29] Interestingly, in the version of *Lycidas* in the Trinity College Manuscript, Milton had included two additional references to hair: he originally described Orpheus' mother as "golden hayrd Calliope," which he then replaced with "the muse her selfe" (line 58), and he referred to Orpheus' "goarie scalpe," which he changed first to "divine head" in the margin, then replaced with "divine visage" on a separate leaf before finally arriving at "gorie visage" (line 59). In the former case, the muse's golden hair would have underscored the irony that even such a powerful figure could not save her own son; in the latter case, referring to Orpheus' gory hair would have more forcefully set off the redemption that Lycidas achieves as he washes his own "oozy locks" (line 175). See *John Milton Poems Reproduced in Facsimile from the Manuscript in Trinity College, Cambridge* (Menston, Eng.: Scolar Press, 1970).

"A superfluitie of members"

It is in this context, I suggest, that we should turn to Milton's image of Adam and Eve in book IV of *Paradise Lost*. In Adam's case, the specific detail that his "hyacinthine locks" do not hang "beneath his shoulders" (IV.301–03) adheres to the Pauline prohibition and distinguishes Adam's innocence from both courtly luxury and Puritans' postlapsarian strictures. As commentators have observed, Adam also resembles – and presumably surpasses – Odysseus on Skhería Island when Athena makes "him seem / taller, and massive too, with crisping hair / in curls like petals of wild hyacinth."[30] And if we have any remaining doubts about how seriously Milton might have approached the subject of hair in his poetry, Roland Frye notes that Adam's "parted forelock" (IV.302) sets him apart from the "overwhelming majority of historical and legendary characters whose portraits have been preserved for us." Frye identifies only two historical figures who wore their hair this way, Oliver Cromwell and Milton himself.[31]

The description of Eve's hair, by comparison, has generated more commentary and raised doubts about her virtue. While some critics such as Michael Lieb have argued that the image of her "unadornèd" and "Disheveled" tresses (IV.305–06) illustrates a "playful but innocent dalliance," others have found troubling Eve's "wanton ringlets" (IV.306).[32] Catherine Belsey, for example, has argued that Eve's hair serves as a metonym for her sexuality, "at once God-given and dangerous"; Robert Newman concludes more emphatically that Eve's disheveled hair "nullifies the prospect of her innocence"; and J. Hillis Miller suggests that, even before Eve eats the forbidden fruit, her "disheveled wantonness means that she is in effect already fallen."[33]

---

[30] Homer, *The Odyssey*, trans. Robert Fitzgerald (New York: Vintage, 1989), VI.243–45 (Greek, VI.230–32).

[31] Roland Mushat Frye, *Milton's Imagery and the Visual Arts* (Princeton: Princeton University Press, 1978), p. 272. Commenting on Adam and Eve's hair, Thomas Newton in 1757 first suggested that Milton "drew the portrait of Adam not without regard to his own person" and may have "intended a compliment to his wife in the drawing of Eve." See Newton, ed., *Paradise Lost*, by John Milton, 4th edn., 2 vols. (London, 1757), I: 282.

[32] Michael Lieb, *Milton and the Culture of Violence* (Ithaca: Cornell University Press, 1994), p. 150.

[33] Catherine Belsey, *John Milton: Language, Gender, Power* (Oxford: Basil Blackwell, 1988), p. 66; Robert D. Newman, "Entanglement in Paradise: Eve's Hair and the Reader's Anxiety in *Paradise Lost*," *Interpretations* 16.1 (1985): 112–15 (p. 114); and J. Hillis Miller, "How Deconstruction Works," in *Theory Now and Then* (Durham: Duke University Press, 1991), pp. 293–94 (p. 294). Sandra M. Gilbert and Susan Gubar, *The Madwoman in the Attic* (New Haven: Yale University Press, 1979), similarly argue that Eve's hair possesses "at least a sinister potential" (p. 199), while William Empson, *Some Versions of Pastoral* (New York: New Directions, 1974), blames Eve for having entangled Adam in her golden curls (p. 177).

All these readings of Eve's "unadornèd ... tresses," however, overlook Satan's potential influence in this scene. While we need not insist along with Michael Wilding that readers should "take the description of Adam and Eve as recording Satan's interpretive vision" – just the word "God" (IV.299), as Fowler notes, instead suggests the narrator's perspective – the details of Adam and Eve's appearance nevertheless occur within a larger survey of Paradise that Milton clearly frames as conveying what Satan views.[34] As Irene Samuel puts it, readers first behold Paradise "not through the distorting lens of Satan's eyes ... but over his shoulder."[35] Thus, immediately before introducing Adam and Eve, the poet announces that "the fiend / Saw undelighted all delight" (IV.285–86), and the scene similarly concludes with a reminder of Satan's abiding presence: "Satan still in gaze, as first he stood" (IV.356). One need not be an avid reader-response theorist to accept that our view of Eden – and, more specifically, of Adam and Eve – is accordingly colored by our alliance with Satan's voyeuristic perspective: unlike Satan, we are able to take delight in the delightful landscape, but our view is restricted to what he is able to see.

Any hints of corruption in the description of Eve's hair as "Disheveled" and "wanton" (IV.306) could then reflect not, as Stanley Fish has argued, the reader's own sinfulness, but may instead convey Satan's contaminating influence and our apparently limited perspective.[36] Here again we might apply Christopher Ricks' idea about the use of corrupted words in *Paradise Lost* to depict prelapsarian innocence.[37] "Dishevelled" and "wanton" fit with other equivocal terms in book IV, as discussed in the preceding chapter, which underscore Edenic purity by foreshadowing its destruction. In the particular case of Eve's hair, "dishevelled" anticipates both the description of her "tresses discomposed" when she awakens from her "irksome" dream (V.10, 35) and the image of her "tresses all disordered" when after the Fall she seeks Adam's forgiveness and falls "humble" at his feet (X.911, 912). The refrain of "dishevelled," "discomposed," and "disordered" allies these three disparate moments in counterpoint to the couple's lost innocence:

[34] Michael Wilding, "'Thir Sex Not Equal Seem'd': Equality in *Paradise Lost*," in *Of Poetry and Politics: New Essays on Milton and His World*, ed. P. G. Stanwood (Binghamton, NY: Medieval and Renaissance Texts and Studies, 1995), pp. 171–85 (p. 174); and Fowler, p. 237. Diane K. McColley, *Milton's Eve* (Urbana: University of Illinois Press, 1983), also argues that "the narrative voice is at this point telling us what Satan saw" (p. 40).

[35] Irene Samuel, "*Paradise Lost* as Mimesis," in *Approaches to "Paradise Lost": The York Tercentenary Lectures.*, ed. C. A. Patrides (London: Edward Arnold, 1968), pp. 15–29 (p. 20).

[36] See Stanley Fish, *Surprised by Sin: The Reader in "Paradise Lost,"* 2nd edn. (1967; Cambridge: Harvard University Press, 1997), p. 102.

[37] Christopher Ricks, *Milton's Grand Style* (Oxford: Oxford University Press, 1963), p. 111.

because Eve's hair does not ostensibly change – except for the possible postlapsarian intensification of "all" (X.911) – readers can better appreciate how everything else does.

I would also suggest that Satan may be right to judge Adam and Eve according to their appearance. Milton invites us to understand the couple's relationship in terms of their hair because this description is not merely superficial, nor even merely symbolic. Instead, in the context of Milton's dynamic philosophy of matter, it literally embodies Adam and Eve's marriage: their clustering and curling locks indicate their spiritual union. If we return to Raphael's explanation that body and soul are different degrees of the same original substance – "one first matter all, / Endued with various forms, various degrees / Of substance, and in things that live, of life" (V.472–74) – then Adam and Eve's experience is inseparably both material and spiritual. Raphael, as we saw in the Introduction, specifically uses a plant metaphor to illustrate the hierarchy of God's creations: the least refined correspond to a plant's roots, more spiritous creations correspond to the green stalk, even more spiritous creations correspond to the leaves, and the most spiritous creations correspond to a flower and its aroma. While Raphael introduces this image to explain angelic digestion, his metaphor as an expression of monism is also literally true. The philosophy he attempts to describe collapses the space between vehicle and tenor; if the distinctions between God's creations reside in their form, so do the distinctions between the parts of God's creations. In *Paradise Lost*, in other words, a flower would consist of the same matter as a plant's roots, stem, or leaves, but the flower would be "more spiritous, and pure" than these other parts (IV.475).

I recount Raphael's speech at such length because, as applied to Adam and Eve, it suggests that their hair may be the most spiritous and pure part of their bodies; in terms of Raphael's plant metaphor, their tresses correspond to "the bright consummate flow'r" that "Spirits odorous breathes" (V.481–82). Milton encourages this alliance by describing the couple's hair as plants: Adam's hyacinthine locks and Eve's vine-like curls. But also recommending such a reading, as we have seen, were the early modern traditions that identified hair as the source of a person's vitality. If, as Raphael asserts, a creation's place within the hierarchy of existence depends on the degree "Of substance, and in things that live, of life" (V.474), then the couple's shimmering, vital locks represent their closest link to the supernatural realm.

Also undergirding such a reading of Adam and Eve were early modern theories about hair's etiology. Beginning with the belief that "Nature makes for the body a form appropriate to the character of the soul," Galen suggests that the quantity and quality of a person's hair depends on the person's humoral composition.[38] As Gustav Ungerer explains, "If a man's metabolism produced much heat and plenty of nutritive blood, his head boasted a profusion of curls. However, if coldness prevailed, as it did in the phlegmatic humor, the head displayed a growth of smooth and limp hair."[39] Thus Chaucer's Pardoner, say, or Sir Andrew Aguecheek in *Twelfth Night* suffer from bad hair because of their respective biological deficiencies. Both the Pardoner's smooth, waxy tresses, hanging "by colpons oon and oon," and Sir Andrew's similarly thin hair, hanging "like flax on a distaff," may symbolize their moral weaknesses, but their hair also indicates physiologically the two men's impotence and cowardly predispositions.[40]

In contrast, Adam and Eve's clustering and disheveled locks in *Paradise Lost* reveal their Edenic vitality, virtue, and freedom; we learn about their inner lives from their physical selves. That hair during the early modern period was sometimes called an "excrement" suggests its material basis: "excrement" could mean simply "that which grows out or forth," but could suggest more specifically "superfluous matter thrown off by the bodily organs; an excreted substance."[41] When, for example, Hamlet's "bedded hair, like life in excrements, / Start up and stand an end [*sic*]," Gertrude is afraid because her son's locks appear to come alive supernaturally.[42]

Yet Hamlet's hair also could stand on end because some people believed that hair was alive. How else could one account for its growth and changing color? How else would it appear to continue growing after death? The sixteenth-century anatomist Thomas Vicary accordingly describes hair as both material and spiritous: he refers to hair as "a superfluitie of members, made of the grosse fume or smoke pasing out of the viscoues matter, thickened to the forme heyre."[43] Vicary's

---

[38] Galen, *On the Usefulness of the Parts of the Body*, trans. Margaret Tallmadge May, 2 vols. (Ithaca: Cornell University Press, 1968), II:531–32 (bk. II, sec. 14).

[39] Gustav Ungerer, "Sir Andrew Aguecheek and His Head of Hair," *Shakespeare Studies* 16 (1983): 101–33 (p. 112).

[40] Geoffrey Chaucer, "General Prologue," *The Canterbury Tales*, in *The Riverside Chaucer*, ed. Larry D. Benson, 3rd edn. (Oxford: Oxford University Press, 1989), pp. 23–36 (line 679); and Shakespeare, *Twelfth Night*, ed. Roger Warren and Stanley Wells (Oxford: Oxford University Press, 1998), I.3.96. Ungerer, "Sir Andrew Aguecheek and His Head of Hair," offers an insightful analysis of Aguecheek's hair and character (pp. 101–03).

[41] *OED*, s. v. "excrement," defs. sb.1, sb.2.

[42] Shakespeare, *Hamlet*, ed. Harold Jenkins (London: Routledge, 1994), III.4.121–22.

[43] Thomas Vicary, *The Anatomie of the Bodie of Man, Part I* [1577], ed. Frederick J. and Percy Furnivall, Early English Texts Series 53 (1888; Millwood, NY: Kraus, 1975), pp. 23–24.

physiological explanation seems to dovetail with *Paradise Lost*'s monist premise and corresponds to the depictions of hair's vitality in classical, Christian, and folkloric texts. Although Vicary finds hair "insencible," he elsewhere associates it with a person's soul, asserting "that by the cullour of the heyre is witnessed & knowen the complexion of the Brayne," and that through a person's hair "the fumosities of the brayne might assend and passe lyghtlyer out."[44]

Presumably the physiological significance of hair encouraged the practice of wearing a loved one's locks as a relic or love token. The speaker in Donne's "The Funeral," for example, wears a "subtle wreath of hair" because it represents "my outward Soul, / Viceroy to that, which then to heaven being gone, / Will leave this to control, / And keep these limbs, her provinces, from dissolution."[45] Donne implies that the beloved's locks have the power to preserve and govern the speaker's actions because he associates her hair with the vital force that now resides in heaven. In "The Relic" Donne similarly focuses on a "bracelet of bright hair" that encircles a corpse's bone: "there a loving couple lies, / Who thought that this device might be some way / To make their souls, at the last busy day, / Meet at this grave, and make a little stay."[46] Here Donne suggests not that the couple's hair contains their souls, but that the hair-bracelet can join their souls at the end of time.

In *Paradise Lost*, Milton subtly suggests the fusion of matter and spirit that Adam and Eve's hair embodies through lines whose structure neatly matches their poetic meaning. Perhaps most obviously, Adam and Eve's spiritual marriage finds expression in the parallel constructions that describe their physical appearance: while Adam's "forelock manly hung / Clust'ring, but not beneath his shoulders," Eve "her unadornèd golden tresses wore / Disheveled, but in wanton ringlets" (IV.302–03, 305–06). This echoing gesture fits with other grammatical parallels as the couple first enter the epic – "He for God only, she for God in him" (299) and "by her yielded, by him best received" (309) – lines that enforce a hierarchy while still suggesting Adam and Eve's mutual relationship.

Milton develops this sense of reciprocity through his complex syntax. If we return to the passage in which he introduces Adam and Eve, the placement of "required with gentle sway" seems especially ambiguous:

[44] Vicary, *The Anatomie of the Bodie of Man, Part I*, pp. 26, 25.

[45] John Donne, "The Funeral," in *John Donne*, ed. John Carey (Oxford: Oxford University Press, 1990), p. 127 (lines 3, 5–8).

[46] Donne, "The Relic," in *John Donne*, ed. John Carey (Oxford: Oxford University Press, 1990), p. 130 (lines 6, 8–11).

> She as a veil down to the slender waist
> Her unadornèd golden tresses wore
> Disheveled, but in wanton ringlets waved
> As the vine curls her tendrils, which implied
> Subjection, but required with gentle sway.   (IV.304–08)

Here the simile of the vine, as Peter Demetz has shown, recalls the traditional motif of the bridal vine growing on the marital elm, a classical and Renaissance topos used to signify blissful marriage.[47] Todd Sammons adds that the passage's erotic language alludes to the counter-topos of the ivy and tree, which in Horace's and Ovid's works symbolizes an extramarital sexual relationship. The combination of topos and countertopos, Sammons claims, shows "how special prelapsarian love is" and how "Eve is just as much Adam's lover as she is his wife."[48] What has gone unnoticed, though, is that Milton enacts the reciprocity that these natural topoi imply by then inviting two seemingly contradictory readings. On the one hand, the phrase "but required with gentle sway" could describe Adam's power over Eve: as a participial modifying the "Subjection" that Eve's hair suggests, it signifies that only Adam's persuasion can prompt Eve to respond meekly – that is, her hair implies subjection, but it is a subjection that Adam alone gently elicits.[49] On the other hand, the phrase just as plausibly indicates Eve's authority over Adam: both "implied" and "required" could describe the action of Eve's "wanton ringlets" – that is, Eve's hair seems to suggest meekness, but in fact it expresses what she herself with gentle persuasion requires. In this latter case, the most likely object for the transitive "required" would elliptically be Adam's own "Subjection." Like the action of Adam and Eve's hair, the line's meaning gently sways between two opposing possibilities – either Eve or Adam requires subjection – and dramatizes the couple's mutual attraction.

Yet, as this description of Adam and Eve progresses, readers may begin to question whether Milton still literally refers to the couple's hair. The tangled syntax in the passage that introduces Adam and Eve seems to confuse hair, sex, and marriage, most notably in the series of hard

---

[47] Peter Demetz, "The Elm and the Vine: Notes toward the History of a Marriage Topos," *PMLA* 73.5 (1958): 521–32.

[48] Todd H. Sammons, "'As the Vine Curls Her Tendrils': Marriage Topos and Erotic Countertopos in *Paradise Lost*," *Milton Quarterly* 20 (1986): 117–27 (p. 120).

[49] The structure of the simile, "As the vine curls her tendrils, which implied / Subjection, but required with gentle sway" (IV.307–08), also momentarily raises the possibility that the adjectival clause ("which implied") modifies how a vine curls around itself and not how Eve's hair is shaped. But the shift in tense from historical present ("curls") back to the narrative's past ("implied") more likely indicates that the clause directly modifies Eve's ringlets.

enjambments that stretch the meaning from one line to the next –
"declared / . . . rule" (IV.300–01), "wore / Disheveled" (IV.305–06), and
"implied / Subjection" (IV.307–08). The continuation of thought
expressed by these enjambments both evokes Adam and Eve's prolonged
"amorous delay" and suggests the long tresses that they literally describe. In
like manner, the separation of subject and verb – "*She* as a veil down to the
slender waist / Her unadornèd golden tresses *wore*" (IV.304–05, emphasis
added) – dramatizes both the couple's long hair and their protracted love-
making. And, while "gentle sway" (IV.308) could signify a "mild influence"
as part of the couple's innocent flirtation, these same words also suggest a
swinging motion and thus limn the action of Eve's long hair as it gently
moves back and forth across her shoulders.

By the time readers reach the parallel clauses, "by her yielded, by him best
received" (IV.309), the description seems to have swung completely away
from the couple's hair and settled on Adam and Eve themselves. Even if
we can visualize Eve's disheveled hair as somehow expressing her innocent
desire, surely her hair does not literally yield "with coy submission, modest
pride, / And with sweet reluctant amorous delay" (IV.310–11). As in the lines
from *A Mask* that Leigh Hunt highlighted in which Milton suggests the
vigorous sexuality and generative power of Bacchus' tresses (lines 53–55), this
passage from *Paradise Lost* invisibly elides Adam and Eve's hair with their
love-making, and, perhaps, as the introduction of "waist" hints (IV.304), no
longer refers only to the hair on top of their heads.[50]

Also helping to dramatize the alliance between the couple's hair and sex
are the passage's end-rhymes. As commentators have observed, the post-
poned rhyme of "sway" and "delay" enacts the sweet reluctance of Adam
and Eve's amorous pleasure – and, I would add, the passage's elongated
construction once again may allude to the pair's long tresses. But we should
also note that the rhyme of "pride"/"implied," together with "sway"/
"delay" and the slant rhyme "waved"/"received," corresponds to a common
form of the sestet in an Italian sonnet (*cde, cde*).[51] Given that Milton
dismisses the "jingling sound of like endings" in the note on the verse
that he added to a reprint of the poem's first edition (*CPEP* 291), his
decision to incorporate the second half of a sonnet to introduce Adam and

---

[50] In the specific expression "sweet reluctant amorous delay" (IV.311), B. A. Wright has detected,
moreover, an allusion to Ovid's *Art of Love* (II.718): *sensim tarda prolicienda mora* ("gently, slowly
drawn out"). This shows, he argues, that in Milton's view "physical love is an essential and
inseparable part of human love at its best." See Wright, "Note on *Paradise Lost*, IV.310," *Notes
and Queries*, ser. 5, 203 (1958): 341.

[51] See also Erik Gray, "Severed Hair from Donne to Pope," *Essays in Criticism* 47.3 (1997): 220–39 (p. 221).

Eve seems especially meaningful. In Paradise, the poet has no need for the sonnet's octave, which typically poses a problem, or for the *volta*, which signifies a sudden change in tone or thought. In Paradise, the resolution revealed in the sestet encompasses the prelapsarian lovers' entire range of experience. Through this stanzaic allusion, Milton implies, we are witnessing the origin of all future lovers and all future love poetry.

The poetic tradition

That the embedded sestet in *Paradise Lost* focuses specifically on Adam and Eve's hair also anticipates a common conceit in Renaissance sonnet sequences. The crucial difference once again is that Milton portrays prelapsarian hair, whereas other early modern poets use the beloved's hair, as they use the sonnet, to depict love in a fallen world. By comparing Eve's hair to a vine and veil, Milton naturalizes the action of her curly tresses and evokes St. Paul's ideal that a woman's "hair is given her for a covering." In contrast, other early modern sonnet sequences emphasize the threatening, trap-like qualities of a woman's hair as a metonymy for her amorous embrace. Samuel Daniel in *Delia* (1592), for example, compares his beloved's "snary locks" with "nets ... / Wherewith my liberty thou didst surprise"; Henry Constable in *Diana* (1594) describes how his beloved captures "so many harts bound in thy haires as thrall"; and Edmund Spenser in *Amoretti* (1595) tells his beloved that only "the fayre tresses" of her "golden hayre" can "tye" his heart "with servile bands."[52] Spenser develops this idea most fully, calling attention to the ominous power of his mistress' "golden snare" with such words as "craftily," "cunningly," "entangle," "entrapped," and "fetters."[53]

I do not mean to suggest, however, that this conceit had a strictly pejorative connotation. Whereas a woman's long hair in the medieval period often signified lasciviousness, the snare metaphor, as appropriated and developed by European Renaissance writers, lost much of its moral tenor.[54] Writing about love in *The Anatomy of Melancholy* (1660), for

---

[52] Samuel Daniel, *Delia,* in *The Complete Works in Verse and Prose of Samuel Daniel,* ed. Alexander B. Grossart (1885–96; New York: Russell and Russell, 1963), sonnet 14, lines 1–2; Henry Constable, *Diana,* facsim. edn. (London, 1594; Menston, Eng.: Scolar, 1973), fourth decade, sonnet 2, line 3; and Edmund Spenser, *Amoretti,* in *"Amoretti" and "Epithalamion": A Critical Edition,* ed. Kenneth J. Larsen (Tempe, AZ: Medieval and Renaissance Texts and Studies, 1997), sonnet 73, lines 2–3. Subsequent quotations of Spenser's *Amoretti* are taken from this edition.

[53] Spenser, *Amoretti,* sonnet 37.

[54] Ungerer, "Sir Andrew Aguecheek and His Head of Hair," p. 117. Lisle Cecil John, *The Elizabethan Sonnet Sequence* (New York: Columbia University Press, 1938), adds that the comparison of hair to

example, Robert Burton sounds appreciative, not accusatory, when he describes "*the hairs*" as "Cupid's *nets, to catch all comers, a brushy wood, in which* Cupid *builds his nest, and under whose shadow all Loves a thousand several ways sport themselves.*"[55] Nevertheless, when Bassanio correctly chooses the leaden casket in *The Merchant of Venice*, we cannot help detecting a disparaging undertone: "Here in her hairs / The painter plays the spider, and hath woven / A golden mesh t'entrap the hearts of men / Faster than gnats in cobwebs."[56] Even as Bassanio praises Portia's beauty and her portrait's verisimilitude, his diction betrays a latent anxiety about his personal freedom and aptly foreshadows Portia's ring trick.

The significance of Eve's hair in *Paradise Lost* thus stems in part from what Milton does not say about it: Eve's curly locks contain no trap, no fetters. On the contrary, the description of her waving ringlets as "wanton" suggests that they are not only "robust" and "amorous" but also "free, unrestrained."[57] Her hair may have "implied / Subjection," but this subjection remains a mere implication, and, as we have seen, we cannot know whether that subjection is hers or Adam's.

Writing about the origin of literary conceits, M. B. Ogle notes that the comparison of hair to a snare does not occur in ancient literature; he offers as a likely precedent Greek and Roman poetry that casts love as a huntress who entraps lovers in a net. Ogle also observes that Greek poets sometimes depict the gaze of the beloved's eyes – not her hair – as the snare that captures the lover's heart, an idea that he traces to Alexandrian poetry and a fragment by Ibycus.[58] The first poet to modify the conceit and associate hair with a snare seems to have been Petrarch. In sonnet 197 of the *Canzoniere* Petrarch refers to Laura's "golden hair" as his soul's "curly snare" (line 9), and in sonnet 198 he describes how "with her lovely eyes and hair she binds / my weary heart and lifts my vital spirits" (lines 3–4).[59] Both of these sonnets illustrate the paradoxical status of a woman's hair in early modern love poetry: not only do the beloved's soft locks exert an

---

golden wires or sunbeams occurs as early as Lydgate (?1370–1449) and became a commonplace in Elizabethan sonnets (p. 144); he cites *The King's Quair*, Henryson, Lyndsay, and Gascoigne.

[55] Robert Burton, *The Anatomy of Melancholy*, ed. A. R. Shilleto, 3 vols. (London: George Bell and Sons, 1893), III: 92 (part iii, sec. ii, mem. ii, subs. ii).

[56] Shakespeare, *The Merchant of Venice*, ed. M. M. Mahood (Cambridge: Cambridge University Press, 1987), III.2.120–23.

[57] *OED*, s. v. "wanton," defs. A.2, 7.b, 3.c.

[58] M. B. Ogle, "The Classical Origin and Tradition of Literary Conceits," *American Journal of Philology* 34.2 (1913): 125–52 (especially pp. 129–30).

[59] Petrarch, *The Canzoniere*, trans. and ed. Mark Musa (Bloomington: Indiana University Press, 1996). In sonnet 196, Petrarch similarly writes, "in still tighter knots time wound her hair / and bound my heart with cord that is so strong / that only Death can free it from such ties" (lines 12–14).

incongruously strong hold on the poet's affection, but the poet also feels both delighted and trapped by his beloved's hair – or, as Petrarch puts it, her hair both "lifts" (*cribra*) and "binds" (*stesse lega*).

Milton in *Paradise Lost* seems keenly aware of these paradoxical implications. Introducing Adam and Eve by emphasizing something as fragile as their hair, he underscores the paradox of their strong but vulnerable position in Eden before the Fall: if the couple's luxuriant locks convey their virtue and vitality, they simultaneously symbolize how easily Adam and Eve can break God's sole command and how quickly they can lose their paradisal marriage. That this initial description of Adam and Eve's hair occurs, as we have seen, in the context of Satan's larger survey of Paradise enhances the couple's frangible state. Focusing on Adam and Eve's vital but fragile hair suggests the perspective from which Satan recognizes the power inherent in the pair's "divine resemblance" but nevertheless views the pair as "ill secured" and "Ill fenced" (IV.364, 370, 372).

Various other seventeenth-century English poets also explore the paradoxical implications of hair, but, as with Petrarch's description of Laura's golden locks, these writers specifically delight in their beloved's entrapping tresses. In "To Althea. From Prison," for example, Richard Lovelace contrasts his actual incarceration with the "Liberty" he enjoys when Althea visits: "When I lye tangled in her haire, / And fetterd to her eye," he insists, "Stone Walls doe not a Prison make, / Nor Iron bars a Cage."[60] Whereas Milton in *Paradise Lost* uses Adam and Eve's hair to depict the harmony of their spiritual and physical lives, Lovelace uses this image of entanglement to express the pleasing pain of fallen desire and to point up the disjunction between his physical and spiritual experience: he escapes his actual prison through a metaphor of erotic entrapment.

Lovelace's desire for Althea's "tangled" tresses also reflects the early modern aesthetic of *sprezzatura*, an artful nonchalance, or, as Baldesar Castiglione defined it, "art which does not seem to be art."[61] Writing about *The Book of the Courtier*, Wayne Rebhorn has explained *sprezzatura* as "an art of suggestion, in which the courtier's audience will be induced by the images it confronts to imagine a greater reality existing behind them."[62] As applied to standards of feminine beauty, this aesthetic would suggest that a woman

---

[60] Richard Lovelace, "To Althea. From Prison," in *Lucasta: Epodes, Odes, Sonnets, Songs, &c.* (London, 1649), H11r–v (lines 8, 5–6, 25–26). Subsequent quotations of Lovelace's poetry are taken from this edition and cited parenthetically.

[61] Baldesar Castiglione, *The Book of the Courtier*, trans. Charles S. Singleton, ed. Daniel Javitch (New York: Norton, 2002), p. 32 [book 1, chap. 26]).

[62] Wayne Rebhorn, *Courtly Performance: Masking and Festivity in Castiglione's "Book of the Courtier"* (Detroit: Wayne State University Press, 1978), p. 38.

with disheveled hair appears more alluring because her beauty seems effortless. The greater reality implied by her unkempt tresses includes the possibility that with effort she could look even more enticing, but it also hints at potentially promiscuous behavior: the woman who lets down her hair signals her sexual availability by conjuring up related images of preparing for bed or hurrying away from a romantic liaison. When, for example, Robert Herrick in "Delight in Disorder" catalogues the various aspects of his mistress' tousled attire – "An erring Lace," "A Cuffe neglectfull" – his moralizing diction invites us to wonder how this woman's clothes became so tousled.[63]

The paradox of *sprezzatura* arises from the care required to create an attractive carelessness: although poets say they want women who look natural, their language suggests that they actually desire some control and restraint. Thus, in "Still to be neat, still to be dressed," Ben Jonson dismisses the "adulteries of art" in favor of "Robes loosely flowing, hair as free," yet his aesthetic of "sweet neglect" may imply a manipulated or "sweetened" beauty as opposed to a genuinely carefree appearance.[64] In "To Amarantha, That She Would Dishevel Her Hair," Lovelace similarly fetishizes Amarantha's "neatly tangled" and "excellently ravelled" tresses; he implores her to "brade no more that shining haire" and to "Let it flye as unconfin'd / As it's calme Ravisher, the winde" (lines 10, 12, 2, 5–6). But for Amarantha not to braid her hair at the poet's request represents just as deliberate a style as wearing her hair in braids. Lovelace's oxymora expose the paradoxical nature of his fantasy: his desire that Amarantha's hair be tangled, but neatly, and that she look ravished, but calmly, indicates the restrictions he tries to impose on her free expression of sexuality.[65]

In *Paradise Lost*, by comparison, Milton offers a version of feminine *sprezzatura* with his description of Eve's "disheveled" curls, but he does not specifically incorporate Lovelace's ideal of calm ravishment or Jonson's notion of a "sweetened" beauty. Attempting to depict pre-lapsarian beauty, Milton evokes but then redirects the paradoxical energies that fascinate and reassure Herrick, Lovelace, and Jonson.

[63] Robert Herrick, "Delight in Disorder," *Hesperides* (London, 1648), C6v (lines 5, 7). Subsequent quotations of Herrick's poetry are taken from this edition and cited parenthetically.

[64] Ben Jonson, "Still to be neat, still to be dressed," in *Ben Jonson*, ed. Ian Donaldson (Oxford: Oxford University Press, 1985), p. 491 (lines 9, 10).

[65] While Herrick explores this same aesthetic, he approaches it with the opposite emphasis, praising his mistress' "wild civility" (as opposed to her "civil wildness"); this phrase occurs in both "Delight in Disorder" (line 12) and "Art above Nature, to Julia" (line 14). If Jonson desires sweetly neglected locks and Lovelace enjoys neatly tangled tresses, Herrick savors the merest trace of wildness in his mistress' otherwise refined appearance; he takes delight in disorder, but only when he can contain it within the strict measure of his own poetic lines.

Milton's metaphors of the hyacinth and vine, for example, illustrate the natural (as opposed to artful) quality of Adam and Eve's physical allure, and even the apparently contradictory detail that Eve's hair is "Disheveled, but in wanton ringlets waved" helps to smooth out any inconsistency in her appearance: while "but" implies a contrast, the meanings of "Disheveled" and "wanton" overlap, sounding almost synonymous. And instead of following cavalier poetic conventions and imagining Adam entangled by Eve's tresses, or Eve constrained by Adam's aesthetic demands, Milton describes the hair of both as mutually unbound – Adam's long, clustering locks, and Eve's disheveled, waving curls.

Also missing in *Paradise Lost* is the greater reality of promiscuity that disheveled hair could imply. If, as Frank Whigham has observed, the modesty of a courtier's *sprezzatura* "arouses inference in excess of the facts," in Paradise before the Fall Milton presents the facts so plainly – Adam and Eve are naked, and they have sex nightly – that readers must willfully read against the text to infer that Eve's hair indicates fallen sexual desire.[66] Her and Adam's hair naturally looks natural; she cannot have deliberately disheveled her hair because she has no knowledge, let alone means, to wear it any other way. Following God's instruction before the Fall to "till and keep" "This Paradise" (VIII.320, 319), Adam and Eve perform the "delightful task" of pruning and lopping Eden's "growing plants" (IV.437–38), but God's injunction does not seem to extend to their personal grooming. On the contrary, the Pauline prescription for men and women's appropriate hair length bases its authority on what "nature itself teach[es] you," which suggests that Adam and Eve's prelapsarian hair would naturally require no cutting or clipping. Whereas the tangled tresses of, say, Lovelace's Amarantha raise provocative questions about how and why her hair became unbraided, Adam's clustering locks and Eve's disheveled tresses precede any such possible narrative. Their hair is unadorned not by artful design but because God created them that way.

Instead of depicting the couple's artful artlessness, Milton conveys contrastively the unique innocence of Adam and Eve's marriage by once again appropriating the paradoxical presentation of women's hair in early

---

[66] Frank Whigham, *Ambition and Privilege: The Social Tropes of Elizabethan Courtesy Theory* (Berkeley: University of California Press, 1984), p. 99. Kent Lehnhof and Thomas Luxon have separately questioned – unpersuasively, I think – whether Adam and Eve have sex before the Fall. Both Lehnhof and Luxon, though, ultimately seem to reach the more modest conclusion that prelapsarian intimacy is not merely genital, a point that, I would add, the spiritual implication of the couple's hair illustrates. See Lehnhof, "'Nor Turnd I Weene': *Paradise Lost* and Pre-Lapsarian Sexuality," *Milton Quarterly* 34.3 (2000): 67–83; and Luxon, *Single Imperfection: Milton, Marriage and Friendship* (Pittsburgh: Duquesne University Press, 2005), pp. 127, 145.

modern love poetry. That the passage in which he introduces the couple concludes with the oxymoronic "coy submission" and "modest pride" does not pertain to Adam and Eve's physical appearance, but rather fits with the other seemingly contradictory descriptions of their prelapsarian experience that I discussed in the previous chapter, expressions such as "hand in hand alone" (IV.689).[67] The image of Adam and Eve's locks at their first appearance, I would suggest, not only brings together the couple synecdochically but also, prefiguring both their hand-holding and their sexual union, symbolizes the reconciliation of these apparent contradictions. As the lines of verse knit themselves into the tight, alternating pattern of an Italian sonnet, so the description of the couple's clustering and curling locks signifies the strength of their marital bond.

Throughout the epic, Milton thus continues to associate the couple's hair with their marriage. As we saw in the preceding chapter, when Eve concludes the story of how she first met Adam, she echoes the gesture of "his gentle hand / Seiz[ing]" hers (IV.488–89) by initiating the contact with her body. In another of the epic's striking visual images, she "half embracing leaned / On our first father, half her swelling breast / Naked met his under the flowing gold / Of her loose tresses hid" (IV.494–97). The parallel of Adam's gentle handclasp and Eve's leaning embrace indicates the lovers' reciprocity. That her disheveled tresses conceal and facilitate her erotic play suggests once again hair's significance for innocently joining the couple and expressing their conjugal desire. The specific detail of "flowing gold" underlines Eve's virtuous power as it figuratively complements and literally covers the eroticism of her "swelling breast."

Later, when Eve awakens from Satan's tempting dream, her hair more subtly implies the spiritual and sexual nature of her and Adam's marriage: Eve "silently a gentle tear let fall / From either eye, and wiped them with her hair" (V.130–31). Anticipating the gospel passage where a woman washes Jesus' feet with her tears and wipes them with her hair, Eve's humble gesture seems to ally her with the remorseful woman and, perhaps surprisingly, Jesus himself (Luke 7:37–38).[68] Given, as we have seen, that hair in early modern England was often associated with a person's soul, Eve's use of her own hair to wipe her tears suggests her individual power to overcome Satan's temptation.

---

[67] Surveying early modern matrimonial handbooks, John Halkett also detects in these paradoxes the "mixture of retirement, love, modesty, sense of equality, and sense of shame which the matrimonial writers attributed to the ideal wife." See Halkett, *Milton and the Idea of Matrimony* (New Haven: Yale University Press, 1970), p. 104.

[68] Milton's simile, "As the vine curls her tendrils" (IV.307), could also subtly ally Eve with Jesus, who in the Gospel of John describes himself as "the vine" (15:1–8).

More generally, analyzing the image of Adam and Eve's hair in *Paradise Lost* illustrates the value of exploring how Milton's philosophy of matter affects his depiction of material objects and physical gestures. Once again, examining the cultural context of *things* in the poem, we discover that they possess greater, spiritual significance than has previously been thought. In the specific case of hair, the image of Adam and Eve's clustering and disheveled locks not only draws on the power of hair in the early modern imagination, but, published seven years after the Restoration, also challenges the extravagant, Parisian fashions introduced at Charles II's court. As women in the late 1600s adopted increasingly elaborate coiffures – such as the aptly named hurly-burly – and men began shaving their heads to accommodate ever more sumptuous wigs, Milton's epic emphasizes his first couple's unadorned majesty. If Adam and Eve's natural, flowing hair expresses their vitality, it also highlights the vanity and triviality of seventeenth-century hair culture.

Fittingly, after Eve separates from Adam in order to garden alone, he wreathes a simple coronet "Of choicest flow'rs . . . to adorn / Her tresses, and her rural labors crown" (IX.840–41). Adam's love token once again indicates the couple's physical and spiritual power: a symbol of fecundity and a celebration of Eve's gardening, Adam's garland refocuses our attention in this decisive moment on the couple's tresses, which, we have seen, embody their marriage and, according to Raphael's plant metaphor, may represent the most spiritous and pure part of their physical selves. Simultaneously, though, Adam's garland corresponds to and is cancelled by Eve's deadly gift, for as she returns from the tree she also carries something: "in her hand / A bough of fairest fruit that downy smiled" (IX.851–52). That Adam then lets his crown fall – "From his slack hand the garland wreathed for Eve / Down dropped, and all the faded roses shed" (IX.892–93) – surely emblematizes the Fall of humankind. But, in the context of the value Milton assigns the couple's locks, the gesture of Adam's dropping the garland also suggests that he and Eve lose the physical and spiritual bond that their hair enacted. If, as Samson laments in *Samson Agonistes*, "God, when he gave me strength, to show withal / How slight the gift was, hung it in my hair" (lines 58–59), so Adam and Eve's hair contains the consecrated gift of their prelapsarian marriage and, with their Fall, it too slips from their grasp.

CHAPTER 8

Images of the future and the Son

There would seem, at first sight, to be no more in his [Milton's] words than in other words. But they are words of enchantment. No sooner are they pronounced, than the past is present and the distant near. New forms of beauty start at once into existence, and all the burial-places of the memory give up their dead.

— Thomas Babington Macaulay[1]

[O]f our conceptions of the past, we make a future.

— Thomas Hobbes[2]

Arguably the best-known image in *Paradise Lost* occurs at the end, as Michael dismisses Adam and Eve from Paradise and the couple makes its way into a fallen world. As we saw in chapter 6, the detail of Adam and Eve's handedness in the final scene — "They hand in hand with wand'ring steps and slow, / Through Eden took their solitary way" (XII.648–49) — expresses the couple's physical and spiritual re-pairing, while the description of their gait and way — "wand'ring," "slow," and "solitary" — suggests the enormous difficulties that await them and their offspring, which the archangel has foretold.

But, aside from the striking final image as Michael silently slips away and the remaining cherubim guard Paradise's gates with firey swords, critics have traditionally bemoaned the quality of the epic's conclusion — "not generally reckoned among the most shining Books of this Poem," as Joseph Addison observed in 1712.[3] C. S. Lewis also stands out as one of the final books' detractors in part because, like Addison, he was otherwise such an ardent admirer of Milton's and because Lewis so thoroughly dismissed the

---

[1] Thomas Babington Macaulay, "Milton," in *Critical and Historical Essays*, 2 vols. (London: Dent; New York: Dutton, 1951), I: 150–94 (p. 158).
[2] Thomas Hobbes, *The Elements of Law, Natural and Politic*, 2nd edn., ed. Ferdinand Tönnies (New York: Barnes and Noble, 1969), p. 15.
[3] Joseph Addison, *Criticism on Milton's "Paradise Lost,"* ed. Edward Arber (London, 1869), p. 144.

epic's concluding overview of sacred history. He called books XI and XII "an untransmuted lump of futurity," and then went further, complaining that he found the final 1,000 lines "dry," "cumbrous," and "curiously bad."[4]

Subsequent attempts to reclaim the epic's last two books – in Lewis' terms, to "transmute" the "lump" – have mostly relied on redefining Adam's development, the poem's structure, and the value and achievement of Michael's prophecy, especially in terms of typology and readers' experience.[5] F. T. Prince, to take one example, ingeniously argued that Milton exploits the process of reading any long work, which inevitably involves the "feeling of imagination satisfied ... hardly distinguishable from a loss of interest."[6] In *Paradise Lost*, Prince contends, this natural change sets off the mood and matter of books XI and XII, and highlights Adam and Eve's fallenness as the poem "for the first time begins to deal with the world as we know it."[7]

Following the thesis laid out in the preceding chapters, we might expect the epic's conclusion to be dominated by imagery of Milton's own experience. Where better for the author to draw on his lived culture than in showing us a version of "the world as we know it"? And, if God's creations in the epic may improve in their material form, so that a sinless Adam and Eve might have ultimately ascended to heaven – as Raphael explains, "from these corporal nutriments perhaps / Your bodies may at last turn all to spirit, / Improved by tract of time" (V.496–98) – we would conversely expect the couple to decline physically with their transgression and to become more visibly accessible. God thus explains in material terms to Michael that Adam and Eve must leave Paradise:

---

[4] C. S. Lewis, *A Preface to "Paradise Lost"* (1942; London and Oxford: Oxford University Press, 1961), p. 129.

[5] The narrative of the final books' critical history – an initial disparagement, followed by studious recuperative efforts – has become a commonplace of Milton studies; virtually every treatment of books XI and XII published after 1950 retraces the same plot points. Stanley Fish, writing in the mid-1980s, used this debate over the function and quality of the epic's final books to show how the critical history of any literary work should not be treated as "a record of discrete insights" but instead as "a linked and dynamic sequence of constitutive acts" enabled by political and ideological conditions (p. 251). See Fish, "Transmuting the Lump: *Paradise Lost*, 1942–1979," in *Doing What Comes Naturally: Change, Rhetoric, and the Practice of Theory in Literary and Legal Studies* (Durham and London: Duke University Press, 1989), pp. 247–93.

[6] F. T. Prince, "On the Last Two Books of *Paradise Lost*," *Essays and* Studies, n.s. 11 (1958): 38–52 (p. 50).

[7] Prince, "On the Last Two Books of *Paradise Lost*," p. 51. Prince further defended books XI and XII (again, ingeniously) on the grounds that they emulate the type of reverse *in medias res* that Homer and Virgil invented in the conclusions of their long poems: just as an epic's opening implies prior events, the conclusion hints at much more to come (p. 48).

> Those pure immortal elements, that know
> No gross, no unharmonious mixture foul,
> Eject him, tainted now, and purge him off,
> As a distemper, gross, to air as gross.   (XI.50–53)[8]

In these lines, according to the precedent of Satan and the bad angels (as discussed in chapters 4 and 5), human beings after the Fall seem to be degenerating substantially and becoming gross, less airy. Similarly, we would anticipate that the incarnate Son, on display at last in book XII, should be more physical and thus more visible than the First Created who resides in heaven at God's right hand. Given the long-standing promise made in the proem to book I – that "one greater man" will "Restore us, and regain the blissful seat" (lines 4–5) – readers could reasonably hope to glimpse the "greater man" before the epic's close.

In this final chapter, I wish to show how Milton both fulfills and defies such expectations. Whereas each of the previous chapters emphasized a visual image or motif of a single object or gesture, here I examine the various ways that Milton depicts the future through physical details. Imagery in the epic's concluding books has been addressed previously: H. R. MacCallum suggested that visual patterns – in particular, of clouds – reinforce the typological signifi-cance of Michael's prophetic vision, while Kathleen Swaim discussed how solar and vegetative images illuminate the contrast between Raphael's divine revelations and Michael's description of a "dynamic continuing process."[9] I argue instead that the epic's last angelic messenger grounds his scriptural overview in literal imagery which becomes more conspicuous in its accommodating effect when such visualizations then disappear from the second half of his prophecy. The angel's final turn from imagery to narration also means that the incarnate Son – from nativity through death and resurrection – remains mostly invisible at the end of *Paradise Lost*, an absence that Milton then fills by visually transferring the role of mediator from the Son to Michael.

---

[8] Here I am following A. W. Verity's modern punctuation, which I think clarifies the passage's meaning. See Milton, *Paradise Lost*, ed. Verity, 2 vols. (1910; Cambridge: Cambridge University Press, 1934), I: 314.

[9] H. R. MacCallum, "Milton and Sacred History: Books XI and XII of *Paradise Lost*," in *Essays in English Literature from the Renaissance to the Victorian Age Presented to A. S. P. Woodhouse*, ed. Millar MacLure and F. W. Watt (Toronto: University of Toronto Press, 1964), pp. 149–68; and Kathleen M. Swaim, *Before and After the Fall: Contrasting Modes in "Paradise Lost"* (Amherst: University of Massachusetts Press, 1986), pp. 47–90 (p. 89).

Visual learner

Even before the angel Michael begins his biblical picture-show, Milton emphasizes Adam and Eve's visual experience. Adam thinks that he *sees* God's receptiveness to the couple's prayers – "Methought I saw him placable and mild, / Bending his ear" (XI.151–52) – and, as discussed in chapter 2, Adam and Eve also have their Fall and punishment confirmed by a series of natural "signs" (XI.182). The sky grows dark, an eagle swoops onto "birds of gayest plume" (XI.186), and a lion chases a deer and dog, "a gentle brace, / Goodliest of all the forest" (XI.188–89). Adam likewise laments his impending departure from Paradise because he will be denied the sight of God's former environs:

> This most afflicts me, that departing hence,
> As from his face I shall be hid, deprived
> His blessed count'nance; here I could frequent,
> With worship, place by place where he vouchsafed
> Presence divine, and to my sons relate,
> "On this Mount he appeared, under this tree
> Stood visible, among these pines his voice
> I heard, here with him at this fountain talked." (XI.315–22)

Not only does this response to Michael's news that the couple must leave Paradise cast the loss of divine contact in largely visual terms ("As from his face I shall be hid"), but also Adam mourns a mode of visual learning similar to the one that, I have been arguing, Milton himself pursues. The theological lessons that Adam wishes he could share with his offspring would depend on remembered sightings, just as Milton in writing his epic theodicy seems to draw on visual recollections of his own world.

That Michael then informs Adam and Eve about their descendants through a series of connected images of the fallen world recalls a style of presentation used in some early modern paintings, altar pieces, and printed illustrations: these depictions of history often combine various episodes in a single composition, what C. A. Patrides called "continuous narration."[10] Yet many of the specific details in the scenes that Michael presents to Adam seem wholly original; they have no imagistic parallels in Milton's source texts and, as Roland Frye has shown, they also have no "rewarding analogues" in the visual tradition.[11] Surveying European pictorial narratives

---

[10] C. A. Patrides, *The Grand Design of God: The Literary Form of the Christian View of History* (London: Routledge and Kegan Paul; Toronto: University of Toronto Press, 1972), p. 53.

[11] Roland Mushat Frye, *Milton's Imagery and the Visual Arts* (Princeton: Princeton University Press, 1978), p. 298.

of Hebrew Scriptures and the New Testament, Frye concluded that portrayals of Adam and Eve after the Fall "are not uncommon" in Western art, but he deemed the uniqueness of some of Milton's images "extraordinary in the extreme."[12]

I wish to stress here two points: one, that Milton (pace Lewis) did transmute the sacred history that his angel foretells; and, two, that Milton did so – as we have seen in different ways in the preceding chapters – by braiding details from his biblical sources with allusions to his contemporary culture. The resulting images once again accommodate seventeenth-century readers and help to make the story Milton's own. Thus, the angel Michael offers a compelling description of the flood that never appears in Genesis:

> the south wind rose, and with black wings
> Wide hovering, all the clouds together drove
> From under Heav'n; the hills to their supply
> Vapor, and exhalation dusk and moist,
> Sent up amain; and now the thickened sky
> Like a dark ceiling stood; down rushed the rain
> Impetuous, and continued till the earth
> No more was seen; the floating vessel swum
> Uplifted, and secure with beakèd prow
> Rode tilting o'er the waves, all dwellings else
> Flood overwhelmed, and them with all their pomp
> Deep under water rolled; sea covered sea,
> Sea without shore.   (XI.738–50)

While early modern travel books might have provided the background for such imagery, Milton, as J. B. Broadbent first proposed, could have observed flooding almost anywhere – a garden in Hammersmith, a steep mew in London, or a poorly drained country road.[13] At least two large-scale floods occurred in Britain in the years when Milton began composing *Paradise Lost*. In 1651, a "great and terrible Inundation of Water" caused the Thames to overflow Lower Deptford, Ratcliff Marshes, and Greenwich's Meadows; and in 1655, the rivers of Trent, Dove, and Severn overflowed their banks and reportedly "swept away many heads of Cattle, as Horses, Cows, Hogs, and sheep, who floting [*sic*] so far as strength would support them, at last perished in the turbulent streams."[14] Admittedly, Milton could have been influenced by published reports of these catastrophes or

[12] Frye, *Milton's Imagery and the Visual Arts*, pp. 298, 302.
[13] J. B. Broadbent, "Milton's Paradise," *Modern Philology* 51.3 (1954): 160–76 (p. 163).
[14] *A True Relation of the Great Terrible Inundation of Waters* (London, 1651), A1r; and *The Sad and Dismal Year. Or, England's Great and Lamentable Flood* (London, 1655), A2v–A3r.

by a more closely related poetic account that scholars have yet to discover; the final phrase, "Sea without shore," for example, echoes Ovid's diction in *Metamorphoses*, "*deerant quoque litora ponto*."[15] But, the cumulative effect of the convincing details in the depiction of Noah's watery cataclysm suggests that its principal source was more immediate than a description that Milton had read. The wind's "black wings / Wide hovering," the "thickened sky / Like a dark ceiling," or the simplicity of "the earth / No more was seen" – all of these visual details sound as if they benefit from direct observation.

Even the first, relatively straightforward image that Michael shows Adam – a "field, / Part arable and tilth" (XI.429–30) – seems to reflect Milton's contemporary culture. In contrast to the terse narrative in the Bible, which tells us only that "Abel was a keeper of sheep, but Cain was a tiller of the ground" (Gen. 4:2), Milton brings the two brothers' story before readers' eyes; he shows us a "sweaty reaper" and a "More meek" shepherd making sacrifices on a "Rustic" altar of "grassy sward" (XI.433–34, 437). The angel also dramatizes Cain and Abel's differences through the image of divided land: on one side "were sheaves, / New reapt, the other part sheep-walks and folds" (XI.430–31). This image of the land's mixed character, the combining of the arable and pastoral, corresponds to a real agrarian practice that emerged in England in the late fifteenth and early sixteenth centuries.[16] As the country's manorial system of agriculture gradually vanished, owners divided lands that had once been used exclusively for crops into fields for both livestock and planting. The dramatic increase in English sheep-farming during Milton's lifetime also encouraged land-holders to adopt a system known as convertible or up-and-down husbandry: fields were divided into arable and pasture lands, as in Milton's image, and then alternated in subsequent years so as to provide a convenient form of fertilizer and to reduce the strain on the soil.[17]

Especially the phrase "sheep-walks and folds" alludes to early modern animal husbandry. Sheep-walks, as the name suggests, were tracts of grass for pasturing sheep. *The Oxford English Dictionary* records the first use of

[15] Ovid, *Metamorphoses*, trans. Frank Justus Miller, rev. G. P. Goold, 3rd edn. (Cambridge: Harvard University Press, 1977), I. 292 (p. 22).

[16] Peter Bowden, "Agricultural Prices, Farm Profits, and Rents," in *The Agrarian History of England and Wales*, 7 vols., gen. ed. Joan Thirsk (Cambridge: Cambridge University Press, 1967–2000), IV: 593–695 (pp. 654–55); and Ordelle G. Hill, *The Manor, the Plowman, and the Shepherd: Agrarian Themes and Imagery in Late Medieval and Early Renaissance English Literature* (Selinsgrove: Susquehanna University Press; London and Toronto: Associated University Press, 1992), pp. 129–30.

[17] *Studies of Field Systems in the British Isles*, ed. Alan R. H. Baker and Robin A. Butlin (Cambridge: Cambridge University Press, 1973), pp. 389–90; Hill, *The Manor, the Plowman, and the Shepherd*, p. 129; and Christopher Taylor, *Fields in the English Landscape* (Gloucestershire: Sutton, 2000), pp. 119, 133.

sheep-walk in print about eighty years before the publication of *Paradise Lost*. In *The Description of England* (1586), William Harrison complains that towns were repeatedly "pulled downe for sheepe-walks" – that is, he explains, the land was "converted in such sort from the furniture of mankind, into the walks and shrowds of wild beasts."[18] Three years after the first edition of Milton's epic, John Evelyn in *Sylva, or A Discourse of Forest-Trees* (1670) similarly uses the term to make a practical point about contemporary planting and shepherding. Among the various ways that Evelyn offers "for improving of *Sheep-walks, Downs, Heaths, &c.*," he proposes that land-owners should plow up twenty-acre plots, each of which would serve for keeping 500 sheep, and then sow the land with fruit and nut trees – a division of use that echoes Milton's image of Cain and Abel's partitioned field.[19]

In all such instances, Milton's visual details seem influenced, consciously or unconsciously, by the contemporary more than the classical, by the observed more than the biblical or literary. Once again, memory or published accounts such as Harrison's could have informed the epic's imagery, but regardless of how Milton's contemporary culture found its way into the poem's prophetic visions, Milton was adapting episodes from Genesis by incorporating topical concepts and images. If the author's political opposition to kingship during the civil wars helped him to imbue Satan's rebellious rhetoric with passion and conviction, so Milton's more mundane cultural experiences seem to have informed and enhanced the final books' quotidian descriptions.

Yet, more important than the mere inclusion of contemporary images in Michael's picture-show – and they continue so that, for example, Adam also sees an early modern blacksmith draining "liquid ore . . . / Into fit molds prepared" (XI.570–71) – the angel's visual survey of biblical history in book XI is notable for its literalness. Whereas Milton imagines Satan's followers in hell building the "ascending pile" of Pandemonium from

---

[18] William Harrison, *The Description of England*, in Ralph Holinshed, *Chronicles* (London, 1586), vol. II, chap. 19, p. 205. Slightly earlier, in 1549, Hugh Latimer used the shorter term *walk* in one of his sermons to signify "land, or a tract of land used for the pasture of animals." See *OED*, s. v. "walk, n.1," def. III.14; and Latimer, *The Fyrste Sermon of Mayster Hughe Latimer, whithe [sic] He Preaced before the Kynges Maiest* (London, 1549).

[19] John Evelyn, *Sylva, or A Discourse of Forest-Trees*, 2nd. ed. (London, 1670), Ff4v (chap. XXXIV). George Bomford Wheeler's use of sheep-walk in his "literal translation" of Virgil's *Georgics* is misleading. According to Wheeler's translation, Virgil encourages readers to reject a white ram with a black tongue and "look out for another over the well-stocked sheep-walk" (book III, lines 389–90). But the Latin word here is *campo*, which simply means "field" and does not literally refer to the English "sheep-walk." See Wheeler, trans., *A Literal Translation of the Works of Virgil* (London: William Tegg, 1853), p. 63.

molten gold – from "veins of liquid fire" – now, after the Fall, a real blacksmith works less grandly to create tools from brass and iron (I.722, 701). Critics such as Addison and Lewis might have found Michael's sacred overview aesthetically deficient in part because it is more direct than, say, the metaphorical imagery that reveals the bad angels' appearance or the allusive depiction of Adam and Eve that appropriates cultural and poetic assumptions about hair and hand-holding. Book XI still includes a few allusions and metaphors: most notably, Adam and Eve in their improving demeanors resemble the devout couple Deucalion and Pyrrha from Ovid's *Metamorphoses*, and the "amorous net" spread by the "bevy of fair women" who seduce the race of Cain (XI.586, 582) recalls the tradition of erotic entrapment discussed in the preceding chapter. Yet most of the images that Michael presents to Adam remain insistently literal: Milton draws on his and his readers' actual experience so as to anticipate actual details about Adam and Eve's descendants.

We read in Genesis, for example, that Jubal, one of Cain's lineage, was "the father of all such as handle the harp and organ" (4:21), and Milton in *Paradise Lost* then portrays a musician who literally handles a harp and organ, two instruments that had ancient Greek precursors but which were popular in seventeenth-century England.[20] Whereas earlier Milton had described the building of Pandemonium by comparing the devils' conveyance of melted gold into "each hollow nook" with the way "in an organ from one blast of wind / To many a row of pipes the soundboard breathes" (I.707–09), now after the Fall the representation of the organ has become literal. As Adam hears a "melodious chime" and "resonant fugue," the player "who moved / Their stops and chords was seen," and Milton

---

[20] During the Commonwealth period, organs were removed from both college and parishes churches, and the instruments were sold, hidden, or partially or totally destroyed. An ordinance dated 9 May 1644 prohibited music in divine worship except for the singing of psalms and stipulated "that all Organs, and the Frames or Cases wherein they stand in all Churches or Chappels aforesaid, shall be taken away, and utterly defaced." With the Restoration, however, enthusiasm for organs "revived in a bewildering burst," and "it became a matter of prestige to dignify sanctuaries, meeting places, and even homes with them." One organ, built in 1637 and initially housed in Magdalen College, Oxford, evidently escaped the 1644 ordinance and was moved to Hampton Court Palace by order of Oliver Cromwell sometime between 1654 and 1660. Milton, according to tradition, played on this organ; as one early biographer, John Aubrey, recorded, Milton "had an Organ in his house: he played on that most." See "An Ordinance for the Further Demolishing of Monuments of Idolatry and Superstition," in *Acts and Ordinances of the Interregnum, 1642–1660*, ed. C. H. Firth and R. S. Rait (London: Her Majesty's Stationery Office, 1911), pp. 425–26; James Boeringer, *Organa Britannica: Organs in Great Britain 1660–1860*, 3 vols. (Lewisburg: Bucknell University Press; London and Toronto: Associated University Press, 1983), I: 27; Cecil Clutton and Austin Niland, *The British Organ* (London: B. T. Batsford, 1963), p. 5; Stephen Bicknell, *The History of the English Organ* (Cambridge: Cambridge University Press, 1996), p. 104; and *The Early Lives of Milton*, ed. Helen Darbishire (London: Constable, 1932), p. 6.

spotlights the musician's nimble fingers, the "volant touch" that moved "Instinct through all proportions low and high" (XI.559–63). The difference in style between the two passages – the shift from the metaphorical in hell to the literal in the fallen world – reflects the epic's changing subject: through most of *Paradise Lost*, Milton strives to depict the unseen and unseeable, but with the prophetic visions in the final books he turns to a remote yet more recognizable world. The resulting inclusion of literal images also subtly suggests the diminishment that marks and is caused by humankind's Fall. If readers experience an emotional letdown as the epic draws to a close, it may stem in part from the flattening effect of dwindling metaphor and the final books' relative straightforwardness.

Even images without clear connections to Milton's experience or culture are remarkable for their literalness. The Bible states, for example, that "Cain rose up against Abel his brother, and slew him" (Gen. 4:8), and the visual tradition that grew up around the story mostly depicted the murder weapon as a club or an animal's jawbone.[21] In book XI, however, Michael shows Adam that the reaper Cain confronted the shepherd Abel and "Smote him into the midriff with a stone" (line 445). This version of events recalls the imagery in Abraham Cowley's *Davideis*. More than twenty years earlier, Cowley also depicted Cain murdering his brother with a rock, but in *Davideis* Cain "fling[s] the *stone*" at Abel, which Cowley immediately converts into a symbol, "as if he meant, / At once his *Murder*, and his *Monument*."[22] By comparison, Milton's stony image remains literal and, in its awkward violence, seems to me more disturbing. Although some Judaic exegesis also refers to Cain's weapon as a stone, midrash expositors claim that Cain struck Abel in the forehead.[23] Milton's unique image is probably easier for readers to picture than to understand: how do you "beat out life" from someone by throwing a rock into the person's midriff (XI.446)? If the image has symbolic significance, it derives from the way "midriff" might focus attention on Abel's navel and thus his status as Adam and Eve's offspring – a point which Michael then underscores: "These two are brethren, Adam, and to come / Out of thy loins" (XI.454–55). But Milton in this scene mostly emphasizes the brother's physical act of

[21] Frye, *Milton's Imagery and the Visual Arts*, p. 302.

[22] Abraham Cowley, *Davideis*, in *Poems* (London, 1656), Aaaa4v. In *Milton's Imagery and the Visual Arts*, Frye notes that the image of Abel's murder in *Paradise Lost* is also supported by representations in the visual arts but only "by an extraordinarily narrow stream" of this tradition – namely, Byzantine caskets made of ivory that date between the tenth and twelfth centuries (p. 303). We don't know whether Milton had ever seen such ivories.

[23] Golda Werman, *Milton and Midrash* (Washington, DC: Catholic University of America Press, 1995), p. 227.

violence and so continues to concentrate on its literal, visual qualities: we read how "gushing blood effused" from Abel's wound, for example, and how "deadly pale" he fell to the ground (XI.446–47).

The hospital full of suffering patients that Michael then shows Adam also appears to be literal, but here Milton more clearly draws on his experience in early modern London. The angel reveals to Adam, "A lazar-house it seemed, wherein were laid / Numbers of all diseased, all maladies" (XI.479–80). Although the specific choice of "lazar-house" might have recommended itself to Milton because of the allusion to the biblical beggar Lazarus, which could subtly anticipate the incarnate Son (Luke 16:19–31), the term more specifically refers to a type of hospital for treating leprosy which was founded in medieval times and continued to operate in seventeenth-century England. In *A Survey of London* (1603), John Stow devotes a section to "of Leprose people, and Lazar houses" and counts five such establishments in and around the city.[24] The modern historian F. P. Wilson refers more generally to "various lazar-houses" in the vicinity of London during the 1600s; we know, for example, that two were connected to St. Bartholomew's Hospital near West Smithfield, a neighborhood where Milton resided between May and August 1660.[25] In the summer of 1603, the masters of the city's lazar houses evidently presented a petition, now lost, in which they objected to the practice of sending patients with plague to them, but, as historians note and as Milton's passage also indicates, lazar houses by the start of the seventeenth century admitted people with all kinds of chronic illnesses, not just leprosy.[26]

Milton goes on to describe these patients' maladies and symptoms with almost clinical precision:

> Of ghastly spasm, or racking torture, qualms
> Of heart-sick agony, all feaverous kinds,
> Convulsions, epilepsies, fierce catarrhs,
> Intestine stone and ulcer, colic pangs,
> Demoniac frenzy, moping melancholy
> And moon-struck madness, pining atrophy,
> Marasmus, and wide-wasting pestilence,
> Dropsies, and asthmas, and joint-racking rheums.   (XI.481–88)

---

[24] John Stow, *A Survey of London*, 2nd edn. (London, 1603), Kk2r–v.

[25] F. P. Wilson, *The Plague in Shakespeare's London*, 2nd edn. (Oxford: Oxford University Press, 1963), p. 81.

[26] Norman Moore, *The History of St. Bartholomew's Hospital*, 2 vols. (London: C. Arthur Pearson, 1918), II: 296.

Certainly literary tradition may have influenced such imagery. Dick Taylor first detected a precedent, for example, in Guillaume de Saluste Du Bartas' more expansive troop of ills in *Le Sepmaine* (1578) – Cankers, Colick, Dropsie, Thirst, and so on – which collectively represent the army of the Fury Sickness.[27] But, unlike Du Bartas' allegorical catalogue, Milton's illnesses are literal; we're invited, along with Adam, to see the suffering of the many patients lying in the seeming lazar-house so that we can appreciate the terrible consequences of Adam and Eve's disobedience. That Milton added three lines to this list of diseases – one of only six such substantive revisions between the epic's first and second editions[28] – suggests the importance that he attached to the catalogue. The added diseases graphically emphasize the horrible physical suffering that the Fall will bring.

When Adam then asks Michael a follow-up question about death, whether "there yet [be] no other way, besides / These painful passages" (XI.527–28), the angel offers another dismal image:

> Thy youth, thy strength, thy beauty . . . will change
> To withered weak and gray; thy senses then
> Obtuse, all taste of pleasure must forgo,
> To what thou hast, and for the air of youth
> Hopeful and cheerful, in thy blood with reign
> A melancholy damp of cold and dry
> To weigh thy spirits down, and last consume
> The balm of life.　　　　　　　　　　　　　(XI.539–46)

Here Milton might have had in mind some of the language in Cicero's essay *On Old Age*, but once again the force of the description suggests that Milton was writing from his own experience. Suffering from painful fits of gout and having witnessed the death of his father at age eighty-five, Milton need not have researched the effects of aging: he knew firsthand about its hardships. More important, Michael's vision of senescence, like

[27] Dick Taylor, Jr., "Milton's Treatment of the Judgment and the Expulsion in *Paradise Lost*," *Tulane Studies in English* 10 (1960): 51–82 (p. 63).

[28] For the second edition of *Paradise Lost* (1674), Milton restructured his epic according to the *Aeneid*'s twelve-book model. He thus divided the original book VII into books VII and VIII and the original book X into books XI and XII. He also added eight lines (VIII.1–3; XII.1–5), revised one line (VIII.4), and fixed or enhanced three other substantive passages in addition to the list of diseases (I.504–05, V.636–41, XI.551). Other comparatively minor changes (approximately thirty-seven) made between the first and second edition might or might not have been authorial. See R. G. Moyles, *The Text of "Paradise Lost": A Study in Editorial Procedure* (Toronto: University of Toronto Press, 1985), pp. 21–28. I also discuss these changes in Dobranski, "Editing Milton: The Case against Modernization," in *The Oxford Handbook of Milton*, ed. Nigel Smith and Nicholas McDowell (Oxford: Oxford University Press, 2009), pp. 480–95 (pp. 482–83).

the list of maladies, both illuminates the horror of death and paradoxically limits its potency. Whereas at the start of *Paradise Lost* Milton had allegorized Death as "The other shape, / If shape it might be called that shape had none" (II.666–67), here he uses Michael to present the "many shapes / Of Death" (XI.467–68). The threat of death, though still "many," seems lessened by becoming known and defined. Similarly, in John Donne's *Holy Sonnet 6*, the speaker tells a personified death to "be not proud" in part because he can mark out the scope of its power: "Thou art slave to fate, chance, kings, and desperate men, / And dost with poison, war, and sickness dwell."[29] Earlier in *Paradise Lost*, Milton also depicts specific types of death, as we saw with the image of the "waves" that "o'erthrew / Busiris and his Memphian chivalry" when they attempted to pursue the Israelites across the Red Sea (I.306–07) or the reference to "that Serbonian Bog / . . . / Where armies whole have sunk" (II.592–94). But these and the epic's many other fatal allusions appear as the vehicles of metaphors, whereas the "many shapes" from the fallen world that Michael shows Adam are not just horrible, but unrelentingly literal. As with the calcifying forms of Satan and the bad angels, the Fall again finds expression in the solidifying of shapes and the dwindling of metaphor.

In the case of Paradise, Milton suggests a similar sense of loss by showing how God will strip away prelapsarian splendor. The scenes of Adam and Eve before the Fall lavish attention on the couple's "blissful bower" (IV.690), depicting it much more vividly than, say, the colorful but generic "tents of various hue" (XI.557) belonging to Cain's descendants that Michael reveals to Adam. Thus we read how the bower's

> roof
> Of thickest covert was inwoven shade
> Laurel and myrtle, and what higher grew
> Of firm and fragrant leaf; on either side
> Acanthus, and each odorous bushy shrub
> Fenced up the verdant wall; each beauteous flow'r,
> Iris all hues, roses, and jessamine
> Reared high their flourished heads between, and wrought
> Mosaic; underfoot the violet,
> Crocus, and hyacinth with rich inlay
> Broidered the ground, more colored than with stone
> Of costliest emblem.   (IV.692–703)

---

[29] John Donne, *Holy Sonnet 6* ("Death be not proud"), in *John Donne*, ed. John Carey (Oxford: Oxford University Press, 1990), pp. 175–76 (lines 1, 9–10).

While critics have discussed natural, poetic, and biblical sources for the poem's rich flower imagery, I wish to emphasize the abundance and specificity of the bower's floral design. Just in this short passage, Milton includes "Laurel," "myrtle," "Acanthus," "Iris," "roses," "jessamine," "violet," "Crocus," and "hyacinth."[30] The succession of hard enjambments in these lines also dramatizes the garden's fecundity; the meaning in almost every verse stretches into the next like a vine's groping tendrils.

By comparison, as Michael informs Adam and Eve after the Fall that they must depart Paradise, the angel succinctly describes how the mountain on which he and Adam stand will turn into a desert island:

> then shall this mount
> Of Paradise by might of waves be moved
> Out of his place, pushed by the hornèd flood,
> With all his verdure spoiled, and trees adrift
> Down the great river to the op'ning gulf,
> And there take root an island salt and bare,
> The haunt of seals and orcs, and sea-mews' clang.   (XI.829–35)

Again, enjambment conveys a sense of movement, but here the emphasis falls on displacement, not exuberant growth, as Paradise, like Adam and Eve, will "be moved / Out of his place" and set "adrift / Down the great river." More notable, the simple image of "an island salt and bare" contrasts sharply with Edenic splendor, in particular the bower's overgrown foliage. If "bare" describes a loss of vegetation, "salt" augments the image's desolation by hinting that the briny soil will prevent prelapsarian plants from ever regrowing. Eve had presciently imagined such a loss when Michael first announced that she and Adam must leave Paradise: "O flow'rs, / That never will in other climate grow" (XI.273–74). But Eve implies that the plants will wither because of her absence: "Who now shall rear ye to the sun, or rank / Your tribes, and water from th' ambrosial fount?" (XI.278–79). Michael's image, by comparison, suggests an inherent physical deterioration. Whereas Adam and Eve before the Fall enjoyed tremendous freedom and mutual companionship, now the land itself is

---

[30] Critical discussion of Milton's Paradise has become an industry unto itself. See, for example, A. Bartlett Giamatti, *The Earthly Paradise and the Renaissance Epic* (Princeton: Princeton University Press, 1966), pp. 295–330; John R. Knott, Jr., *Milton's Pastoral Vision: An Approach to "Paradise Lost"* (Chicago: University of Chicago Press, 1971), pp. 109–26; Charlotte F. Otten, "'My Native Element': Milton's Paradise and English Gardens," *Milton Studies* 5 (1973): 249–67; Diane Kelsey McColley, *Milton's Eve* (Urbana: University of Illinois Press, 1983), pp. 115–19; and Karen L. Edwards, *Milton and the Natural World: Science and Poetry in "Paradise Lost"* (Cambridge: Cambridge University Press, 1999).

rooted, isolated, and haunted, and its barrenness reverberates in the reduction of "Paradise" to a nameless "island."

All of these contrastive images once again help to dramatize the world's fallenness so as to drive home the real consequences of Adam and Eve's disobedience. Even Eden's prelapsarian menagerie – the "unwieldy elephant," "bended dolphins," "tawny lion," "swift stag," and "scaly crocodile" (IV.345; VII.410, 464, 469, 474) – has been reduced to a few monstrous and noisy scavengers – seals, orcs, and sea-mews. And although Paradise's spoiled verdure may symbolize the many trials that Adam and Eve's descendants will now confront, the metaphorical has again calcified to the literal. Satan in hell, as we saw in chapter 4, resembles "that sea beast / Leviathan" (I.200–01), but here the beast has become an actual orc, most often identified as a killer whale, while the evocative "soft lays" (VII.436) and "amorous descant" (IV.603) of the prelapsarian nightingale, that "wakeful bird" with which the poet in his blind inspiration identified (III.38), has been superseded after the Fall by the shrill cries – the "clang" – of gulls or sea-mews.

Incarnate and invisible

The sense of loss and diminishment in Michael's sacred overview increases as the angel then abandons the visual altogether to summarize the next 2,200 years of biblical history. Although Addison, faulting the turn to narration in the poem's final book, conjectured that Milton would have found it too difficult "to have shadowed out so mixt and complicated a Story in visible Objects," later critics have more often defended the lack of imagery in book XII.[31] Wayne Shumaker, for example, argued that Michael's new, narrative tactic allows Milton to admit "more judgmental phrases" that consistently give a "recountal human warmth" to the angel's descriptions; and David Loewenstein has traced a deliberate demythologizing pattern whereby books I–X are superseded first by *tableaux* in book XI, then by book XII's tragic narrative of human history.[32] Perhaps most persuasively, Jameela Lares has attributed the poem's change in mode to a prevailing homiletic tradition.

---

[31] Addison, *Criticism on Milton's "Paradise Lost,"* p. 145. For similar explanations, see Dunster in *The Poetical Works of John Milton*, ed. Henry John Todd, 2nd edn., 7 vols. (London: J. Johnson, 1809; New York: AMS Press, 1970), IV: 377–78; and H. Stebbing, ed., *The Complete Poetical Works of John Milton* (New York: Daniel Appleton, 1843).

[32] Wayne Shumaker, *Unpremeditated Verse: Feeling and Perception in "Paradise Lost"* (Princeton: Princeton University Press, 1967), p. 218; and David Loewenstein, *Milton and the Drama of History: Historical Vision, Iconoclasm, and the Literary Imagination* (Cambridge: Cambridge University Press, 1990), pp. 91–125.

Following the two-part structure of some early modern sermons, Michael first uses imagery to foment feelings of sorrow, then turns to narration and the protoevangelium to console Adam.[33]

One apparently unfortunate consequence of the final book's narrative style is that Milton renders the story of Jesus with less force and emotion than he depicts the earlier image-laden scenes from Genesis. Even within book XII, Michael's lengthy account of Nimrod and the Tower of Babel eclipses the angel's succinct overview of the Messiah's life. Literal-minded readers could be forgiven for agreeing with Milton's former student, Thomas Ellwood, an earnest, 26-year-old Quaker, who after perusing a manuscript copy of *Paradise Lost* in 1665, claimed to have asked the author, "Thou hast said much here of *Paradise lost*, but what hast thou to say of *Paradise found?*"[34] In the end, Michael repeats that the Son will "bruise" the enemy's head through "Obedience" and "by obedience and by love" (XII.391, 397, 403), but largely absent from the angel's prophecy are specific details of the Son's incarnation and the redemption that he achieves through suffering.[35]

Critics have traditionally explained the epic's relatively brief account of the incarnate Son in terms of reformed religious practices. A reformist author such as Milton might have found the subject of Christ's suffering "distasteful," as Roy Flannagan puts it, because the Crucifixion was associated with Catholic iconography.[36] Contempt for external signs of worship in favor of inward acts of the spirit as well as the rejection of the doctrine of real presence presumably contributed to the difficulty that English writers after the Reformation experienced in representing the body of Christ. In particular, early modern religious verse tends to dwell more on authors' inability to respond appropriately to the Crucifixion than on Christ's actual sacrifice.[37] George Herbert, for example, increasingly

---

[33] Jameela Lares, "*Paradise Lost*, Books XI and XII, and the Homiletic Tradition," *Milton Studies* 34 (1996): 99–116.

[34] Thomas Ellwood, *The History of the Life of Thomas Ellwood*, ed. S. Graveson, with an intro. by W. H. Summers (London: Headley Brothers, 1906), p. 199.

[35] Michael also refers to "thy great Deliverer, who shall bruise / The serpent's head" (XII.149–50); "that destined seed to bruise / The serpent" (XII.233–34); the "One greater" than Moses, the "great Messiah" (XII.242, 244); "Some blood more precious . . . paid for man" (XII.293); "His name and office bearing who shall quell / The adversary serpent" (XII.311–12); and the figure "of the royal stock / Of David . . . / A son, the woman's seed to thee foretold" (XII.325–27).

[36] Roy Flannagan, *The Riverside Milton* (Boston: Houghton Mifflin, 1998), p. 50.

[37] See Michael Schoenfeldt, "'That Spectacle of Too Much Weight': The Poetics of Sacrifice in Donne, Herbert, and Milton," *Journal of Medieval and Early Modern Studies* 31.3 (2001): 561–84. More specifically, Dick Taylor, surveying hexameral and dramatic works that depict Adam and Eve's expulsion from the garden, concluded that in earlier treatments the Messiah is "mentioned so briefly, or so abstractly" and the tone is almost always "harsh and grim, without much mitigation or hope." See Taylor, "Milton's Treatment of the Judgment and the Expulsion in *Paradise Lost*," p. 70.

portrays Christ in *The Temple* as an abstract participant in an internal dialogue – a friend, a whisperer, or, finally, Love itself.[38] Donne, by comparison, literally and figuratively averts his gaze from the face of Christ in such devotional poems as "Good Friday, 1613. Riding Westward" and "A Hymn to Christ, at the Author's Last Going into Germany." In the latter poem, the speaker can see God's face only in "disguise" and concludes, "Churches are best for prayer, that have least light: / To see God only, I go out of sight."[39] This aphoristic formulation suggests that the speaker cannot experience God through imagery but instead must prayerfully isolate himself and shut his eyes.

In *Paradise Lost*, Milton's treatment of the incarnate Son seems similarly oblique. After Michael explains that the Son can save Adam and Eve's descendants by "coming in the flesh" and enduring their punishment (XII.405), the angel describes the Son's suffering, death, and resurrection in a fast fifteen lines:

> For this he shall live hated, be blasphemed,
> Seized on by force, judged, and to death condemned
> A shameful and accursed, nailed to the cross
> By his own nation, slain for bringing life;
> But to the cross he nails thy enemies,
> The law that is against thee, and the sins
> Of all mankind, with him there crucified,
> Never to hurt them more who rightly trust
> In this his satisfaction; so he dies,
> But soon revives, Death over him no power
> Shall long usurp; ere the third dawning light
> Return, the stars of morn shall see him rise
> Out of his grave, fresh as the dawning light,
> Thy ransom paid, which man from death redeems,
> His death for man. (XII.411–25)

This concise account contains little visual imagery, and its few concrete details soon fade into abstractions. The body "nailed to the cross" almost immediately becomes a symbol of retribution, the "cross" on which the Messiah figuratively "nails thy enemies"; and the "stars of morn" that witness how the Son will "rise / Out of his grave" are outshone in the same line by the resurrected Son's figurative illumination, "fresh as the dawning light."

---

[38] See Judith Irvine, PhD dissertation, "Christ in Speaking Picture: Representational Anxiety in Early Modern English Poetry" (Georgia State University, 2014).

[39] Donne, "A Hymn to Christ, at the Author's Last Going into Germany," *John Donne*, pp. 283–84 (lines 5, 29–30).

Living in seventeenth-century London, Milton must have had ample knowledge of corporal punishment. If he enhanced the scenes that Michael initially shows Adam with visual details from early modern culture, certainly Milton could have also applied firsthand observations about violent forms of justice to a visual depiction of the Son's suffering on the cross. Public executions by hanging occurred regularly in England in the early modern period, sometimes attracting crowds of more than 2,000. J. A. Sharpe offers the "conservative estimate" that, in London alone, 150 felons were hanged each year during the reign of James I, which means that by the age of fifteen Milton could have attended more than 2,250 executions.[40] Other forms of corporal punishment such as pillorying and whipping were also commonly doled out until the late eighteenth century, and historians note that it was "not unknown" for angry crowds to stone to death men who had been pilloried for sodomy or the rape of a child.[41] After the Restoration, Milton, though blind, must have known of the brutal retributive justice suffered by his friends and collaborators for their opposition to the monarch. In 1661, the newsbook *Mercurius Publicus* lauded the "glorious memory" of the punishment inflicted on the bodies – the "odious Carcasses" – of Oliver Cromwell (who died in 1658), Henry Ireton (who died in 1651), and John Bradshaw (who died in 1659). On 30 January 1661, the anniversary of Charles I's execution, the three men's corpses were "pull'd out of their Coffines and hang'd at the several angles of that Triple Tree, where they hung till the Sun was set; after which they were taken down, their heads cut off, and their loathsome Trunks thrown into a deep hole under the Gallows."[42] The common hangman subsequently set the heads on poles on the top of Westminster Hall.

Perhaps influenced by a culture that tolerated and sometimes celebrated such horrible spectacles, Milton in his other works returns to graphic images of bodily suffering. Especially the Chorus' description of corporal punishment in *Samson Agonistes* seems informed by the aftermath of the civil wars. Samson's friends complain that God abandons those whom he has "solemnly elected" (line 678) and "Oft leav'st them to the hostile sword / Of heathen and profane, their carcasses / To dogs and fowls a

---

[40] J. A. Sharpe, *Crime in Early Modern England, 1550–1750*, 2nd edn. (London and New York: Longman, 1999), p. 92; and Philip Jenkins, "From Gallows to Prison? The Execution Rate in Early Modern England," *Criminal Justice History* 7 (1986): 51–71 (pp. 54–61).

[41] John Briggs, Christopher Harrison, Angus McInnes, and David Vincent, *Crime and Punishment in England* (New York: St. Martin's, 1996), p. 78.

[42] *Mercurius Publicus*, 24–31 Jan. 1661 (London, 1661), H4v.

prey, or else captíved" (lines 692–94). But even much earlier, Milton in his poetry and prose often incorporates images of mythic violence. In *Lycidas* he imagines how "the rout that made the hideous roar" dismembered Orpheus and sent "His gory visage down the stream" (lines 61–62).[43] Or, in *Areopagitica*, he appropriates the story of Osiris and personifies truth as a dismembered virgin. Milton wants English men and women who will persevere in their reading, "imitating the carefull search that *Isis* made for the mangl'd body of *Osiris*" by "gathering up limb by limb" the "dissever'd peeces" of Truth "scatter'd" in books (*CPW* II: 549, 550–51).

Given such disturbing somatic imagery, and given the violent punishments that all early modern English citizens would have witnessed, John Rumrich has concluded that the lack of imagery accorded the Passion and Crucifixion in Milton's works probably indicates the author's sense of decorum, not his diffidence: "we should not think it odd that he never found the public execution of Jesus to be a congenial subject for poetry. It would be frightening if he had."[44] Not only does Milton understate the suffering of the incarnate Son in *Paradise Lost*, but he also left his early poem "The Passion" unfinished as the speaker becomes increasingly entangled in images of thwarted representation, and in *Paradise Regained* Milton focuses on Jesus' temptation in the wilderness instead of the sacrifice on the cross. Such limited portrayals of the incarnate Son's suffering might also reflect Milton's deep-seated resistance to an Augustinian concept of self that emphasizes an individual's unworthiness. Milton in the autobiographical digressions in his works, as Stephen Fallon has shown, stresses his exceptional virtue, not his sin.[45] The poet accordingly may have downplayed the Passion because it points to humanity's depravity and implies dependence on Christ for liberation.[46]

Yet the incarnate Son's relative invisibility in *Paradise Lost* extends beyond the lack of imagery for his suffering and death. Even if Milton had reason for not depicting the Passion and Crucifixion, he could have found ways to visualize the Son's "Poor fleshly tabernacle," as he more fully describes the Messiah's body in both "The Passion" (line 17) and *Paradise*

---

[43] As we saw in the previous chapter, the version of *Lycidas* in the Trinity College Manuscript contains an alternative, equally graphic image: Orpheus' "goarie scalpe." See *John Milton Poems Reproduced in Facsimile from the Manuscript in Trinity College, Cambridge* (Menston, Eng.: Scolar Press, 1970).

[44] John Rumrich, "Milton's *Theanthropos*: the Body of Christ in *Paradise Regained*," *Milton Studies* 42 (2002): 50–67 (p. 58).

[45] Stephen M. Fallon, *Milton's Peculiar Grace: Self-Representation and Authority* (Ithaca and London: Cornell University Press, 2007).

[46] See James Holly Hanford and James G. Taaffe, *A Milton Handbook*, 5th edn. (New York: Appleton-Century-Crofts, 1970), p. 115.

Regained (IV.599).[47] "The Passion," unfinished and deeply flawed, nevertheless offers a compelling vision of the Son at the moment of his incarnation. He humbly enters his corporal host, "stooping his regal head / That
dropped with odorous oil down his fair eyes" (lines 15–16), an image that
conflates weeping and baptism so as to suggest the relation between
Christ's abasement and humankind's renewal.

Milton's earlier poem "On the Morning of Christ's Nativity" also
visually depicts the Incarnation as an act of humiliation. In the stanzas
preceding the section labeled "Hymn," Milton describes how the Son
relinquishes "the courts of everlasting day" so that he can settle in a
"darksome house of mortal clay" (lines 13–14). The subsequent images in
the Hymn support this pattern of abasement – from light to dark, and
from "courts" to a single "house" – by underscoring Christ's vulnerable
corporality. Milton does not include a complete portrait of the infant
Messiah, but instead offers a limited, synecdochic representation: we
glimpse the "smiling" babe "All meanly wrapped" (lines 151, 31) as well
as "his blessèd feet" (line 25), "swaddling bands" (line 228), and the
"dreaded infant's hand" (line 222). This final paradoxical image neatly
captures the poem's larger visual strategy; just as the small child embodies
divine power – able to intimidate a long list of false gods merely by raising
his tiny hand – so the ode's brief physical descriptions contain the
magnitude of the Son's glory. The Hymn thus concludes with another
striking image encapsulating the paradox of the hypostatic union: we first
see Christ's tender humanity as "the virgin blest, / Hath laid her babe to
rest" (lines 237–38), but the poem quickly tracks back to reveal the latent
power of the infant's divine nature, as "all about the courtly stable, /
Bright-harnessed angels sit in order serviceable" (lines 243–44).

The same paradox informs much of the imagery in Milton's "Upon the
Circumcision," although this poem, as the title indicates, more emphatically focuses on Christ's physical shape. On the one hand, Milton – like
Richard Crashaw, Robert Herrick, Francis Quarles, and George Wither –
was participating in a broad artistic and poetic tradition of celebrating
the Feast of the Circumcision, a liturgical calendar day that typically
took place on 1 January. On the other hand, that Milton chose this
particular event and wrote another poem about Jesus' somatic experience
suggests the author's ongoing fascination with the Son's corporality. In
"Circumcision," Milton once again relies on synecdoche to dramatize the
idea of divinity confined in a finite form. Specifically, a brief image of the

---

[47] Milton appropriated this metaphor of the human body as a tabernacle from the Bible: see 2
Corinthians 5:1, and 2 Peter 1:13–14.

surgical wound in the first verse prefigures Christ's tremendous redemptive sacrifice:

> He who with all Heav'n's heraldry whilere
> Entered the world, now bleeds to give us ease;
> Alas, how soon our sin
>   Sore doth begin
>   His infancy to seize! (lines 10–14)

The second verse paragraph again visualizes the Son's enormous achievement in limited, somatic terms: "for us frail dust" he "Emptied his glory, ev'n to nakedness" (lines 19–20) and "seals obedience first with wounding smart" (line 25). Clearly the stress in both sets of lines falls on bodily suffering – the infant "bleeds," feels "Sore," and experiences "nakedness" and a "wounding smart." But all of these physical details point to the infant's simultaneously divine achievement as Milton attempts to connect surgical pain with both the Son's glory in heaven and his future salvific suffering.

That Milton focuses this poem on the human act of circumcision, as opposed to Christ's sacrifice on the cross, might anticipate the poet's mature theology and his emphasis on the redemptive efficacy of each individual's virtuous obedience.[48] But while Milton as a young poet mostly still portrayed Christ in accordance with an orthodox view of the Trinity – in the Nativity Ode, for example, he envisions the Son sitting at "Heav'n's high council table" in "trinal unity" (lines 10–11) – by the time that Milton composed *Paradise Lost* he had come to espouse a heretical, Arian concept of the Son.[49] The author did not go as far as the Socinians who held that Christ was "a mere man" (*CPW* VI: 419), but he no longer thought that a "begotten" Son could be co-eternal, co-essential, and self-existent. As Milton repeatedly asserts in *De Doctrina Christiana*, "nothing can be said of the one God that is inconsistent with his unity, and which makes him both one and not one" (*CPW* VI: 148). Thus, in *Paradise Lost*, Milton dramatizes the Son's heroic volunteering to die for humankind (not the Son's passive acceptance of death on the cross), because, as Gregory Chaplin has argued, Milton understood the Messiah primarily as an

---

[48] So argues John Rogers, "Milton's Circumcision," in *Milton and the Grounds of Contention*, ed. Mark R. Kelley, Michael Lieb, and John T. Shawcross (Pittsburgh: Duquesne University Press, 2003), pp. 188–213.

[49] On Milton's Arianism, see Maurice Kelley, "Milton's Arianism Again Considered," *The Harvard Theological Review* 54.3 (1961): 195–205; and Michael Bauman, *Milton's Arianism* (Frankfurt and New York: P. Lang, 1986).

embodiment of divine obedience (not as God himself).[50] The Son's willingness to empty himself, the *kenosis*, represents the type of heroism that
Milton believed available to all of God's creations – including the Son as
the First Created – all of whom must actively collaborate with God's will
and strive to reflect God's glory.[51]

Yet, even as Milton rigorously pursued a rational approach to scripture
and disavowed the orthodoxy that the Son shared God's essence, the
author maintained a remarkably consistent position on the paradox of
Christ. Milton continued to believe that the incarnate Son somehow
contained a "mutual hypostatic union of two natures, . . . of two essences,
of two substances and consequently of two persons" (*CPW* VI: 424). And,
uncharacteristically, Milton accepted the Incarnation as a mystery: "As
God has not revealed to us how this comes about it is much better for us to
hold our tongues and be wisely ignorant" (*CPW* VI: 424).

Milton goes on to reason in *De Doctrina Christiana* that Christ, posses-
sing two persons, did not embody a generic human nature at the
Incarnation. Instead, Milton argues, Christ existed as an ordinary human
being, "[f]or human nature, that is, the form of man contained in flesh,
must, at the very moment when it comes into existence, bring a man into
existence too, and a whole man, with no part of his essence or his
subsistence (if that word signifies anything) or his personality missing"
(*CPW* VI: 422). This belief in the inseparability of human nature and
manhood would seem to invite a visual representation of the incarnate Son.
In arguably the best example of the complex fusion of matter and spirit that
informs much of the imagery in *Paradise Lost*, the hypostasis of the
Messiah, simultaneously divine and human, should manifest itself not
only in "his essence or his subsistence" but also in his corporal shape. As
with the imagery of hands and hair that expresses Adam and Eve's spiritual
and physical marriage, or the metaphorical and metonymic imagery that

---

[50] Gregory Chaplin, "Beyond Sacrifice: Milton and the Atonement," *PMLA* 125.2 (2010): 354–69. By
comparison, Erin Henriksen, *Milton and the Reformation Aesthetics of the Passion* (Leiden and
Boston: Brill, 2010), argues that Milton did not omit the subject of Christ's suffering from his
prose and poetry but instead portrayed what she calls an "alternative passion" that "redirects our
attention to the incarnation and even the pre-incarnate Christ" (pp. 67, 69).

[51] Bryan Adam Hampton also discusses Milton's emphasis on striving toward divinity, which
Hampton connects to what he identifies more broadly as an "Incarnational poetics" that shaped
Milton's works as well as the writings of some of his radical contemporaries. Hampton argues that
the paradox of the Incarnation – the combining of the human and divine – not only served as an
aspirational model for imitating God but also helped to shape theories of reading and preaching.
Language during the seventeenth century was thus thought to be a practical means of effecting
transformation and helping readers and auditors to achieve divine participation in their everyday
lives. See Hampton, *Fleshly Tabernacles: Milton and the Incarnational Poetics of Revolutionary
England* (Notre Dame, IN: University of Notre Dame Press, 2012).

helps to dramatize Satan and the bad angels' ontological and moral decline, so a visual representation of the Son on earth should capture his uniquely double nature as a god-man. Milton in *De Doctrina Christiana* rejects alternative explanations of Christ's appearance – that his divine form was destroyed at the Incarnation, that his human form was destroyed, or that Christ had two external forms. Instead, Milton explains, "if the divine nature and the human nature coalesced in one person, that is to say, . . . in a rational being numerically one, then they must have coalesced in one external form as well" (*CPW* VI: 424). Any images of this "one external form" in *Paradise Lost* would accordingly have to reflect the Son's double union – that is, both spiritually and physically – as god and man.[52]

But if the appearance of the Son on earth provided a marvelous opportunity for Milton to explore the theological implications of his heterodox monist philosophy, in *Paradise Lost* he demurs, and the angel Michael, as we have seen, relates the Incarnation only briefly and with almost no visual details. Perhaps Milton's reticence grew out of a commitment to veracity and his respect for the Incarnation as a singular mystery. How could he hope to describe more fully the historical, yet divine figure of the Messiah without introducing something that was potentially untrue? As Stephen Fallon has argued, "*Paradise Lost* stands out among seventeenth-century long poems for its attention to the truth of not only its central themes, but also its myriad details."[53] Or, perhaps because the Bible already includes considerable visual detail about the Nativity, Passion, and Crucifixion, Milton chose not to add more. At the start of *Paradise Regained*, the poet announces that he wants to write what is missing, "to tell of deeds / Above heroic, though in secret done, / And unrecorded left through many an age, / Worthy t' have not remained so long unsung" (I.14–17). By comparison, the four Gospels so vividly record Jesus' birth, death, and resurrection that Milton might have decided in *Paradise Lost* to focus instead on the Son's heroic *kenosis*. Perhaps Milton thought that Jesus' life and suffering had already been adequately sung.

Instead, *Paradise Lost* includes more, direct visual imagery of the Son's heavenly figure than his earthly form. Raphael refers to the Son's "right hand" and "puissant thigh" during the war in heaven (VI.835, 714), and both the angel and epic narrator frequently describe the Son's countenance in the divine council. On the final day of the war, for example, Raphael lingers on the Son's angry expression, "too severe to be beheld / And full of wrath bent on his enemies" (VI.825–26), and when the Son volunteers to

---

[52] See also Rumrich, "Milton's *Theanthropos*," p. 59.
[53] Fallon, *Milton among the Philosophers* (Ithaca: Cornell University Press, 1991), p. 163.

die for humankind, the narrator notes that "his meek aspect / Silent yet spake, and breathed immortal love / To mortal men, above which only shone / Filial obedience" (III.266–69). All of these visual details of the First Created's visage hint at his exalted position in heaven, for he repeatedly embodies God's emotions. As Milton explains in *De Doctrina Christiana*, the Son had existed "in the beginning, under the title of the Word or Logos," which Milton describes as the "word by which God is audible," and only later was the Son granted his role as the "image . . . by which God becomes visible" (*CPW* VI: 206, 297). In *Paradise Lost*, this change in status – from "Word" to God's "image now proclaimed" (V.784) – is marked by the Son's exaltation as God's "right hand," and as the "Lord" and "head" of the angels (V.606, 608), the appointment that both leads to Satan's rebellion and prefigures the Son's earthly incarnation.[54]

Yet, even in the position as the "radiant image" of God's "glory" (III.63), the Son in heaven remains at best an indistinct figure. When God addresses the exalted First Created, he calls him, "Son beloved, / Son in whose face invisible is beheld / Visibly, what by deity I am" (VI.680–82). This highly compressed syntax suggests that in the Son's face God (the "invisible") can be apprehended ("beheld / Visibly"). But Milton's inverted word order also momentarily implies that the Son's face is invisible ("Son in whose face invisible is beheld") – which, literally, it is, because the Son expresses something that Milton never describes. Unlike God, the Son in heaven may have a "conspicuous count'nance, without cloud" (III.385) – and, as we earlier read, "in him all his Father shone / Substantially expressed" (III.139–40) – but just what the Son's face looks like, in heaven or on earth, Milton does not presume to know.

Still, the Son's role as "divine similitude" (III.384), along with his status as humanity's "Patron or intercessor" (III.219), justifies Milton's indirect representation of the incarnate Son in *Paradise Lost*. Instead of a synec-dochic portrayal, as we saw in the poet's early Christic lyrics, Milton now relies on typological substitution, a form of mediation that enacts the Son's own role as divine mediator, both in heaven and on earth. H. R. MacCallum was among the first to discuss how the Pauline and Augustinian emphasis on "lonely men of faith" represents the "dominant feature" of Milton's typology in the epic's concluding books.[55] Beginning

---

[54] Rumrich, "Milton's *Theanthropos*," p. 56. On the relation between the Son's begetting and the Incarnation, see Albert C. Labriola, "'Thy Humiliation Shall Exalt': The Christology of *Paradise Lost*," *Milton Studies* 15 (1981): 29–42 (p. 33).

[55] MacCallum, "Milton and Sacred History: Books XI and XII of *Paradise Lost*," p. 158. See also Prince, "On the Last Two Books of *Paradise Lost*," p. 45.

with Enoch ("daring single to be just," XI.703), Michael's overview of sacred history repeatedly returns to the image of the righteous individual – Noah, Abraham, Isaac, Jacob, Joseph, Moses, Aaron, David, and Solomon. Collectively, these isolated men lend cohesion to the angel's scriptural account and, more importantly, they prefigure the Messiah, with whom Michael's prophecy naturally culminates. But, as I will show in the final section of this chapter, it is the archangel Michael himself who emerges as the exemplary "shadowy type" at the end of *Paradise Lost* (XII.303). Milton in books XI and XII primarily depends on his own angel to signify the incarnate Son.

Angelic surrogate

To understand Milton's indirect visual strategy for depicting the Messiah, we need to return to the explanation that Michael gives for abandoning imagery in favor of narration. Michael, we should remember, proves to be a "gentle angel" (XI.421). Holding a spear and wearing both a "military vest" and sword, he may look "solemn and sublime," not "sociably mild, / As Raphael" (XI.241, 234–36). But the epic's final messenger nevertheless acts with tenderness and compassion, responding with "sweet new speech" when Adam falters (XII.5) and ultimately "In either hand" catching "Our ling'ring parents" and leading them to Paradise's eastern gate (XII.637–38).

Even when Michael first arrives in the garden, he takes into account Adam and Eve's fallen state. Whereas Raphael had approached the pre-lapsarian couple in his heavenly form – as Adam announces, a "glorious shape / Comes this way moving; seems another morn / Ris'n on mid-noon" (V.309–11) – Michael instead greets the sorrowful pair "Not in his shape celestial, but as man" (XI.239). The distance between these two angelic images – "seems . . . morn" and "as man" – measures the decline in Adam and Eve since their sin: the vision of a supernatural midday sunrise is replaced by the familiar reflection of the couple's own less perfect forms. The narrator explains that Adam would have seen that Michael, too, was "A glorious apparition, had not doubt / And carnal fear that day dimmed Adam's eye" (XI.211–12). Yet we should not assume that Michael entirely conceals his majesty. Adam can perceive that the visitor is a highly ranked angel; he just cannot ascertain Michael's exact position in heaven's hierarchy. Thus he tells Eve,

> I descry
> From yonder blazing cloud that veils the hill
> One of the Heav'nly host, and by his gait
> None of the meanest, some great potentate
> Or of the Thrones above, such majesty
> Invests him coming.   (XI.228–33)

Here Adam serves in part as stage manager, helping readers to visualize the epic's unfolding action, but the passage also highlights the angelic messenger's great stature and Adam's perceptiveness. Just as moments earlier Adam ably interpreted the three natural signs that limn his and Eve's imminent punishment, he clearly understands the significance of Michael's heavenly appearance and gait.

The sartorial metaphor in the subsequent phrase – that Michael comes forward "as man / Clad to meet man" (XI.239–40) – suggests that the angel has temporarily chosen a human shape so as to address the fallen couple. If, as I have argued, some of the literal images in the first part of Michael's biblical survey accommodate the poem's seventeenth-century readers, now Milton dramatizes a literal act of accommodation. Because Adam and Eve's sight has been "dimmed" by "doubt / And carnal fear," in other words, Michael, like the Messiah, voluntarily adopts the form of a man. The specific metaphor of "clad" echoes the language of earlier, patristic authorities who described the Incarnation as an act of dressing, God's becoming "clothed with flesh" and "clothed with manhood."[56]

In contrast, Raphael before the Fall had dined with Adam and Eve, warned them of Satan's threat, and told long stories of the war in heaven and the world's creation. But the "sociable spirit" (V.221) still consistently set himself apart from the first couple through his physical presence. When Raphael alights in Paradise, as we saw in chapter 5, he immediately resumes his "proper shape ... / A Seraph" with six pairs of wings "to shade / His lineaments divine" (V.276–78), and even earlier, speeding toward earth, "to all the fowls he seems / A phoenix, gazed by all" (V.271–72). Both of these descriptions emphasize Raphael's preternatural resplendence. Compared to all of the birds in Paradise, Raphael resembles a unique creature, winged and incandescent, naturally an object of rapt fascination whom Adam thus doubts can even eat the same food as humans.

That Michael instead forgoes his heavenly form as he converses with Adam and Eve suggests the angel's importance for the biblical history that he then relates. Of celestial appearance and gait but cladding himself "as

---

[56] See, for example, Tertullian, *Treatise on the Incarnation*, ed. Ernest Evans (London: SPCK, 1956), pp. 11, 39 (sections 3, 10).

man," the angel more than any of the figures in his narrative helps to prepare Adam and the poem's readers for the idea of the incarnate Son. When, accordingly, Michael finally introduces the idea of a messiah whose mother is "A virgin ... but his sire / The power of the Most High" (XII.368–69), Adam never questions the mystery of the Incarnation. Instead, he rejoices to learn that "God with man unites" and readily accepts that from his own "loins" the virgin mother "shalt proceed" and from "[her] womb the Son / Of God Most High" (XII.380–82). Adam has been conversing at length with "One of the Heav'nly host" who appears "as man" and whose name literally means "as God"; why should he now doubt the efficacy of another type of divine–human union?

The imagistic promotion of Michael as a Christic surrogate also fits the antitrinitarian bias of Milton's mature theology. The angel's active acceptance of God's mission dramatizes the availability of virtuous obedience for all of God's created, not just the Son. Already in book VI, Milton had established the precedent for allying Michael and the First Created; in the Judeo-Christian tradition, Michael engages in eternal combat with Satan – see, for example, the Books of Daniel and Revelation – but Milton instead replaces the archangel with the Son as the devil's opponent on the third day of the war. Now, at the end of the epic, Milton effects a substitution in the other direction so that Michael stands in for Christ – not as a redeemer, but instead as the kind of figure that Milton came to understand the Son to represent, namely, a guide and model in striving to reflect God's glory. Thus, when God gives Michael instructions – "this my behest have thou in charge" (XI.99) – the angel immediately acts: "[God] ceased; and th' archangelic power prepared / For swift descent" (XI.126–27). Ultimately, as Michael explains to Adam, the Son will fulfill "The law of God exact ... / Both by obedience and by love, though love / Alone fulfill the law" (XII.402–04). The angel himself in executing his divine mission already embodies these twin ideals: he obediently follows God's commands and, in doing so, shows compassion for the fallen couple.

Near the end of *Paradise Lost*, Michael concludes his long prophecy, and we learn that Eve has also been informed visually of future events. As she tells her husband, "For God is also in sleep, and dreams advise, / Which he hath sent propitious, some great good / Presaging" (XII.611–13). This reference to Eve's prophetic dream seems to return the epic to the imagery that distinguished the first part of the angel's sacred overview and prepares readers for the visual emphasis in the concluding scene as the angel departs. Michael's benign intervention also counterbalances Satan's earlier corrosive intrusion into Eve's unconscious while qualifying Eve's claims of subordination to Adam: her apparently comparable share of visual knowledge suggests equal protection under God's law. Eve's last statement sounds hopeful as she looks forward to the Messiah's redemption – "By me the promised seed shall all restore" (XII.623) – but she offers no additional details, visual or otherwise, about the incarnate Son.[57] Instead, Milton continues to focus on the angel as the epic's Christic surrogate, instructing and attending to the couple.

In *Lycidas*, Milton had also used an image of the archangel Michael to provide resolution and point the way to redemption. As the uncouth swain in Milton's monody tries to imagine what happened to the body of his friend who drowned at sea, he wonders whether Lycidas has sunk "under the whelming tide" somewhere "beyond the stormy Hebrides" (lines 156–57) or whether he might have washed up in Bellerium (that is, whether he now "Sleep'st by the fable of Bellerus old," line 160). The swain then directly addresses Michael, the patron saint of, appropriately, both mariners and Cornwall: "Look homeward angel now, and melt with ruth. / And, O ye dolphins, waft the hapless youth" (lines 163–64). This image of the protecting angel, mourning the loss of Lycidas and turning his gaze inward and away from possible outside threats, forecasts the epic's concluding image of the archangel as a compassionate Christic surrogate. But whereas the swain in *Lycidas* calls on a school of dolphins to convey the shepherd's body safely to land – Milton links the angel's compassion with a traditional symbol of resurrection through the snap of a couplet – now at the end of *Paradise Lost* Michael himself brings the sorrowful first parents safely out of Paradise:

> In either hand the hast'ning Angel caught
> Our ling'ring parents, and to th' eastern gate
> Led them direct, and down the cliff as fast
> To the subjected plain; then disappeared.   (XII.638–40)

In contrast to the extended syntax in the first, long sentence ("In either hand . . . the subjected plain"), the brevity of "then disappeared," set off by a strong caesura, jolts readers into recognizing how suddenly Adam and Eve find themselves alone together and how quickly Michael once again acts – "hast'ning," "caught," "direct," and "fast." They also serve who do not stand and wait.

Moreover, the image of the vanishing angel completes the final two books' trajectory of diminishment, beginning, as we have seen, with the

---

[57] *Seed* occurs often at the end of the epic: Milton uses the word four times before the Fall, and twenty-three times after Adam and Eve disobey God (books X–XII) – twelve times in the final book alone.

loss of metaphor and continuing through the removal of visual detail in favor of narration. Finally, as with the swift ascent of Jesus in scripture (Luke 24:50–53, Mark 16:19, Acts 1:9), the angel is gone, and the couple must now rely on each other as they make their way haltingly toward the future that the angel has not only foretold but providentially embodied.

CHAPTER 9

Postscript

When Adam asks Raphael about the creation of the world – "how," "When," "whereof created," and "for what cause" (VII.62–64) – the archangel genially complies but prefaces his remarks by emphasizing the difficulty of his task and the limitations set on Adam and Eve. The couple, Raphael explains, can attain "knowledge within bounds" but must "beyond abstain / To ask, nor let thine own inventions hope / Things not revealed, which th' invisible King, / Only omniscient, hath suppressed in night" (VII.120–23). Raphael's conditional reply might recall the images of heaven's responsive gates and barriers, as discussed in chapter 3, and suggest once again the paradox of divine accessibility and God's unknowableness. In this scene, Raphael gladly tries to satisfy Adam's curiosity about creation but then refuses to answer a follow-up question about the configuration of the earth and sun.

Yet Milton himself in *Paradise Lost*, as the preceding chapters have shown, seems to ignore the divine stricture that Raphael here sets forth. If humankind can attain knowledge only "within bounds," then Milton for his own purposes appears to have redefined those limits: he repeatedly relies on his "own inventions" to illuminate "Things not revealed" in the epic's scriptural source text. Such imagistic innovation, I have argued, not only builds on works by Milton's peers and predecessors, but was also shaped in important ways by the author's firsthand experiences and cultural circumstances.

Thus, the Bible offers a simple account of God creating "the beast of the earth after his kind, and cattle after their kind, and every thing that creepeth upon the earth after his kind" (Gen. 1:25). But Milton in *Paradise Lost* envisions an extraordinary, almost cinematic scene of spontaneous generation as the animals paw and climb out of the earth:

> The grassy clods now calved, now half appeared
> The tawny lion, pawing to get free
> His hinder parts, then springs as broke from bonds,

Figure 9.1 Raphael Sanzio, *The Creation of the Animals*, 1518–1519. Fresco.

> And rampant shakes his brinded main; the ounce,
> The libbard, and the tiger, as the mole
> Rising, the crumbled earth above them threw
> In hillocks; the swift stag from under ground
> Bore up his branching head: scarce from his mold
> Behemoth biggest born of earth upheaved
> His vastness: fleeced the flocks and bleating rose,
> As plants. (VII.463–73)

How could readers of such a passage doubt Milton's visual imagination? Samuel Taylor Coleridge first proposed that the scene resembles the depiction of an emergent bear, elephant, and unicorn in the painting "The Creation of the Animals," one of fifty-two frescoes that the artist Raphael designed for the Loggia in the Vatican, which Milton could have seen during his Grand Tour (see figure 9.1).[1] Martin Evans alternatively offered the possible influence of a similar scene of earth-born animals in Dracontius' fifth-century *Carmen do Deo*; Harinder Singh Marjara detected a possible mythic allusion to the classical earth mother, Gaia or Tellus, who gives birth to God's creations from her fecund womb; and

---

[1] Samuel Taylor Coleridge, *Table Talk* (7 August 1832), in *Coleridge on the Seventeenth Century*, ed. Roberta F. Brinkley (Durham: Duke University Press, 1955), p. 598. Coleridge mistakenly identified the scene as part of the Sistine Chapel.

Karen Edwards, in the spirit of my own method, suggested that Milton's original image could have benefited from firsthand knowledge of exotic felines.[2] Lions, for example, were fairly common animals in early modern Europe, and various other cats – lynxes, tigers, and ounces – were popular displays at the Tower of London beginning in medieval times.

But also notable in Raphael's description of the animals' earthly generation is the way that Milton frames his astonishing description with two comparatively mundane images – of a rodent crawling out of a hole and plants emerging from soil. The use of such familiar things grounds and thus enhances the epic's more marvelous inventions. Even seventeenth-century readers with little knowledge of lions, tigers, and behemoths, or entirely unaware of the passage's classical or artistic precedents, could still have visualized with wonder the animals of Paradise springing up and clawing out from the dirt. As the preceding chapters have attempted to show, the combination of the mythic and real, the literary and the observed, helps to make the poem's imagery powerful.

Yet Raphael's evocative warning to Adam about "knowledge within bounds" could also apply more generally to an imagistic study such as the one that I have undertaken in this book. In addition to the risk of constructing an overarching visual pattern that crushes distinctions among a diverse group of scenes – as M. H. Abrams once cautioned, "The danger is, that the pattern may be largely an artifact of the implicit scheme governing the critical analysis"[3] – imagist critics run the risk of imposing their own cultural assumptions onto a text and envisioning the imagery in terms of their own experience. I have accordingly tried to respect the dramatic and verbal bounds of each of the images that I have examined, often concentrating on individual passages instead of aspiring to harvest the text for a crop of like images. And I have attempted to guard against my inevitable subjectivity by insisting on Milton's own cultural and historical circumstances as the bounds for interpreting the poem's diverse visual depictions.

In pursuing the latter strategy and emphasizing the relation between Milton's observation and imagination, I may seem to have attributed too much artistry to Milton. Did the author of *Paradise Lost* deliberately appropriate contemporary objects or attitudes to depict the epic's unseen

[2] J. M. Evans, *"Paradise Lost" and the Genesis Tradition* (Oxford: Clarendon, 1968), pp. 127–28; Harinder Singh Marjara, *Contemplation of Created Things: Science in "Paradise Lost"* (Toronto: University of Toronto Press, 1992), p. 214; Karen L. Edwards, *Milton and the Natural World: Science and Poetry in "Paradise Lost"* (Cambridge: Cambridge University Press, 1999), p. 230.

[3] M. H. Abrams, "Five Types of *Lycidas*," in *Milton's "Lycidas": The Tradition and the Poem*, ed. C. A. Patrides (Columbia: University of Missouri Press, 1983), pp. 215–35 (p. 225).

characters and deeds? Would he have agreed in principle with modernist arguments against abstraction and believed that artistic expression without reference to real things loses its drama?[4] Certainly, as I have shown, Milton followed out the implications of his heterodox theory of matter and conceived images that capture both the physical appearance and spiritual significance of a wide range of ideas and figures. But the imagistic practices that *Paradise Lost* deploys need not have emerged consistently out of a calculated poetic style. While the manifest self-concern that Milton exhibits in much of his poetry and prose would suggest that his contemporary experience never drifted too far from his consciousness, I do not mean to turn Milton into, say, James Joyce, assembling and transmuting his personal observations into a narrative of Homeric proportions. Instead, Milton's epic reveals an author whose cultural context sometimes had a subtle effect on his imagery, which might or might not have been on purpose. Adam and Eve's European hair and fair coloring, for example, presumably reflect a Western bias instead of a deliberate poetic decision. Confronting such an audacious subject as the Fall of humankind, Milton would naturally have begun, consciously or unconsciously, with things he had read *and* things he had seen.

Yet, for an author who had been suffering from eye problems since 1644 and who lost his remaining sight in 1652 – fifteen years before the publication of *Paradise Lost* – some of the things Milton had seen were probably distant memories; in some places, what I have called his firsthand observations must have been largely or exclusively a remembrance of things past, powerful images recollected in tranquility. This broader subject – memory and perceptions of the past – has emerged as a scholarly field unto itself in the more than three decades since Keith Thomas' influential Creighton Lecture, "The Perception of the Past in Early Modern England."[5] At a time when written and printed documents were becoming more important and more widespread, the mental faculty of memory remained an indispensable quality of social existence for both individuals and communities, although it was rarely treated as definitive and instead came to complement written records, which were also acknowledged as susceptible to error.[6] In the case of Milton, the choice to write an epic – traditionally, the most capacious

---

[4] *Letters of the Great Artists from Ghiberti to Gainsborough*, ed. Richard Friedenthal, 2 vols. (New York: Random House, 1963), II: 256–57.

[5] Keith Thomas, *The Perception of the Past in Early Modern England* (London: University of London, 1983).

[6] Andrew Gordon, *Writing Early Modern London: Memory, Text, and Community* (New York: Palgrave, 2013), pp. 1–10; and Daniel Woolf, *The Social Circulation of the Past: English Historical Culture, 1500–1730* (Oxford: Oxford University Press, 2003), pp. 271–83.

and comprehensive genre – might have encouraged him to think of his poem as, in part, an archive, preserving not just the world's history but also its present knowledge, including cultural and personal recollections of his contemporary world. Given that objects and visible details were, as historians have shown, a primary means for sustaining popular memory in early modern England, Milton might have been conditioned from an early age to turn to such imagery as a way of representing his own experience and incorporating it into his epic.[7]

To develop further the potential significance of personal observation and recollection for Milton's visual imagination would require the examination of additional scenes and objects from *Paradise Lost* and a fuller engagement with his other writings. Much good, early scholarship focused on the image clusters and patterns in Milton's poetry, such as the aquatic, floral, and stellar images that dominate *Lycidas*, and the even wider range of visual depictions in *Samson Agonistes* – of animals, prisons, ships, and storms, for example – which comment on the moral position of the drama's principal characters.[8] More recent critics, anticipating the approach in this book, have expanded and deepened the discussion of Milton's imagery by reconstructing aspects of his history and culture. Lawrence Lipking, for example, has argued that geographical images in *Lycidas* help to challenge the conventions of pastoral elegy while participating in a burgeoning discourse about national identity; Malabika Sarhar has proposed that Satanic images of stars and comets in *Paradise Lost* demonstrate Milton's disillusionment with millennial hopes after the Restoration; and I have suggested elsewhere that images from early modern publishing advance *Areopagitica*'s argument against pre-publication censorship by reminding Parliament of the collaborative creation of books.[9]

As further evidence of how seriously Milton seems to have approached the imagery in his poetry and prose, we should also consider that visual perception itself sometimes emerges as one of his work's themes. In *Paradise Regained*, to take perhaps the most thorough-going example,

---

[7] See Woolf, *The Social Circulation of the Past*, pp. 360–61.

[8] See the overview of imagist studies in, respectively, Mark Womack, "On the Value of *Lycidas*," *Studies in English Literature* 37 (1997): 119–36; and Dobranski, *A Variorum Commentary on the Poems of John Milton: "Samson Agonistes,"* intro. Archie Burnett, ed. P. J. Klemp (Pittsburgh: Duquesne University Press, 2009).

[9] Laurence Lipking, "The Genius of the Shore: Lycidas, Adamastor, and the Poetics of Nationalism," *PMLA* 111.2 (1996): 205–21; Malabika Sarkar, "Astronomical Signs in *Paradise Lost*: Milton, Ophiucus, and the Millennial Debate," in *Milton and the Ends of Time*, ed. Juliet Cummins (Cambridge: Cambridge University Press, 2003), pp. 82–95; and Dobranski, "Principle and Politics in Milton's *Areopagitica*," in *The Oxford Handbook of Literature and the English Revolution*, ed. Laura Lunger Knoppers (Oxford: Oxford University Press, 2013), pp. 190–205.

Jesus' identity and sense of vocation rest on Hebrew scripture (I.207–11), his mother's advice (I.230–58), and God's baptismal pronouncement (I.283–86) – an almost exclusively verbal epistemology reinscribed in the poem's dialogic structure. But while the text repeatedly returns to God's declaration – "the Father's voice / From Heav'n pronounced him his beloved Son" (I.32–33; also I.283–86, II.1–5, II.83–85, and IV.512–13) – Satan cannot fathom the meaning of God's words and strives with increasing desperation for ocular proof of Jesus' status as the Son. The arch-fiend explains,

>   I saw
> The prophet do him reverence, on him rising
> Out of the water, Heav'n above the clouds
> Unfold her crystal doors, thence on his head
> A perfect dove descend, whate'er it meant.   (I.79–83)

The poem's dramatic irony hinges on these last three words: unlike Satan, Milton's readers can confidently understand such visual signs, and, at least with the benefit of hindsight, the images seem so obvious that Satan's befuddlement suggests his impotence even as the signs that he cannot read indicate the Son's merit.

Perhaps equally important, Satan in *Paradise Regained* also proves a poor image-maker. The Son summarily rejects Satan's various visual temptations and quickly sees through the devil's futile disguises, first as "an aged man in rural weeds" (I.314), an apparent parody of the Son's pastoral role, and in the subsequent temptation, "seemlier clad, / As one in city, or court, or palace bred" (II.299–300). When Satan tempts Jesus to expel the emperor Tiberius and rule Rome – even resorting to a supernatural "airy microscope" so that the Son "mayst behold / Outside and inside both" (IV.57–58) – Jesus criticizes Satan for not contriving a more effective visual image: "thou shouldst add to tell / Their sumptuous gluttonies, and gorgeous feasts / On citron tables or Atlantic stone" (IV.113–15). Jesus goes on to demonstrate his own imagist facility as he recommends a better tactic for the arch-fiend:

> Their wines of Setia, Cales, and Falerne,
> Chios and Crete, and how they quaff in gold,
> Crystal and myrrhine cups embossed with gems
> And studs of pearl, to me should'st tell who thirst
> And hunger still.   (IV.117–21)

Yet, even as Satan futilely relies on imagery to tempt the Son, *Paradise Regained* resembles *Paradise Lost* in resisting a straightforward dichotomy that would treat language as divine and imagery as diabolic. On the contrary, if we return to the repeated accounts of Jesus' baptism in Milton's brief epic, stock visual images of a descending dove, parting clouds, and unfolding doors complement and illustrate God's pronouncement (see, for example, I.79–83). Instead of reinforcing a distinction between language and imagery, *Paradise Regained* evokes the Son's status as the flesh made word by privileging God's material depictions of spiritual truth over the devil's tactile but false and worldly visualizations.

A similar type of spiritually and physically unified imagery has been the focus of this book. Milton in *Paradise Lost*, I have argued, can make the invisible visible in part because he believed that spirit and matter were inherently inseparable. Based on a shared etiology, the two states can be used to depict the diabolic and godly, while Adam and Eve's material reality intrinsically contains spiritual significance. Milton's epic also resembles *Paradise Regained* in its representation of seeing and being seen as indications of power. Satan in the earlier poem thus reveals his limited authority by being able to remain unseen only temporarily, as when he briefly disguises himself to deceive Uriel, enter Paradise, seduce Eve, or return to hell. And Satan, for all his chicanery, never escapes the perfect witness of an ever-judging deity, as when "the unsleeping eyes of God" observe the devil fomenting rebellion (V.647) or, as discussed in chapter 2, God's balance weighs the ruinous outcome of Satan's possible fight with Gabriel.

In contrast, I have shown, Milton's God is sometimes associated with physical things but remains permanently inaccessible, most often shrouded by a cloud or flaming mount, or engulfed entirely in "glorious brightness" (III.376). Descriptions of God's own visual ability correspondingly express His omnipotence so that Raphael, recounting the war in heaven, describes God as "th' eternal eye, whose sight discerns / Abstrusest thoughts" (V.711–12), and when Adam and Eve eat the forbidden fruit, the narrator conceives of God's power in specifically visual terms: "what can scape the eye / Of God all-seeing, or deceive his heart / Omniscient" (X.5–7). If we turn once again to Raphael's warning to Adam and Eve about "knowledge within bounds," the angel also explains humankind's limited apprehension by contrasting it with "th' invisible King, / Only omniscient." Only the one who remains invisible, in other words, perceives everything and controls what all other creatures apprehend.

The power of visual perception also plays a significant role in the depiction of Adam and Eve, as discussed in chapters 6, 7, and 8 – from Adam's birth and acceptance of God's existence, to Eve's initial discovery of Adam and her rejection of her own image, to Eve's and Adam's questions (in, respectively, books IV and VIII) about the appearance of the planets, stars, and sun. After the Fall, the couple can still interpret without much difficulty both the natural imagery that foretells humanity's punishment and, as we have seen in the preceding chapter, Michael's status as an angel in human garb. But the Fall, as I have also discussed, has nevertheless occluded the first parents' visual ability. Michael, before he can explain "what shall come in future days" (XI.357), must remove "from Adam's eyes the film . . . / Which that false fruit that promised clearer sight / Had bred" (XI.412–14).

Milton and his readers, as descendants of the first couple, presumably suffer from the same visual impairment, and one way of interpreting the invocations in *Paradise Lost* is that the poet seeks from the heavenly Muse an ocular purgation like the one Michael administers to Adam. Milton in his invocations accordingly emphasizes the ability to see. At the start, he beseeches the Muse, "what in me is dark / Illumine" (I.22–23), and he initially invokes Siloa's brook (I.11), the pool in whose waters Jesus cured a blind man (John 9:7). Later, when Milton complains that "holy light" does not revisit his eyes "that roll in vain / To find thy piercing ray" (III.1, 23–24), he not only refers to his literal blindness but also suggests a lack of prelapsarian perception:

> thou celestial light
> Shine inward, and the mind through all her powers
> Irradiate, there plant eyes, all mist from thence
> Purge and disperse. (III.51–54)

The internal "mist" that Milton wants dispelled resembles the mental darkening that Adam and Eve suffer upon eating the forbidden fruit (IX.1053–54).

Yet, even before the Fall, as Milton takes pains to show, the first parents are limited – "within bounds" – in what they can see, say, and know. Bowing lowly, Adam and Eve thus begin an unmeditated morning prayer by praising but not specifically naming or describing the deity: "Unspeakable, who sit'st above these heavens / To us invisible or *dimly seen / In these thy lowest works*, yet these declare / Thy goodness beyond thought, and power divine" (V.156–59, emphasis added). The couple goes on to propose that angels can "best" comprehend the deity because they alone "behold him" (V.160–61) – although, as we have seen, heaven's attendants must "with both wings veil their eyes" to view God (III.382). Still, Adam and Eve in this prayer hold out hope for their own profound knowledge that will come through glimpsing God in his creations, "these thy lowest works." Milton's use of physical objects and gestures to tell the story of the Fall follows the same logic of second-handedness. It is one of *Paradise Lost*'s pleasing paradoxes that Milton audaciously aspired to soar above the Aonian mount, yet even with the Muse's aid he humbly returned again and again to the "lowest" things to envision his narrative. Surely he would have also appreciated the irony that the visual imagination that he summoned for his epic would both be scorned in later centuries and come to influence the way that generations of readers understand and imagine the Fall.

But even as early as *Il Penseroso*, Milton suggests that he understood poetic inspiration as largely a visual process. That the poem specifically depicts a "dewy-feathered Sleep" bringing the speaker insight in the form of pictures indicates once again the significance that Milton seems to have attached to imagery: "let some strange mysterious dream / Wave at his wings in airy stream, / Of lively portraiture displayed, / Softly on my eyelids laid" (lines 147–50). More important for this book's thesis, Milton in *Il Penseroso* then describes the speaker's inspiration as combining such imaginative "portraiture" with not only religion and study but also his firsthand knowledge. He concludes the poem by explaining that "old experience do attain / To something like prophetic strain" (lines 173–74). While commentators have sometimes glossed "experience" here as a further allusion to the speaker's studies, the word may not be as ambiguous as these editors propose. *Experience* during the seventeenth century referred more simply to knowledge from "actual observation" or the "study or practice, in affairs generally, or in the intercourse of life."[10] Surely Milton drew often on his considerable learning in writing his poetry and prose. But only by also drawing on actual observations, as he forecasts in *Il Penseroso*, can a writer hope to speak prophetically and serve as a mediator between humankind and God.

---

[10] *OED*, s. v. "experience, *n.*," defs. 3, 8.

Index

Abdiel 37, 42, 74, 120
Abel 181, 184–85
Abrams, M. H. 206
accommodation, doctrine of 17–18, 114, 120, 178,
    180, 200
Ad Patrem ("To my Father") 160
Adam and Eve 6, 19, 22–25, 34, 37, 38, 93, 119
    after the Fall (postlapsarian) 6, 16, 50–51, 65,
        74, 86–87, 93, 150–52, 163–64, 175,
        176–78, 179–89, 202–03, 211
    appearance of 153–57, 162–75, 183, 196
    creation of 23–24, 136–37, 147
    descendants 24, 50–51, 74, 136, 146, 176, 179,
        183–87, 189, 191, 211
    education 20, 54, 60, 173, 177–90, 199–203,
        204, 206
    hands, hand-holding 135–39, 146–47, 149–52,
        174, 176, 183, 196
    love and marriage 19, 33, 34, 135–39, 146–52,
        157, 164, 166–69, 171, 173–75
    temptation 24–26, 30–31, 79, 111, 130, 174, 210
    visual experience 32–33, 35, 54, 150, 179–89,
        199–200, 201, 210–11
Addison, Joseph 2, 68, 125, 176, 183, 189
Aeschylus 130
Aesops Fables 103–04
Alciato, Andrea 141
Aleotti, G. B. 70
angels, angelology 19–21, 42, 58, 76, 159, 211; *see*
    also Paradise Lost, war in heaven *and the*
    names of individual angels
    the bad (fallen or rebel) 16, 44–45, 51, 65,
        88–89, 92–94, 101
    appearance of 108–10, 120–34
    transformation of 20–21, 34, 92–93, 110–19,
        135, 178, 187
    the good 16, 52, 55, 60–61, 65, 93–94
    appearance of 44–45, 119–20
    nature of 19–20, 110–11, 116–19
Anne of Denmark 144
anti-Trinitarianism *see* Arian, Arianism

Apollonius of Rhodes 39
Appelbaum, Robert 32
apples *see* Paradise Lost, forbidden fruit
Aquinas, Thomas 116–17, 119
Archer, Ian 79
Areopagitica 34, 49, 76, 193, 208
Arian, Arianism 195–97, 201
Ariosto, Ludovico 39, 157
Aristotle 9, 15
Arminian, Arminianism 34, 36, 38, 47–52, 53, 101;
    see also Paradise Lost, free will in
Arminius, Jacob 49
Arnold, Matthew 2, 90
Asington, John 69
Aubrey, John 159, 183
Augustine 12, 74–75, 193, 198

Bacon, Francis 70–71
balances (early modern) 8, 38, 56–59; *see also* God,
    scales
Banks, Theodore Howard 3, 4, 146
Barbaro, Francesco 151, 152
Barker, Arthur E. 125
Barry, James 98
Bate, John viii, 71, 72
Bauman, Michael 195
Baxter, Richard 48–49
Beelzebub 113, 134
Belsey, Catherine 137, 162
Berg, Charles 159
Bergel, Lienhard 106
Bernheimer, Richard 159
Blake, William 7, 98
Blakemore, David 94–95
Blakemore, Steven 62
Blessington, Francis C. 54
Book of Common Prayer, The 141, 143
Bradshaw, John 192
Bramante, Donnato 64
Brightman, F. E. 141
Broadbent, J. B. 105, 131, 180

Brooks, Cleanth 105
Brown, Cedric C. 131
Brown, Eleanor Gertrude 4
Browne, Thomas 64
Bryer, Robin 154
Bunyan, John, *The Pilgrim's Progress* 63
Burden, Dennis H. 137
Burgesse, Michael viii, 98, 100
Burke, Edmund 124–25
Burton, Robert 64, 71, 169–70
Bush, Douglas 6, 146

Cain 181, 183, 184, 187
Calvin (John), Calvinism 11, 46–50, 51–52;
    see also God, foreknowledge
Cambridge University 81; *see also* Christ's College
Carew, Thomas 82–84, 138
Carlton, Charles 94
Castiglione, Baldesar 171–72
Catholics, Catholicism 49, 190
Chaplin, Gregory 195–96
Charles I 28, 46–48, 81, 154, 155, 156, 192
Charles II 28, 58, 154, 175
Chaucer, Geoffrey 69, 107, 165
Christ's College 28
Chrysostom 23
Cicero 10, 12, 186
cities 77–81, 84; *see also* London
civil wars, British 40–43, 46–48, 52, 94–96,
    154–55, 182, 192
Clark, Stuart 130
Coleridge, Samuel Taylor 4, 205
Como, David 48
Constable, Henry, *Diana* 169
Corbett, Julian 94
Corbould, Richard viii, 98–99
corporal punishment 192–93
Corson, Richard 158
Corum, Richard 149
Cowley, Abraham, *Davideis* 120–21, 184
Crashaw, Richard 194
Cromwell, Oliver 43, 155, 162, 183, 192
Crucifixion *see* Son, incarnate
Cruso, John 95
Cunnar, Eugene 43

da Vinci, Leonardo 10
Dagon 134
Dali, Salvador 7
Dalton, O. M. 144, 156
Daniel, Clay 54
Daniel, Samuel, *Delia* 169
Danielson, Dennis 48, 61
Dante Alighieri 93, 121–22, 130
Daston, Lorraine 69

De Doctrina Christiana (*Christian Doctrine*) 18, 20,
    23, 33, 40, 44, 50, 51, 118, 195, 196, 197, 198
Death (personified) *see* Sin and Death
Defoe, Daniel 14
Demetz, Peter 167
Dennis, John 109–10
Di Cesare, Mario A. 136
di Valvasone, Erasmo 122, 130
Diodati, Charles 146
Doctrine and Discipline of Divorce, The 49, 148–49
Donne, John 62, 139–40, 147, 166, 187, 191
Donnelly, Phillip J. 19, 21, 22, 24, 118
Doré, Gustave 7
Dracontius, Blossius Aemilius 205
Dryden, John 3, 14, 55
Du Bartas, Guillaume de Saluste 186
Du Fresony, Charles Alphonse 14
DuBois, Page 84
Duran, Angelica 56
DuRocher, Richard J. 30

Edda 158
Edwards, Karen 25, 27, 85, 87, 103, 188, 206
Eikonoklastes 158
ekphrasis 12
elegies, Milton's 78
Eliot, T. S. 3, 5, 7, 17, 27, 105
Elizabeth I 48
Ellwood, Thomas 190
Empson, William 38, 40, 162
enargeia 12, 15
Episcopacy 11, 158, 161
Epitaphium Damonis ("Epitaph for Damon") 146
Euripides 13
Evans, J. Martin 205, 206
Eve *see* Adam and Eve
Evelyn, John 30, 182

faeries 129–31
Fairfax, Thomas 155
Fallon, Stephen M. 20–22, 39, 68, 92, 193, 197
Farnell, Lewis Richard 157
Fiennes, Celia 30
"Fifth Ode of Horace, The" 156
Firth, C. H. 94. 95
Fish, Stanley 59, 90, 106, 127, 163, 177
Flannagan, Roy 105, 190
Fleming, James Dougal 115
flood, flooding 180–81
Forsyth, Neil 110, 117, 130, 131
Fowler, Alastair 27, 37, 56, 156–67, 163
Franz, Wolfgang 104
Freeman, James A. 45, 90, 105
Fresch, Cheryl H. 147
Friedman, Donald 105

Frye, Roland Mushat 5, 28, 64, 120, 124, 162, 179–80, 184
Fumerton, Patricia 8
Furman-Adams, Wendy 7
Fuseli, John Henry 98

Gabriel 34, 36, 38–45, 46, 51–62, 120, 149, 210
Galen 165
Galileo Galilei 105–06
gates *see* Paradise Lost, heaven, depiction of *and* hell, depiction of
Gellius, Aulus 144
Giamatti, A. Bartlett 27, 188
Giese, Loreen L. 143
Gilbert, Sandra M. 162
Giorgi, Alessandro 70
Gitter, Elizabeth 158, 159
God 11–12, 18, 44–45, 195–98
    and creation 19–21, 22–23, 36, 43, 67–68, 76, 88, 136, 147, 204–05; *see also* monism
    appearance of 11, 23, 34, 36–37, 64, 191, 204, 210, 211–12; *see also* Paradise Lost, heaven, depiction of
    foreknowledge 36, 38, 45–54; *see also* Calvin (John), Calvinism
    scales 34, 36–39, 43–46, 51–61, 62, 64; *see also* balances (early modern)
Goodyer, Henry 140
Gordon, Andrew 207
Goslee, Nancy M. 6
Gray, Erik 168
great houses 77, 81–84
Greville, Fulke 96
Gubar, Susan 162
Guillory, John 91, 153

hair culture
    biblical 154, 157–58, 166
    classical 157, 162, 166, 170
    folkloric 158–59, 166
    seventeenth-century 154–56, 162, 164–66, 169–72, 173–74, 175, 183; *see also* Adam and Eve, appearance of
Hall, James 154
Hampton, Bryan Adam 196
hands *see* Adam and Eve, hands, hand-holding
Hanford, James Holly 94, 193
Hanmer, Thomas 29
Harding, Davis P. 30
Harris, Neil 105
Harrison, William 182
Hartlib, Samuel 29
Hartman, Geoffrey 109
Henderson, Paula 81
Henriksen, Erin 196

Henslowe, Philip 69
Herbert, George 140–41, 152, 190–91
Herman, Peter C. 110
Hero of Alexandria viii, 70–73
Herrick, Robert 172, 194
Hesiod 74
Heywood, Thomas 116–17
Hill, Christopher 40, 48
History of Moscovia, The 78
Hobbes, Thomas 176
Hogarth, William 98
Homer 38, 39, 40, 110, 131, 177, 207
    Iliad 35, 52–53, 54, 57, 68, 69, 91, 93, 96, 98, 101–02, 105, 107, 157
    Odyssey 30, 68, 162
Horace 130, 167
    Ars Poetica 8–10, 13–14, 15; *see also* "Fifth Ode of Horace, The"
Howard, George Elliott 143, 144
Hughes, Merritt Y. 53, 121
Hume, Patrick 112–13
Hunt, Leigh 153, 156, 168
husbandry 181–82
Hutchinson, Lucy 94–95

idolatry, idols 11, 34, 74, 110, 115, 132–34, 135, 139, 155, 183
Il Penseroso 156, 212
image, imagery 3 (defined), 22–24, 208; *see also* Paradise Lost, metonymy in *and* metaphors (similes) in
    literal 178, 180–89, 200, 203
    poetic theories of 8–17, 206
    religious 10–11, 210
In quintum Novembris ("On the fifth of November") 123
Incarnation, the *see* Son, incarnate
Ireton, Henry 155, 192
Irwin, M. Eleanor 157

James I 48, 144, 192
Jebb, R. C. 131
Johnson, Samuel 1, 2, 3, 7, 17, 18, 45
Jonson, Ben 14, 79, 82–84, 172
Jonston, Joannes 102–03
Joyce, James 207
Justice (personified) 56

Keats, John 6
Kelley, Maurice 49, 195
Kerrigan, William 39
Kilgour, Maggie 138
Knott, John R., Jr. 188
Koehler, G. Stanley 27
Kosslyn, Stephen Michael 4

Krieger, Murray 14
Krouse, F. Michael 158

L'Allegro 159
Laking, Guy Francis 94, 107
Landy, Marcia K. 146
Lares, Jameela 189–90
Latham, Minor White 131
Lau, Beth 6
Laud, William 11, 19, 46–48, 133, 144
Lawrence, Henry 43
lazar-house 185
Le Comte, Edward 146
Leavis, F. R. 4, 27
Lehnhof, Kent 173
Lennon, John 138
Leonard, John 31, 39, 137
Lewalski, Barbara K. 52, 133
Lewis, C. S. 89, 176–77, 180, 183
Lieb, Michael 85, 162
Lightsey, Scott 69
Lilburne, John 56
Lipking, Lawrence 208
Lisle, George 95–96
Lockhart, William 95
Loewenstein, David 189
London 2, 8, 18, 57, 64, 78–81, 180, 185, 192;
    see also cities
Longinus, *On the Sublime* 13, 14, 16, 17
Louden, Bruce 40, 53
Lovelace, Richard 171, 172, 173
lovelock 154–55
Luther, Martin 147
Luxon, Thomas 173
Lycidas 1, 156, 160–61, 193, 202, 208

Macaulay, Thomas Babington 176
MacCallum, H. R. 178, 198
McCartney, Paul 138
McColley, Diane Kelsey 6, 104, 137, 163, 188
Machacek, Gregory 52
MacKenzie, Phyllis 17
Mackworth-Young, Robin 81
Macrobius 144
Mansus ("Manso") 160
Marjara, Harinder Singh 205, 206
Marlowe, Christopher 70, 108
marriage 141, 143–44, 147, 148–49, 151; *see also*
    Adam and Eve, love and marriage
Martin, John viii, ix, 98, 126–28
Marvell, Andrew 152
marvels, mechanical 68–75
Mask Presented at Ludlow Castle, A (also known as
    Comus) 123, 146, 156, 168
materialism, animist *see* monism

Medusa 114–15
memory 4–5, 129, 176, 182, 192, 207–08
Michael 37, 42, 45, 92, 120, 151, 176, 199–200
    as narrator 189–91, 197, 199
    as surrogate 34, 178, 198–203
    as visual teacher 35, 50, 74, 177, 180–90, 199,
        201–02, 211
Miller, J. Hillis 162
Milner, Andrew 45
Milton, John 159–60, 183, 185, 192, 206–08; *see
    also the titles of individual works and the
    names of characters*
    blindness 1–2, 4–5, 7, 35, 146, 207, 211
    continental journey 5–6, 64, 77, 127, 129
    on himself 1–2, 106–07, 162, 193
    Secretary for Foreign Tongues (Latin
        Secretary) 81, 183
Mitchell, W. J. T. 14, 23
Mollenkott, Virginia 38
monism 18–24, 27, 35, 88–89, 91–92, 118–19,
        132–34, 135–37, 147–52, 164–66, 175,
        177–78, 196–97, 207, 210
Moore, Norman 185
More, Ellen 48
More, Henry 116–16
Morrill, John 133
Moyles, R. G. 186

Nashe, Thomas 116–17
Nativity Ode *see* "On the Morning of Christ's
    Nativity"
natural world 91, 102–07, 173, 187–89, 204–06;
    see also husbandry *and* Paradise Lost,
    forbidden fruit
Naturam non pati senium ("That Nature Is Not
    Subject to Old Age") 46
New Criticism 3–4, 105, 109
Newman, Robert 162
Newton, Isaac 29
Newton, Thomas 162
Nicolson, Marjorie Hope 5–6, 38
Norbrook, David 16

objects, object studies 3, 4, 6, 8, 9, 10, 12–14, 16, 31,
        33, 37, 70, 89, 92, 106, 110, 132–34, 175,
        189, 206, 208, 212; *see also* monism *and the
        names of individual things*
Ogle, M. B. 170
"On Shakespeare" 92–93
"On the Morning of Christ's Nativity" 77, 123,
        194, 195
"On Time" 72–74
optics 10–11, 13, 211
Origen 117
Otten, Charlotte F. 188

Ovid 167, 168
  Metamorphoses 30, 68–69, 85, 130, 139, 157, 160,
    181, 183
Oxford University 81, 183

Paradise Lost
  chaos 17, 37, 60, 62, 84, 88, 130
  creation in 6, 19–24, 25, 46, 76, 88
  final books 16, 34, 50–51, 61, 74, 151, 176–203
  forbidden fruit 24–33
  free will in 19, 36, 38, 45–46, 51–58, 61, 64, 118,
    147–52; *see also* Arminian, Arminianism
  heaven, depiction of 34, 62–65, 67–68, 72,
    74–77, 81, 84–89, 204
  hell, depiction of 5–6, 16, 65–68, 76, 77, 88,
    108, 114
  illustrations of 7, 98–100
  invocations 1–2, 7, 31, 42, 211
  metaphors (similes) in 109–10, 114, 126–32, 135,
    167, 173, 174, 183–84, 187, 189, 191, 200,
    203, 206, 212
  metonymy in 108–09, 125–26, 134, 135, 183
  Pandemonium 62, 64, 65, 129–32,
    182–83
  Paradise, depiction of 34, 77, 85–86,
    88, 163, 169, 173, 176, 187–89, 202,
    204–06
  seizing in 136–39, 146–52, 174
  war in heaven 2, 6, 17, 20–21, 40, 42–45, 51, 85,
    93–94, 107, 197, 201; *see also* weaponry
    *and the names of the epic's individual
    characters*
Paradise Regained 41, 42, 78, 79, 95, 193–94, 197,
    208–10
Park, Katharine 69
Parker, William Riley 4
Parkinson, John 28–29
"Passion, The" 7–8, 193–94
Patrides, C. A. 179
Peacham, Henry (the elder) 13
Pepys, Samuel 80
Perry, Mary Phillips 55, 57
Peter, John 38
Petrarch, Francesco 170–71
Philaras, Leonard 35
Plato 9, 115–16
Plutarch 9
Poole, William 25
predestination *see* Calvin (John), Calvinism
Prince, F. T. 177, 198
Pro Populo Anglicano Defensio Secunda (*Second
    Defense*) 43, 106–07
Prolusions 77–78
Prynne, William 154–55
Puttenham, George 15

Quarles, Francis viii, 58–59, 194
Quintilian 12, 13, 16

Rajan, Balachandra 130
Raleigh, Walter 110
Randall, Dale B. J. 144
Raphael 17, 37, 40, 51, 54, 65, 68, 88, 89, 118, 121,
    136, 147–48, 152, 177, 178, 197, 200, 204,
    206, 210
  appearance of 119–20, 199, 200
  his plant metaphor 17–22, 25, 60, 67, 91, 118,
    164, 175
Rathborne, Isable E. 131
Raymond, Joad 114, 117, 118, 120
Rebhorn, Wayne 171
Restoration 41, 42, 58, 131, 156, 175, 183, 192, 208
Revard, Stella Purce 6, 42, 43, 93, 121, 122, 125, 160
Richardson, Catherine 8
Ricks, Christopher 32, 110, 149–50, 163
Rivetus, Andreas 48
Roberts, Lewes 57
Robinson, Henry 158
Rogers, John 154, 195
Romance of the Rose 69
Romney, George 98
Rumrich, John 39, 193, 197, 198
Rupert, Prince of the Rhine 81
Ruskin, John 4, 124
Ryken, Leland 4, 27

St. Agnes 159
St. Paul 11, 12, 92, 107, 154, 162, 169, 173, 198
St. Paul's School 10
St. Peter 86
Sammons, Todd H. 167
Samson Agonistes 41, 78, 101, 102, 145–46, 156,
    157–58, 160, 175, 192–93, 208
Samuel, Irene 163
Sandys, George 14
Sanzio, Raphael ix
Sarhar, Malabika 208
Satan 36–37, 76, 85–87, 94, 96–109, 126–34, 163,
    164, 171, 182, 189
  in *Paradise Regained* 41, 78, 79, 95, 209–10
  material degeneration of 26–27, 34, 88–89,
    90–93, 104–05, 113–14, 116, 124–25, 135,
    178, 187, 210
  residual goodness of 111–12
  temptation of Eve 27, 30–31, 104, 111, 125, 174,
    201, 210
  versus Death 39, 40
  versus Gabriel 36, 38–45, 51–62; *see also*
    weaponry
Sawday, Jonathan 70
scales *see* balances (early modern) *and* God, scales

Schoenfeldt, Michael 140, 190
Shakespeare, William
   Cymbeline 70
   Hamlet 165
   King John 138
   Love's Labour's Lost 160
   Measure for Measure 80
   Merchant of Venice 170
   Much Ado About Nothing 158
   Richard II 36
   Romeo and Juliet 138
   Tempest, The 70
   Twelfth Night 135, 165
   Venus and Adonis 138–39, 147
Sharpe, J. A. 192
sheep-walks 181–82
Sherbo, Arthur 150
shields *see* weaponry
Shore, Daniel 133
Shumaker, Wayne 70, 189
Sidney, Philip 96
   Defense of Poesy, The 15–16
Sidney, Robert 82, 83
Simonides of Ceos 9
Simpson, James 134
Sin and Death 39–40, 62, 65–66, 67, 121, 151,
   186–87
Sleeman, Margaret 156
Socinian, Socinianism 195
Son 86, 197–98; *see also the titles of individual*
   poems
  and creation 88
  in *Paradise Regained* 41–42, 79, 193,
   209–10
  incarnate 34, 151, 178, 190–99, 201, 210
  versus rebels 42–43, 45, 85, 92, 197
sonnets, Milton's
  Sonnet 7 "How soon hath Time" 49–50
  Sonnet 20 "Lawrence of virtuous father" 43
Speed, John ix, 144–45
Spenser, Edmund
   Amoretti 169
   Faerie Queene, The 62–63, 70, 74, 83–84, 91,
   96, 101, 159
   Fowre Hymnes 120
sprezzatura 171–73
Spurgeon, Caroline 3
Steadman, John M. 121, 125
Stebbing, H. 189
Stein, Arnold 150
Sterry, Peter 42–43
Stock, Richard 41
Stone, Lawrence 144
Stothard, Thomas 98
Stow, John 185

Strong, Roy 70, 141
Sugimura, N. K. 17, 21–22, 92, 113
Sumner, Graham 97
Swaim, Kathleen M. 178
Swinburne, Henry 144

Taaffe, James G. 193
Tasso, Torquato 39, 84
Taylor, Dick, Jr. 186, 190
Taylor, John 156
Tertullian 117, 200
Tetrachordon 22
Theis, Jeffrey S. 62, 67
Thomas, Keith 207
Thomson, Thomas 144
Tillyard, E. M. W. 4, 146
Todd, Henry John 189
Topsell, Edward 103
Trapp, J. B. 160
Treatise of Civil Power, A 40
Treip, Mindele Anne 38
Trinity College Manuscript 73, 161
Trissino, Gian Giorgio 53
Tufte, Virginia James 7
Turner, J. M. W. 7
Turner, James Grantham 150
Tuve, Rosemond 3, 31
Tyacke, Nicholas 46

Ullyett, Kenneth 73
Ungerer, Gustav 165, 169
"Upon the Circumcision" 194–95
Uriel 60, 119, 120, 159, 210

Valla, Lorenzo 70
van den Vondel, Joost 122–23, 130
Van Dyck, Anthony ix, 154, 155
Verity, A. W. 178
Vicary, Thomas 165–66
Virgil 38, 177, 182
   Aeneid 12, 35, 52–55, 57, 83, 97, 99, 186
visual arts 5, 6, 7, 8–12, 14, 28, 43, 55, 56, 57, 120,
   155, 157, 159, 179–80, 184, 205

Waldock, A. J. A. 125
walls *see* Paradise Lost, heaven, depiction of *and*
   hell, depiction of
Warren, Robert Penn 3
Warton, Joseph 27
weaponry 8, 34, 90–102, 104–07, 108, 109,
   124, 126
Webber, Joan 105
Werman, Golda 184
West, Robert H. 117
Westall, Richard 98

Whaler, James 109
Wheeler, George Bomford 182
Whigham, Frank 149, 173
Whitgift, John 144
Wilding, Michael 163
Wilson, F. P. 185
Winn, James A. 93

Wither, George ix, 141, 142, 194
Womack, Mark 208
Woolf, Daniel 4, 207, 208
Wordsworth, William 2
Wright, B. A. 168

Zupko, Ronald Edward 57

Lightning Source UK Ltd.
Milton Keynes UK
UKOW06n2047060316

269711UK00003B/104/P